This Way to BOOKS

For Johanna Hurwitz, with love—
This should be worth at least three hundred letters.

This Way

Caroline Feller Bauer

Drawings by Lynn Gates

to BOOKS

This is especially for Rosemary
1983
Hope this is the way to ideas.
Lots of Love,
Caroline Feller Bauer

THE H. W. WILSON COMPANY • 1983

Library of Congress Cataloging in Publication Data

Bauer, Caroline Feller.
  This way to books.

  Bibliography: p.
  Includes index.
  1. Children—Books and reading—Handbooks, manuals.
etc. I. Title.
Z1037.B37 1983 [PN1009.A1] 028.5′5 82-19985
ISBN 0-8242-0678-9

International Standard Book Number 0-8242-0678-9

Printed in the United States of America

Acknowledgments

The author is grateful for permission to quote the following copyrighted material:

"Eats" and "I Am Learning" from *Eats* by Arnold Adoff. Copyright © 1979 by Arnold Adoff. By permission of Lothrop, Lee & Shepard Company (A Division of William Morrow & Co.).

"Money" from *An Armoury of Light Verse* by Richard Armour. Copyright © 1942, 1964 by Bruce Humphries. Reprinted courtesy of Branden Press, 21 Station Street, Brookline, MA.

Excerpt from *Mr. Popper's Penguins* by Richard and Florence Atwater. Copyright © 1938 by Richard and Florence Atwater. Reprinted by permission.

"Give a Quote" by Caroline Feller Bauer reprinted from *Cricket, The Magazine for Children*, Vol. 7, No. 4, December 1979, © by Open Court Publishing Company.

"Pockets" from *Story-teller Poems* by Rowena Bennett, published by Holt, Rinehart & Winston, Inc. By permission of Kenneth C. Bennett.

"Caps 'n Hats" and "Lincoln Penny" by Nonie Borba. Courtesy of the author.

"Dinnertime" from *Rhymes About Us* by Marchette Chute. Copyright © 1974 by Marchette Chute. Reprinted by permission of the publisher, E. P. Dutton.

"Dogs" from *Rhymes About the City* by Marchette Chute. Copyright 1946 (Macmillan), renewal copyright © 1974 by Marchette Chute. Used by permission of the author.

"First Day of Spring" from *A Bunch of Poems and Verses*, by Beatrice Schenk de Regniers. Il. by Mary Jane Dunton. Houghton/Mifflin/Clarion Books, 1977. Copyright © 1977 by the author.

"Lunchbox" from *Poems for Children Only* by Susan Cohen Field. By permission of the author.

Text excerpts from *Harriet the Spy* by Louise Fitzhugh. Copyright © 1964 by Louise Fitzhugh. By permission of Harper & Row, Publishers, Inc. and Victor Gollancz Ltd.

"Blowing Bubbles" from *Stilts, Somersaults, and Headstands*, by Kathleen Fraser. Copyright © 1968 by Kathleen Fraser. Reprinted by permission of Curtis Brown, Ltd.

Excerpt from *My Father's Dragon* by Ruth Stiles Gannett. Copyright © 1948 by Ruth Stiles Gannett. Reprinted by permission of Random House, Inc.

v

Contents

INTRODUCTION

Miss Stevenson
Sixth Grade
Glenwood Landing School
Long Island, New York

Dear Miss Stevenson:

I'm sorry I haven't written you for the last thirty-five years, but I've been so busy. Just wanted to say thanks for the best present a teacher can give a student: the gift of reading.

You were the one who took me, a non-reader—after all, I was passed into third grade on probation because of my lack of reading skills—and turned me into a confirmed, lifetime reader.

How did you do that? I can't remember all the things you did, but I do know you read aloud to us every day. And I still remember and love the books you personally recommended to me.

Anyway, thanks.

Yours sincerely,

Caroline Feller Bauer '47

I don't really feel so bad that it took me thirty-five years to get around to thanking Miss Stevenson. Most teachers don't expect to get thank-you notes from their former students. The satisfaction of introducing students to the pleasures of reading is probably sufficient reward for many years.

Maybe it was easier for kids to get involved with books in those days, before television had taken over. But I guess that isn't fair to say. There were just as many outside demands on our time then as there are on our children's time today. In fact, my daughter Hilary, who is in the eighth grade, takes exactly the same after-school lessons I did: piano and ice-skating.

When I look back at everything I learned in my years of formal and informal education, I realize that reading is the one thing that has lasted as a lifetime "sport." And that's because an adult, my teacher Miss Stevenson, took the time to convey to us students her own involvement with and enthusiasm for books.

I don't say that any adult can do for children what Miss Stevenson did for us in the sixth grade, but I do know that ideas and techniques like hers for getting young people and books together really do work and that those of us who are teachers, librarians, counselors, and parents can use those techniques to imbue children with that all-important love of reading.

This Way to Books is a collection of ideas, programs, techniques, and activities designed to involve children in books and to extend their reading experience by making reading so much fun that a child cannot resist. I feel strongly that adults who work with children should be thinking "books" and "reading" throughout the day, not just between 2:00 and 3:00 on Tuesdays. Of course, I don't expect everybody to be as devout as I am in the pursuit of reading as an integral part of life—I set my table with book dishes and book placemats, wear clothing and jewelry with book themes and designs, and sleep between Paddington Bear sheets!

I spend a great deal of my time—both personal and professional—with books. You may not think you have that much time to spare from your busy schedule—and you might be right—but I have found that once reading becomes a habit it also becomes a priority activity. Those who "suffer" from bibliomania need to have words in front of them all the time. They read ads on the subway, the backs of breakfast cereal boxes—they even reread books they disliked, if nothing else is available. Best of all for these bibliomaniacs, they have plenty of books around at all times. A common complaint among non-readers is that they "don't have time" to read. I can't accept this excuse, since I know from my own experience that we always manage to find the time to do the things we really want to do. For instance, when I was supposed to write my Ph.D. dissertation, I just couldn't find the time to sit down and write (I wish I approached writing with the same enthusiasm I have for reading). Then I learned that if I didn't finish my dissertation within three months, I would have to take my comprehensive exams over (an unspeakable fate!). Suddenly, I had loads of time for writing.

When I married Peter he read only professional journals and never had time for books. He is one of my outstanding successes. Now he feels extremely uncomfortable if he doesn't have a book with him and a back-up book to start as soon as he finishes the first one. I must be truthful and point out that one drawback to our family's reading addiction is that on trips we have to carry an extra suitcase for our library.

When does our family read? Anytime, all the time, that we are not engaged in other activities. We read during all those waiting periods that seem to afflict modern life: we read while waiting in the doctor's office; while waiting in the check-out line at the supermarket; while waiting at the gas station; while waiting for the spaghetti sauce to cook; while waiting for an order in a restaurant. We read instead of watching television. We even read in the bathtub (switch to baths if you usually take a shower).

We also have a special Bauer family tradition known as the "flood book." Whenever any of us leaves the house, no matter what the reason—"Just going to pick up my ice skates at Jeannine's" (Hilary), "Be back in ten minutes, going to pick up the cleaning" (Peter), "Going to the store to get some milk" (Caroline)—we bring a "flood book" with us. Who knows, there might really be a flood (or a flat tire or a revolution), and so we are prepared to pass the time reading. As a reminder to you and your family, put up a small sign near your usual exit door:

REMEMBER YOUR FLOOD BOOK.

This Way to Books isn't meant to be the sort of book you cuddle up with in front of a roaring fire on a winter's day to read from beginning to end like a thrilling novel. In some respects it's a grab bag of ideas, suggestions, and techniques that I have encountered or used myself. Conveying enthusiasm about books is not a scientific exercise, and the organization of this book tends to allow a good deal of overlapping. Probably you will want to page through the book to get a feel for it and its organization, then return to it for specific ideas or for inspiration for your own programs.

The book is divided into seven major sections, each representing a method or theme for bringing books and children together.

I. STORYTELLING

In a previous book, *Handbook for Storytelling*, I devoted four hundred pages to the basic techniques of storytelling. In this present volume, I've suggested a few ways of extending these techniques. There is an outline course designed to teach students or volunteers how to tell stories; a summary presentation of how to create multi-media storytelling packets; a few easy-to-duplicate presentation ideas; and a collection of story programs. The programs are meant to promote reading; they involve telling or reading a story aloud and then suggesting other books that relate to the story theme for leisure reading. The activities described are meant to extend the enjoyment of the storyhour after the story is over.

II. PROGRAMS

This section shows how to create and present book programs in your classroom, library, or clubhouse. After a short introduction on methodology, I've included sample programs which you can reproduce in their entirety or from which you can take selected ideas.

I've tried to include a variety of subjects and presentations. There are programs that you might use just once, or once a year, like the program on teeth. There are ongoing programs, like the summer reading ideas. I think celebrating holidays real (Thanksgiving and Halloween) or imagined (Balloon Day, Fairy Tale Day) is one of the most appealing and effective ways of bringing books into the lives of children. This section also includes a list of possible program ideas for you to develop and another list of sources for further inspiration.

III.   BOOKTALKS

I've included four traditional booktalks for you to use verbatim or as models for your own talks. I've also included ideas for presenting books with visual aids or with dramatic "come-ons."

IV.   PRESENTING POETRY

This section—the result of my disappointment in the effort our schools have made ("not made" is more accurate) in giving children an appreciation of this genre—attempts to present interesting and amusing ways of bringing poetry to the attention of children. There are practical, easy-to-reproduce ideas for activities and exhibits that include actual poems.

V.   GAMES

The games in this section are meant for the reading or game corner. Some are meant to be played by children, others involve both children and an adult. Some of the games are simply packaging ideas for book reports, but call it a "game" and children will enjoy playing; call it a "book report" and you might get a few groans. Make several of these games for your reading center so there is a choice.

VI.   CRAFTS

This section is for those adults or children who like to make things. And if you are going to make something it might as well be book-oriented or decorated with a book theme—for instance, a lampshade to use with bedtime stories, or a bank to hold money for new books.

xiii

VII.   EXHIBITS

Bulletin boards and exhibits are almost always popular and successful ways of introducing books. Most of these ideas, such as the chalkboard special and picture pocket smock, can be used virtually all the time. Some, such as bringing a tarantula to the library or exhibiting a pet rock, are suggested for occasional use.

BIBLIOGRAPHIES

Subject bibliographies appear throughout *This Way to Books*. They can be used as reading lists or as aids in setting up book exhibits. They are an integral part of each project and, *no cheating,* you are not allowed to tell a story or practice a craft unless you also READ a book or books!

TIME AND MONEY

An attempt has been made to include ideas that will not take a lot of time to carry out or be terribly expensive. However, for those who are interested in more elaborate craft projects or can find budget money for permanent exhibits and programs, there are ideas here for you, too. Please remember that if you begin working at the age of twenty-five (late to begin these days) and retire at the age of sixty-five (early to retire these days), you will have worked for forty years. If you make one project each year of your working life, you will have a lovely collection of forty book ideas.

LIBRARIANS, TEACHERS, PARENTS

Obviously, it's impossible to read the nearly 2,000 juvenile books that are published every year, not to mention those classics that remain in print. But in order to acquaint children with what you think may be of interest to them, you must read as much as possible. Unless you have read a book you will be unable to compose a booktalk about it, relate it to crafts, or make an exhibit featuring its theme. Fortunately, in most areas of the United States, children's books are available at a school or public library.

Explore your library's shelves for the books you read as a child and remember with warmth (if you're lucky, some of them might still be in print). Consult with the librarian. Look for books you missed reading and read as many as you can of the recent titles. Ask colleagues, friends, and children what books they have enjoyed reading.

And to help you keep up with the abundance of books, consult Appendix X for the names of organizations that compile lists of recommended titles—and often review them as well.

Teachers will find that many of these projects are not listed in their curriculum or job description. You will simply have to find the time. If you have only a few minutes, tell a story, present a poem, or introduce one or two books in a booktalk. If you have a little more time, you can add an activity to your story, present more poems, or speak longer about books. If you have *no* time, use the exhibit ideas or put the titles from a subject bibliography in an obvious place and let the children discover books on their own.

I hope that at least some of the ideas in this book turn you or your children on to books. Don't wait thirty-five years to write me if they do!

Portland, Oregon   CAROLINE FELLER BAUER

I STORYTELLING

Telling a story is one of the most personal ways of introducing books to children. Begin by choosing a story to learn from the numerous collections of folklore in your library. Learning a story will take time, but the pleasure you will get from audience reaction is well worth the effort. Traditional storytelling, or telling a story without props or a book, requires the highest skill in telling as well as sophisticated listening skills on the part of the audience. Many children today, who are used to the visuals of television, are not ready to concentrate on simply listening to longer complicated stories, but they will absorb shorter tales, and you can use these as stepping stones to more involved stories. Children used to television might also be ready to "see" a story as well as hear it if you use one of the many media techniques available to us, such as slides, film, transparencies, and Velcro boards. In this section I have included several successful storytelling ideas that would be useful to anyone planning continuing storytelling programs.

Story Programs

The collection of story programs that follows shows how to expand the traditional storyhour into a full-fledged program. Each program includes the bibliographic information for a story to tell or read aloud, a list of related leisure-reading books to exhibit, and instructions for an individual or group activity. As the story leader, you may or may not wish to lead the group in a book-related craft or activity, but you could suggest follow-up activities for the children to try at home.

The cores of these programs originally appeared in a manual accompanying a fifteen-minute storytelling television series used for in-school viewing. The series was designed for 4th to 6th graders, but many younger children happily watched the shows too.

These stories may be read aloud, of course; however I heartily recommend that you attempt to learn and tell as many of the stories as you can for a more effective presentation.

These are proven programs, but obviously you can use your own storytelling repertoire in the same way. Whichever you use, it is very important that you make the books available and suggest other books for outside reading, in addition to the book from which the story comes. One of the major objectives of storytelling should be to get children to read on their own. If you find that a book you want is out of print or not in your library, try to get it through interlibrary loan.

WHAT'S IN A NAME?

STORIES TO TELL

These are three short, easy-to-learn stories in which the search for a name is important.

"The Ogre Who Built A Bridge," *in* Yoshiko, Uchida. *The Sea of Gold, and Other Tales From Japan*. il. by Marianne Yamaguchi. Scribner, 1965.

"Tiki, Tiki Tembo," *in* Jeanette Perkins Brown, *The Storyteller in Religious Education: How to Tell Stories to Children*. Pilgrim Press, 1951. *See also* Arlene Mosel, *Tikki Tikki Tembo*. il. by Blair Lent. Holt, 1968.

"Yung-Kung-Pung," *in* Philip M. Sherlock. *Anansi, the Spider Man; Jamaican Folk Tales.* il. by Marcia Brown. Crowell, 1954.

SOMETHING TO READ These are other stories in which the search for a name is important.

Babbitt, Natalie. *The Search for Delicious.* il. by author. Farrar, Straus, 1969. Young Gaylen sets out to find the definition of *delicious* in this novel.

Farjeon, Eleanor. *The Silver Curlew.* il. by Ernest H. Shepard. Viking, 1954.
The young queen must guess Spindle-Imp's name or lose her beautiful baby. A book-length version of Tom Tit Tot.

Master of All Masters; an English Folktale. il. by Marcia Sewall. Little, 1972.
See also Joseph Jacobs, ed., *English Folk and Fairy Tales.* il. by John D. Batten. Putnam [n.d.]
". . . get out of your barnacle and put on your squibs and crackers. White-faced Simminy has got a spark of hot cockalorum on her tail" . . . and other nonsense in this short story.

"Rumpelstiltzkin," by the Brothers Grimm, *in* Andrew Lang. *The Blue Fairy Book.* Ed. by Brian Alderson. il. by John Lawrence. Viking, 1978.
In the Grimms' version of this story, a queen must guess the name of a funny little man, who says:

> "Today I brew, tomorrow I bake,
> And then the child away I'll take;
> For little deems my royal dame
> That Rumpelstiltzkin is my name!"

"Tom Tit Tot," *in* Joseph Jacobs, *English Folk and Fairy Tales.* il. by John D. Batten. Putnam [n.d.].
The amusing English story in which a young girl must discover the name of an impet:

> "Nimmy nimmy not
> My name's Tom Tit Tot."

Weiss, Joan Talmadge. *Home for a Stranger.* Harcourt, 1980.
"Who Am I? Nobody Knows." A child living in a Mexican orphanage searches for her mother and her name.

Zemach, Harve. *Duffy and the Devil; a* Cornish Tale Retold *by Harve Zemach.* il. by Margot Zemach. Farrar Straus, 1973.

A picture-book version of a Cornish tale. Duffy must find the devil's name:

"Tomorrow! Tomorrow! Tomorrow's the day!
I'll take her! I'll take her! I'll take her away!
Let her weep, let her cry, let her beg, let her pray—
She'll never guess my name is . . ."

ACTIVITIES

1. Name scramble. Scramble the name of each person in the group in a list. The first to unscramble the list wins (e.g., Eraoilnc = Caroline).

2. Look up the names of your family and friends in a "What to Name the Baby" book to find their original meanings.

3. Try to say this name jingle quickly:

    Betty Botter bought some butter.
    Bosh! said she, the butter's bitter.
    If I put it in my batter
    My batter will be bitter.
    But a bit of better butter
    Will make the batter better.
    Then she bought a bit of butter
    Better than the bitter butter
    Then she put it in her batter
    And the batter was not bitter.

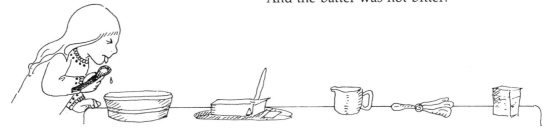

4. Make up a story title using each letter in your name as the first letter in each word. Here's an example: Hilary = How inconsiderate, Larry ate Ron's yo-yo. Write a story to go with the title.

5. Write your name. How many words can you make using the letters in your name?

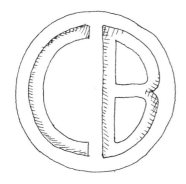

TO MAKE

1. A DESIGN USING YOUR INITIALS

YOU NEED: cardboard   glue
yarn   a safety pin

HOW TO: Write your initials, making your design as attractive as possible. Draw the design on a small piece of cardboard. Glue yarn on your design. Paste a safety pin on the back to make a pin.

2. A NAME POSTER

YOU NEED: colored paper or foil
colored cardboard

HOW TO: Fold a piece of colored paper or foil in half lengthwise. Write your name in script just above the fold. Cut out each letter and open the paper up. The name will become a lively design. Paste it on a piece of colored cardboard to hang in your room.

5

"1 + 1 = 2"

STORIES TO TELL

"The Leopard's Daughter," by Harold Courlander, *in* Virginia A. Tashjian, *With a Deep Sea Smile: Story Hour Stretches for Large or Small Groups.* il. by Rosemary Wells, Little, 1974.
A new way of counting wins a bride.

"Two of Everything," *in* Alice Ritchie, *The Treasure of Li Po.* il. by T. Ritchie. Harcourt, 1949.
Mr. Hak Tak finds a magic pot that produces two of everything.

SOMETHING TO READ

Burns, Marilyn. *The I Hate Mathematics! Book.* il. by Martha Hairston. Little, 1975.
An attractive collection of games, facts, and tricks to make math fun.

Dodgson, Stuart, ed., *Diversions and Digressions of Lewis Carroll.* Collingwood, Dover, 1961.
You may remember that Lewis Carroll, author of *Alice's Adventures in Wonderland* and *Through the Looking Glass* was a mathematician. Some of Carroll's mathematical puzzles appear in this collection.

"The Doughnuts," *in* Robert McCloskey. *Homer Price.* il. by author. Viking, 1943.
In this chapter, a doughnut machine continues to produce doughnuts until an entire luncheonette is overflowing with them.

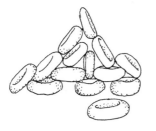

"Gallons of Guppies," *in* Beverly Cleary. *Henry Huggins.* il. by Louis Darling. Morrow, 1950.
In this chapter, Henry's guppies multiply until glass jars of swimming guppies fill his bedroom.

Juster, Norton. *The Phantom Tollbooth.* il. by Jules Feiffer. Random, 1961.
In this fantasy, Milo journeys to Digitopolis, where everything is logical and mathematical.

Nye, Robert. *The Mathematical Princess, and Other Stories.* il. by Paul Bruner. Hill and Wang, 1971.
The problem of finding a husband for a princess who knows more about math than all her tutors times six is solved by a charming shepherd.

St. John, Glory. *How to Count Like a Martian.* Walck H. Z., 1975.
A puzzle-solving device is used to explain number series and counting systems.

ADULT REFERENCE: **Young, Sharon.** *Mathematics in Children's Books: An Annotated Bibliography Preschool Through Grade 3.* Creative Publications (Box 10328, Palo Alto, CA 94303).
Books listed are annotated and arranged by subject: numbers, arithmetic operations, measurement, geometry, sets, etc.

ACTIVITIES

NUMBER GAMES

1. Find out your friend's age without asking her directly.
    a. Ask her to silently multiply her age by 3.
    b. Ask her to add 6 to the answer.
    c. Ask her to divide her answer by 3.
    d. Ask her to tell you this total.
    e. You subtract 2 from her answer.
    f. Now you know her age.

    Your friend is 10 years old.
    a. $10 \times 3 = 30$
    b. $30 + 6 = 36$
    c. $36 \div 3 = 12$
    d. 12
    e. $12 - 2 = 10$ years old

2. a. Choose three successive digits under 10 and arrange them in descending order to form a number.
    b. Reverse the digits and subtract this number from the first number.
    c. The answer will always be 198.
        Example: a. 765
                  b. 567
                  c. 198
    Try it!

3. a. Think of a number.
    b. Double it.
    c. Add 6.
    d. Divide by 2.
    e. Subtract the number you first thought of.
    f. Your answer is 3.
        Example: a. Your number is 5.
                  b. $5 + 5 = 10$
                  c. $10 + 6 = 16$
                  d. $16 \div 2 = 8$
                  e. $8 - 5 = 3$

7

4. a. Write down any number with two or more digits.
    b. Mix up the digits any way you like to create a new number.
    c. Subtract the smaller number from the larger.
    d. Add up the digits in the answer.
    e. If your result contains 2 or more digits, add those numbers until you're left with one number.
    f. The number is always 9.

$$843675$$
$$-\,347586$$
$$496089$$

$4+9+6+0+8+9=36$
$3+6=9$

5. Magic squares.

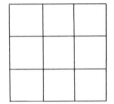

The object of this game is to fill in the squares so that the numbers in each row (vertical, horizontal, and diagonal) add up to 15.

Fill in each square above with a number from 1 to 9. Do not use the same number twice. There are several ways to solve this puzzle:

8	3	4
1	5	9
6	7	2

2	7	6
9	5	1
4	3	8

6	1	8
7	5	3
2	9	4

8	1	6
3	5	7
4	9	2

THE APPROACH OF WINTER

STORY TO TELL

"The Silver Hen," by Mary E. Wilkins *in* Eulalie Steinmetz Ross. *The Lost Half Hour.* il. by Enrico Arno. Harcourt, 1963.
A group of children searching for a lost hen meet the snowman's family.

SOMETHING TO READ

Other good stories and books that take place in the cold of winter:

Andersen, Hans Christian. *The Snow Queen.* Tr. by R. P. Keigwin. il. by June Atkin Corwin. Atheneum, 1968.
This is a longer story by the Danish storyteller.

Aurembou, Renée. *Snowbound.* Tr. by Anthea Bell. il. by Douglas Bisset. Abelard-Schuman, 1966.
Four children are stranded when snow buries their house.

Benchley, Nathaniel. *Gone and Back.* Harper, 1971.
Obediah's family travels from Nantucket to Kansas to Oklahoma for the great land rush. Obediah and his friend Lennie are stranded in a Plains blizzard.

Fife, Dale. *North of Danger.* il. by Haakon Saether. Dutton, 1978.
Arne attempts to journey 200 miles over frozen Norwegian wasteland to warn his father, a scientist, that the Nazis are looking for him.

George, Jean. *My Side of the Mountain.* il. by author. Dutton, 1959.
Sam spends a year all alone in the woods of the Catskills.

Haar, Jaapter. *Boris.* Tr. from the Dutch by Martha Mearns. il. by Rien Poortliet. Delacorte, 1970.
A Dutch author relates a Russian war story that takes place during a cold winter.

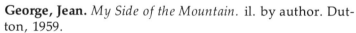

Lawson, Robert. *The Tough Winter.* il. by author, Viking, 1954.
A sequel to the author's animal fantasy *Rabbit Hill.*

Lewis, C. S. *The Lion, The Witch and the Wardrobe: A Story for Children.* il. by Pauline Baynes. Macmillan, 1950.
Behind the wardrobe lies Narnia, inhabited by talking beasts and a cold forest.

London, Jack. *The Call of the Wild.* il. by Karel Kezer. Macmillan, 1963.
This is the story of Buck, an Alaskan sled dog, who learns the "law of club and fang" during the time of the gold rush.

Morey, Walt. *Canyon Winter.* Dutton, 1972.
Peter is forced to spend a winter with an old "canyon rat" when the private plane in which he is traveling crashes in the wilderness.

Moskin, Marietta. *Day of the Blizzard.* il. by Stephen Gammell. Coward, McCann & Geoghegan, 1978.
A young girl's adventures during the great New York blizzard of 1888.

Wibberley, Leonard. *The Epics of Everest.* il. by Genevieve Vaughan-Jackson. Ariel Books, c 1954.
Various attempts to reach the top of the highest mountain in the world are detailed in this absorbing narrative.

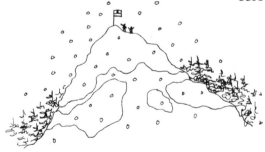

Wilder, Laura Ingalls. *The Long Winter.* il. by Garth Williams. Harper, 1953.
A pioneering family experiences a particularly severe winter.

TO MAKE

1. **CANDLE**

    Make an old-fashioned candle to light up the holiday season and the long winter ahead. The traditional way of making candles is the dipping method. Dipping a candle takes a bit of time, so it's more fun to do it as a group project. Perhaps your school class, Scout, or Campfire Girl group would like to try it during the holiday season.

YOU NEED: 128° candle wax (available at art supply and hobby shops)
a double boiler
wicking (ask the appropriate size at your shop)
a stick or pencil
a can of water
candle dyes or colored crayons (optional)

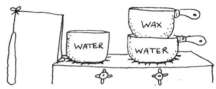

HOW TO: Heat the wax in the top of the double boiler (never over direct heat), and add coloring (if you like). Tie the string to a stick or pencil and simply dip it into the wax. Let it air dry for about 30 seconds before dipping it again. Line up everybody in the group to dip. As they wait their turn after the first dipping, their candles will dry and be ready for the next dipping when they reach the head of the line. Sing Christmas carols or other group songs as you wait in line. The last dip should be into water to smooth the candle. If your candle comes out crooked, roll it between your hands before it hardens completely.

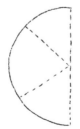

2. **SNOWFLAKE**

    Cut out a snowflake. Draw a 6" circle on plain white paper. Cut it out. Now fold the circle in half, then in thirds. Leaving the circle folded, use scissors to cut out a pattern, plain or fancy. When you open the paper, your snowflake will have a six-sided pattern just like snow from the sky. Decorate the window with a variety of snowflakes.

11

RIDDLES

STORY TO TELL

"The Flea," *in* Phyllis Fenner, ed. *Fools and Funny Fellows: More "Time to Laugh" Tales.* il. by Henry C. Pitz. Knopf, 1947.
"We shall pasture her out, this flea, and feed her enormously until she is as big as a calf." A story from Spain.

You have learned the following Spanish words while listening to "The Flea":

por Dios—"for heaven's sake!"
tortilla—Mexican pancake
Señor Pastor—Mr. Shepherd
la hormiquita—the ant
el escarabajo—the beetle
pobrecito—"poor little thing"

SOMETHING TO READ

STORIES THAT FEATURE RIDDLES:

"The Princess and Jose," *in* Anita Brenner. *The Boy Who Could Do Anything and other Mexican folk tales.* il. by Jean Charlot. W. R. Scott, 1942.
The riddle of the Sphinx is featured in this Mexican story.

"The Riddlemaster," by Catherine Starr, *in* Kathleen Lines. *The Faber Storybook.* il. by Alan Howard. Faber, 1961.
Polly must solve a riddle to keep herself from being eaten by a wolf.

"Riddles in the Dark," *in* J.R.R. Tolkien. *The Hobbit; or, There and Back Again.* il. by the author. Houghton, 1930.
This section will introduce you to a fascinating author.

COLLECTIONS OF RIDDLES:

Aardema, Verna. *Ji-Nongo-Nongo Means Riddles.* il. by Jerry Pinkney. Four Winds, 1978.
African riddles.

Bernstein, Joanne E. *Fiddle With A Riddle: Write Your Own Riddles.* il. by Giulio Maestro. Dutton, 1979.
How to turn jokes, double meanings, and famous names into riddles.

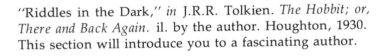

Leach, Maria. *Riddle Me, Riddle Me, Ree.* il. by William Wiesner. Viking, 1970.
Riddles from around the world.

Leeming, Joseph. *Riddles, Riddles, Riddles.* il. by Share Miller. Watts, 1953.
A collection of new and old riddles.

RIDDLES

Can you answer these?

Why are lumberjacks never hungry?

They can always eat their forest preserve.

What gets taken before you get it?

Your picture.

Why is the heart of a tree like a dog's tail?

It's farthest from the bark.

What animal took the most luggage into Noah's ark?

The elephant. He took his trunk.

What did the mother sardine say to her son when they saw a submarine?

Don't be afraid. It's just a can of people.

If you were surrounded by five giraffes, twenty horses, four lions, and six leopards, how would you get away?

Stop the merry-go-round and get off.

What did Ben Franklin say when he discovered electricity in lightning?

Nothing. He was too shocked.

What is always broken before it is used?

An egg.

What has four wheels, six legs, and two wings?

A car with two people and a bird inside.

What can be heard but not seen?

A song.

What's the difference between a lion and a flea?

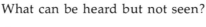

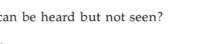

A lion can have fleas but a flea can't have lions.

13

What has 300 feet, is green with stripes and stepped on by people?

A football field.

Why is a baby like an old car?

They both have a rattle.

What kind of shoes would you make out of banana skins?

Slippers.

Where do moths dance?

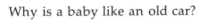

At a mothball.

How do you keep an elephant from charging?

Take away his credit card.

Why is it hard to carry on a conversation with a goat?

He keeps butting in.

What's big, green, and warty, and swims in the sea?

Moby Pickle.

What kind of dog says "meow"?

An undercover police dog.

Can an astronaut do everything a bird can do?

Not unless he can sit on a telephone wire and tuck his head under his wing.

THE SPIDER'S WEB

STORIES TO TELL

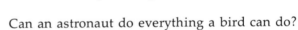

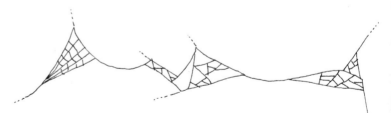

Courlander, Harold (with Albert Kofi Prempeh). *The Hat Shaking Dance and Other Ashanti Tales from the Gold Coast.* il. by Enrico Arno. Harcourt/E. M. Hale, 1962.
Choose one or more of these African stories. Particularly recommended: "Anansi Plays Dead," "Anansi's Hatshaking Dance," and "The Liar's Contest."

McDermott, Gerald. *Anansi the Spider: A Tale from the Ashanti.* il. by author. Holt, 1972.
Picture-book version of how Anansi is saved by his six sons. Gloriously illustrated with stylized symbols. This single tale has also been made into a film. (Texture Films, 1600 Broadway, New York, N.Y. 10019)

SOMETHING TO READ

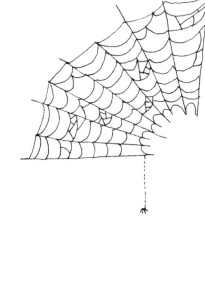

Arkhurst, Joyce Cooper. *The Adventures of Spider; West African Folk Tales.* il. by Jerry Pinkney. Little, 1964.
Trickster tales.

Freschet, Berniece. *The Web in the Grass.* il. by Roger Duvoisin. Scribner, 1972.
Narrative picture book describes the spider's life cycle.

Haley, Gail E. *A Story, A Story; An African Tale Retold.* il. by author. Atheneum, 1970.
Ananse tricks the Sky God into releasing his stories to the world. Picture-book format.

LeGuin, Ursula K. *Leese Webster.* il. by James Brunsman. Atheneum Pubs., 1979.
Leese weaves such beautiful webs that the palace in which she lives becomes a museum.

Ryder, Joanne. *The Spider's Dance.* il. by Robert J. Blake. Harper, 1981.
The life cycle of the spider is explored in this poetic picture book.

Sherlock, Philip M. *Anansi, the Spider Man; Jamaican Folk Tales.* il. by Marcia Brown. Crowell, 1954.
Light-hearted stories about Anansi from Jamaica.

Wagner, Jenny. *Aranea; A Story About a Spider.* il. by Ron Brooks. Bradbury, 1975.
The trails and tribulations of a spider who takes weaving webs seriously. Large black and white illustrations in a picture-book format.

White, E. B. *Charlotte's Web.* il. by Garth Williams. Harper, 1952.
Charlotte the spider saves Wilbur the pig from becoming bacon by weaving urgent messages in her web.

ACTIVITIES

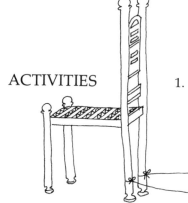

1. SPIDER RACE
Using a heavy grade of paper or posterboard, draw two large spiders on separate 5" cards. Punch a hole in the card and run a six-foot piece of string through the hole.

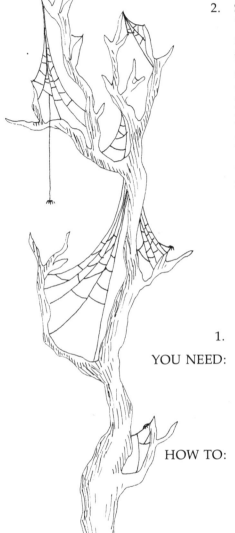

Attach one end to the legs of a chair. You and your friend stand at the other end and maneuver your spiders from you to the chair. First spider to the chair wins.

2. SPIDER WEB HUNT
This is just as much fun to set up as it is to play. You'll need lots of string. Attach one end of a ball of string to the finish point. Run the string all over the room, under chairs, around the furniture, on top of bookshelves. Do the same for each player. The more the merrier. You will have a room crisscrossed with string: a giant spiderweb. Each player takes an end and follows his string to the starting point. Be sure that you rewind the string into a ball when you've finished so that you can reuse it. You can give several small prizes, one large one, or just have fun getting tangled in the web.

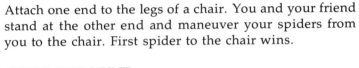

TO MAKE

1. SPIDER WEB DESIGN NAIL BOARD

YOU NEED: A wooden board or découpage board
1″ nails
Hammer
Black spray paint
A selection of colored rubber bands or thread

HOW TO: Hammer nails 1″ apart in rows over the entire board. Spray paint (black makes the best background) and dry. Now make designs by stretching the rubber bands on the nails, or use colored thread for more permanent designs.

2. CATCH A WEB

YOU NEED: Construction paper or poster board (a dark color)
Enamel spray paint (a light color)
Scissors

HOW TO: Find a spider web (outside!). Chase away the spider.
Spray both sides of the web lightly with spray paint. (Do not inhale the paint fumes.)
Hold the paper against the web and cut the guy lines of the web.
Let your spider web dry.

16

TROLLS

Trolls are large, ugly beings that live in the Scandinavian forests. Unlike the smaller Tomtes, who protect households, the trolls are enemies of people and it is rare to find a kind or generous one.

STORY TO TELL

"The Boy and the Trolls, or the Adventure," by Walter Stenstrom in *Great Swedish Fairy Tales*. Tr. by Holger Lundbergh. il. by John Bauer. Delacorte, 1973.
The boy outwits the trolls, but they have plenty of personality and are more interesting than frightening.

SOMETHING TO READ

Asbjørnsen, Peter Christen. *East of the Sun and West of the Moon; Old Tales from the North.* il. by Kay Nielsen. Doubleday, 1977.
Several stories in this collection feature fearsome trolls.

Asbjørnsen, Peter Christen and Jorgen Moe. *Norwegian Folk Tales.* Tr. by Pat Shaw Iversen and Carl Norman. il. by Erik Werenskiold and Theodor Kittelson. Viking, 1960.
Classic collection of folk stories.

Aulaire, Ingri and Edgar Parin d'. *D'Aulaires' Trolls.* Doubleday, 1972.
Full-color lithographs illustrate this encyclopedic work.

Berenstain, Michael. *The Troll Book.* il. by author. Random, 1980.
A large-size picture book details the unique habits and genealogy of trolls.

Dasent, Sir George Webbe. *The Cat on the Dovrefell; a Christmas tale.* il. by Tomie de Paola. Putnam, 1979.
The "cat" is a large white bear that scares away the wild trolls. A picture book for all ages.

De Paola, Tomie. *Helga's Dowry: A Troll Love Story.* il. by author. Harcourt, 1977.
Delightful picture book in which Helga goes off to earn her own dowry.

Krensky, Stephen. *A Troll in Passing.* Atheneum, 1980.
Morgan is a troll whose curiosity gets him into trouble.

Manning-Sanders, Ruth. *A Book of Ogres and Trolls.* il. by Robin Jacques.
Thirteen stories from Europe.

17

ACTIVITIES

1. Make a troll puppet. Use a sock for the head. Sew on yarn hair, felt eyes and ears. Use your imagination. Use your puppet to introduce the subject of trolls to a class of younger children. Learn and tell "The Three Billy Goats Gruff" to them or use a picture-book version illustrated by Marcia Brown (Harcourt, 1957) or by Paul Galdone (Seabury, 1973) in a story hour. Help a child read *Troll Country,* written by Edward Marshall and illustrated by James Marshall (Dial, 1980). This is an "easy-to-read" book in which Elsie Fay insists that trolls really exist. You can use your troll puppet just at the beginning of the story hour to introduce yourself and the story, or throughout.

2. If others in your class have also made puppets, try making up a skit about trolls that suddenly find themselves transported to the 20th century.

TO MAKE

1. A COTTON COLLAGE TROLL

YOU NEED: cotton   glue
            paper   ink
            poster board

HOW TO: Put glue on the poster board and stick on a cotton head. Draw features on paper and glue them on top.

2. A TROLL MEMORY MAGNET

YOU NEED: small magnets (available from a variety or hardware store)
            poster board
            felt-tip pens
            glue

HOW TO: Draw a small picture of a troll on a 1" x 1" piece of poster board. Cut it out and glue it to a magnet. Use the magnet to hold notes to the refrigerator in your kitchen or to a file cabinet.

AMERICANS FROM AFRICA

STORIES TO TELL

"The Goat Well" and "The Farmer of Babbia," *in* Harold Courlander and Wolf Leslau. *The Fire on the Mountain, and Other Ethiopian Stories.* il. by Robert W. Kane. Holt, 1950.
"The Goat Well" is a trickster story, and the "Farmer of Babbia" is a "ridiculous" folktale. Both stories are from Ethiopia, easy to learn, and delightful to tell.

SOMETHING TO READ

The Blacks of the United States have their roots in Africa. These books are about the African and Afro-American experience and heritage.

Adoff, Arnold, comp. *My Black Me: A Beginning Book of Black Poetry.* Dutton, 1974.
A short collection of poems by Blacks.

Bryan, Ashley. *Walk Together Children: Black American Spirituals.* sel. and il. by author. Atheneum, 1974.
Words and music of Black American spirituals illustrated with bold woodcuts.

Bryan, Ashley. *Beat the Story-Drum, Pum-Pum.* il. by author. Atheneum, 1980.
Five animal stories from Africa.

Courlander, Harold. *The King's Drum, and Other African Stories.* il. by Enrico Arno. Harcourt, 1962.
Animals and people are featured in 29 traditional African tales.

Feelings, Muriel. *Moja Means One: Swahili Counting Book.* il. by Tom Feelings. Dial Press, 1971.
Softly illustrated beginner's counting book.

Fox, Paula. *The Slave Dancer.* il. by Eros Keith. Bradbury Press, 1973.
A white boy is kidnapped and forced to play his flute on a slave ship.

Greenfield, Eloise and Lessie Jones Little. *Childtimes: A Three-Generation Memoir.* With material by Pattie Ridley Jones; photos from the authors' family albums. il. by Jerry Pinkney. Crowell, 1979.
Three Black women, a grandmother, mother, and daughter, reminisce about their childhoods.

Hurmence, Belinda. *Tough Tiffany.* Doubleday, 1980.
Tiffany is a spunky 11-year-old growing up in a close-knit family in North Carolina.

Lauré, Jason and Ettagale Lauré. *South Africa: Coming of Age Under Apartheid.* Photographs by Jason Lauré. Farrar Straus, 1980.
The lives of eight South African young adults from different ethnic backgrounds are revealed through interviews in contemporary South Africa.

Lester, Julius. *To Be a Slave.* il. by Tom Feelings. Dial Press, 1968.
Former American slaves record their memories of the "way it was."

McDermott, Gerald. *Anansi the Spider: A Tale from the Ashanti.* il. by author. Holt, 1972.
Kwaku Anansi must decide which of his six sons to reward for a job well done. Stylized drawings. (See the film. Texture Films, Inc. 1600 Broadway, New York, N.Y. 10019.)

Murphy, E. Jefferson. *Understanding Africa.* il. by Louise E. Jefferson. Crowell, 1978.
An overview of Africa today.

Myers, Walter Dean. *It Ain't All for Nothin'.* Viking, 1978.
Twelve-year-old Tippy must make the choice between his father and "right" in New York City's Harlem.

Price, Christine. *Talking Drums of Africa.* il. by author. Scribner, 1973.
How African tribes use drums to speak and sing.

Sebestyen, Ouida. *Words by Heart.* Little, 1979.
The first Black family in a pioneer western farm community pays a tragic price for trying to make a better life.

Smucker, Barbara. *Runaway to Freedom: A Story of the Underground Railway.* il. by Charles Lilly. Harper, 1978.
Two slave girls hide during the day and move at night towards "North" and freedom.

Taylor, Mildred D. *Roll of Thunder, Hear My Cry.* Dial Press, 1976.
Cassie Logan and her family survive in the American South.

ADULT REFERENCE: **Coughlan, Margaret N.** *Folklore from Africa to the United States; an annotated bibliography*. Library of Congress, 1976. Lists sources of African tales and traces their relationship to stories carried to the West Indies and America. Listed by region.

ACTIVITY   Play Kasha Mu Bukondi (pronounced Kah-sha Moo Boo-koh-ndeé) or Antelope in the Net, a game played in Zaire.

Play this game in a gym or outdoors. The larger the group the better. One player is chosen to be the antelope. The others form a net (a circle) around him. They hold hands and shout "Kasha Mu Bukondi! Kasha Mu Bukondi!"

The antelope tries to break out of the net by crawling under, over, or running through the tightly held hands. When he breaks free, the others chase him. The player who succeeds in catching the antelope becomes the new antelope, and the game begins again.

TO MAKE   1.   YOUR OWN AFRICAN BEADS (from American ingredients)

YOU NEED: ½ cup white flour   2 tablespoons vegetable oil
            ¼ cup whole wheat flour   food coloring
            ¾ cup salt   toothpicks
            2 teaspoons powdered   string
            alum (available from a
            drugstore)

21

HOW TO: To make the clay, combine salt, flour, and alum in a pot. Slowly add water and cook over low heat while stirring. The clay will become rubbery. Remove the pot from heat and add vegetable oil. When the mixture is cool, add food coloring and mix with your hands. Shape the clay into round or tubular beads. Use a toothpick to poke a hole large enough to insert string. String the beads while they are still moist on a heavy string to wear as a necklace or bracelet.

2. A SHIELD

YOU NEED: thick cardboard cut from a carton
tinfoil (paperbacked tinfoil, such as that used in Christmas wrap, works best because it takes glue better, but you can use the kitchen kind)
glue
black liquid shoe polish

HOW TO: Cut the background in the shape of a shield from the side of a cardboard box. Then cut simple shapes, also from cardboard, and glue them to the shield. Spread glue over the entire surface of the shield, including the raised portions. Cover it with tinfoil. The shapes will stand out as though carved. Cover the tinfoil with black liquid shoe polish. Spread the shoe polish over the shield and then wipe most of it off to give an antique effect.

SPRING SKIPPING

STORY TO TELL

"Elsie Piddock Skips in her Sleep," by Eleanor Farjeon *in* Association for Childhood Education International. *Told Under the Magic Umbrella: Modern Tales of Fancy and Humor.* il. by Elizabeth Orton Jones. MacMillan, 1967. *Also in* Eileen Colwell, ed. *A Storyteller's Choice: A Selection of Stories with Notes on How to Tell Them.* il. by Carol Barker. Walck, 1965. *Also in* Eleanor Farjeon, *Martin Pippin in the Daisy Field.* il. by Isobel and John Morton-Sale. Lippincott, 1937.
Elsie learns to outskip everyone, even the fairies. This is a long story to learn, but well worth the effort.

SOMETHING TO READ

JUMP ROPE: **Abrahams, Roger D.,** ed. *Jump-Rope Rhymes: A Dictionary.* Pub. for the American Folklore Society by the Univ. of Texas Press, 1969.
A collection of more than 600 authentic jump-rope rhymes.

Mitchell, Cynthia. *Halloweena Hecatee and Other Rhymes to Skip to.* il. by Eileen Browne. Crowell, 1979.
Collection of enchanting rhymes. The author counts how many skips each rhyme contains (*see* p. 246 for a presentation idea).

Skolnik, Peter L. *Jump Rope!* Photographs by Jerry Darvin. il. by Marty Norman. Workman, 1974.
Rope tips, rope play, rope games.

Worstell, Emma Vietor, comp. *Jump the Rope Jingles.* il. by Sheila Greenwald. Macmillan, 1961.
Children's collection of jump-rope rhymes.

OTHER GAME BOOKS: **Arnold, Arnold.** *World Book of Children's Games.* il. by author. World Pubs., 1972.
Directions for hundreds of indoor and outdoor games.

Caney, Steven. *Steven Caney's Kids' America.* il. by Ginger Brown. Photographs by the author. Workman, 1978.
Games, activities, and crafts for children from colonial times to today.

Ferretti, Fred. *The Great American Book of Sidewalk, Stoop, Dirt, Curb, and Alley Games.* Photographs by Jerry Darvin. Workman, 1975.
The rules for many street games, including Cans Up, Pottsie, Giant Steps, and Curb Ball.

Ferretti, Fred. *The Great American Marble Book.* Photographs by Jay Good. Workman, 1973.
Everything you ever wanted to know about playing with marbles. Directions for more than 50 games.

Grunfeld, Frederic V., ed. *Games of the World: How to Make Them, How to Play Them, How They Came to Be.* Design, illustration, and game models by Pieter Van Delit and Jack Botermans. Holt, 1975.
Lavishly illustrated, clearly documented compendium.

Langstaff, John and Carol. *Shimmy, Shimmy Coke-ca-pop! A Collection of City Children's Street Games and Rhymes.* Photographs by Dan Macsorley. Doubleday, 1973.
City games illustrated with black and white photographs.

23

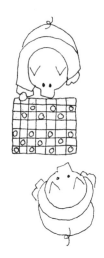

Lombardy, William and Bette Marshall. *Chess for Children, Step By Step: A New, Easy Way to Learn the Game.* Photographs by Bette Marshall. Chess art by John Schnell. Little, 1977.
Easy-to-follow directions teach you how to play chess.

New Games Foundation. *The New Games Book.* Ed. by Andrew Fluegelman; il. with photographs. Dolphin, 1976.
"New" games, created by the New Games Foundation, that emphasize fun, not athletic prowess or competition.

Ravielli, Anthony. *What Are Street Games?* il. by author. Atheneum, 1981.
History of street games and rules for playing them.

Rockwell, Anne. *Games (And How to Play Them).* il. by author. Crowell, 1973.
Big, colorful illustrations show how to play such traditional games as Sardines, Yankee Doodle Cracker, and Coffeepot.

Wagenvoord, James. *Hangin' Out: City Kids, City Games.* Photographs by author. Lippincott, 1974.
Games kids play in the city. Illustrated with black and white photographs.

Weigle, Marta. *Follow My Fancy: Jacks and Jack Games.* il. by Jessica Hoffmann Davis. Dover, 1970.
Rules for games to play with jacks.

Wood, Clement and Gloria Goddard. *The Complete Book of Games.* Doubleday, 1940.
A huge collection of rules for playing indoor and outdoor games.

ACTIVITIES

1. JUMP!
    Begin today to jump rope every day. One hundred jumps will make you feel like a ski racer, prizefighter, or astronaut.

2. COLLECT RHYMES
    The rhymes that youngsters chant while jumping rope are passed from child to child. Your mother may have jumped rope to the same jingle that you know. Collect your own folklore by writing down all the jump-rope rhymes you can remember. Your friends can help you. Make a little book of illustrated rhymes to keep for your children or to publish in your school magazine. If you don't jump rope, try the same thing with cheerleading chants, counting-out rhymes, or any other game rhymes.

3. ALPHABET BALL GAME—the way Susan played it in Brooklyn, New York. My cousin Susan taught me this game when I lived in New York with her family while attending the fifth and eighth grades in Brooklyn. Susan always won. I'm still practicing in hopes that someday I will beat her. It can be played alone or with a friend, indoors or outside. You will need a small ball (about the size of a tennis ball) and lots of imagination. Make up a short jingle for each letter of the alphabet. As you bounce the ball, swing your leg over it while reciting the words beginning with the selected letter.

    Example:

    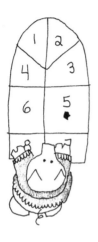

    A my name is *Alice*
    My husband's name is *Abe*
    We come from *America*
    We sell *apples*

    B my name is *Betty*
    My husband's name is *Bob*
    We come from *Barbados*
    We sell *bananas*

    C my name is *Caroline*
    My husband's name is *Carl*
    We come from *Canada*
    We sell *cucumbers*

4. KICK THE CAN—the way we played it in Washington, D.C.
    You will need a can (a big paint can or coffee can works best) and a group of friends.
    Place the can about 10 feet from a home base. One person is "It." "It" faces away from the players and counts to 50 while they run and hide. When "It" has finished counting, he turns around. The object of the game is for the players to get to home base without being tagged by "It." If a player is tagged by "It" before reaching home base, that player is out and must remain a prisoner by the can. However, if another player runs in and kicks the can, any previously tagged prisoners are freed to resume the game, *unless* "It" can grab the can and touch home before the player who kicked the can does.

5. ROADS AND STREETS—the way we played it at camp in Vermont.
    You will need a group of friends.

25

One person is the cat and the other is the rat.
The rest of the group form into lines of at least three each, and hold their arms straight out with hands touching to form roads. The cat chases the rat up and down the roads. At any time the rat can call out "change." The players then turn at a 90° angle, creating the streets so that the rat cannot be tagged.

6. PUMP PUMP PULL AWAY—the way Arvid played it in Owatonna, Minnesota.
"It" stands in the middle of a playing field. All the players stand on one end of the field. "It" yells, "pump, pump, pull away," and all the players try to run past "It" to the other end of the field. Those players that "It" manages to tag then hold hands with "It" in the center of the field for the next run through. The winner is the player who has not been tagged after all the remaining players have been tagged and are forming a wall by holding hands.

DOGS

STORY TO TELL

"Jean Labadie's Big Black Dog," *in* Natalie Savage Carlson. *The Talking Cat, and Other Stories of French Canada.* il. by Roger Duvoisin. Harper, 1952. *Also in* Eileen Colwell. *A Second Storyteller's Choice: A Selection of Stories, With Notes on How to Tell Them.* il. by Prudence Seward. Walck, 1965.
An imaginary dog helps teach a neighbor a lesson. This is a long story and you may want to read it to the children, but try to find the time to learn it. The story is improved when told with a French-Canadian accent.

SOMETHING TO READ

Burnford, Sheila. *The Incredible Journey.* il. by Carl Burger. Little, 1961.
Two dogs and a cat travel 250 miles to reach home and their beloved master.

Cleary, Beverly. *Ribsy.* il. by Louis Darling. Morrow, 1964.
Henry Huggins' dog is lost and finds a variety of new owners.

Cole, William. *Good Dog Poems.* il. by Ruth Sanderson. Scribner's, 1981.
A collection of poems about dogs.

Gipson, Fred. *Old Yeller.* il. by Carl Burger. Harper, 1956.
Old Yeller, a frontier dog, is a companion to Travis while his father is away running herd.

Hall, Lynn. *Dog of the Bondi Castle.* Follett, 1979.
Based on the legend "The Dog of Montargis," this is a story about justice in medieval France.

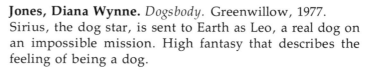

Jones, Diana Wynne. *Dogsbody.* Greenwillow, 1977.
Sirius, the dog star, is sent to Earth as Leo, a real dog on an impossible mission. High fantasy that describes the feeling of being a dog.

Morey, Walt. *Kävik, the Wolf Dog.* il. by Peter Parnell. Dutton, 1968.
A dog makes his way from Seattle to Alaska, returning to the family he loves.

Rawls, Wilson. *Where the Red Fern Grows: The Story of Two Dogs and a Boy.* Doubleday, 1961.
A sad and very popular novel about Billy Colman's yearning for a pair of coonhounds and the fate that awaits them.

Stern, Mark. *It's a Dog's Life.* Atheneum, 1978.
Big Business as seen from a dog's point of view. Picturebook format.

ACTIVITIES

1. Treat a dog extra special this week. Take your own or your neighbor's dog for a particularly long, companionable walk.

2. Hire yourself out as a dog-walker in the neighborhood (put up advertisements). Donate your profits to the local Humane Society.

3. Read aloud to your dog. A good choice is Beverley Conrad's *Doggy Tales: Bedtime Stories for Dogs* (il. by Joel Schick. Dell, 1980).
   I wish I had written this book. Stories included are "Rumpleddogskin," "Jack and the Bonestalk," and "The Story of Little Red Riding Dog."

27

4. Find the dog in the puzzle below by blackening all the squares marked with the numeral 1.

6	8	5	7	9	2	7	3	4	9	6	7
3	9	2	9	3	4	2	9	3	4	5	8
2	8	7	1	1	8	3	8	5	3	9	3
3	9	1	1	1	2	6	7	4	6	5	3
2	8	1	1	1	3	8	9	3	5	1	6
8	2	7	1	1	7	3	8	2	4	1	9
9	3	8	1	1	1	1	1	1	6	1	4
2	4	9	1	1	1	1	1	1	1	8	7
3	5	5	1	1	1	1	1	1	1	6	5
4	6	8	1	1	5	6	2	1	1	4	8
7	3	9	1	1	4	8	3	1	1	3	8
8	4	5	1	1	3	7	8	1	1	2	6
9	3	1	1	1	4	6	1	1	1	5	3
4	6	1	1	1	3	7	1	1	1	6	4
3	7	3	8	6	9	4	3	7	2	7	9

TO MAKE

1. PET PILLOWCASE
Decorate a pillowcase with batiking for your favorite pet—or person. This project will take more than an hour. Put aside an afternoon, or do a little at a time over several days.

YOU NEED: white 100% cotton pillowcase
batiking wax, candle wax, or a mixture of half paraffin and half beeswax
double boiler
paintbrush
fabric dye (available in variety stores) or batik dye (available in art supply stores). Dye should be a cold-water type.
newspapers
iron
baking soda

HOW TO: Spread the pillowcase on a thick layer of newspapers, or on a piece of cardboard on newspapers. Gently heat the

wax in a double boiler with water in the bottom (never heat wax directly over a flame). When the wax is hot enough, it will lose its milky appearance. Do not let it become so hot that it smokes. Always keep baking soda nearby in case of fire.

Paint a design with the wax on the pillowcase. Make sure that you saturate the fabric on both sides with the wax. The dye will not stick to the wax.

When the wax has dried, pull the pillowcase away from the newspapers. In a sink or pan, dip it into the dye bath that has been mixed according to directions on the package. Some of the dye will rinse out later, so dye it a shade darker than you desire.

If you want a two-color pillowcase, reheat the wax and paint another design. Then wet the pillowcase and add a second color. This color will mix with the first one. For instance, blue on top of yellow will make green.

Let the pillowcase air-dry completely. Then remove the wax by ironing the fabric between two pieces of newspaper or paper towels. As each newspaper or towel becomes saturated with wax, replace it with a fresh one. Iron the pillowcase until the paper no longer absorbs wax. Won't your dog, or your friend's dog, be excited?

HINT: Don't have enough time, or not feeling artistic enough for batik? Decorate a pillowcase with permanent felt-tip pens.

2.   ORIGAMI DOG
Make an origami head of a dog. Use a square piece of paper and fold it according to the diagram below.

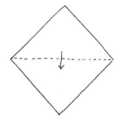 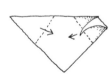 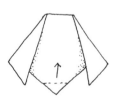 

3.   BISCUIT BOX
Decorate a box or a big tin can, such as a coffee can, to hold dog kibble or dog biscuits. Give it to your favorite dog.

4.   PET ACCESSORIES
Make a gift for a dog using this book for ideas: *Make Your Pet a Present*, by Eve Barwell (il. by Giulio Maestro. Lothrop, 1977). In it, directions are given for simple gifts, such as a quilt, a dinner mat, and a braided leash.

29

TREAT   COOKIES FOR DOGS

YOU NEED: 3½ cups all-purpose flour   1 package dry yeast
           1 cup rye flour   2 cups chicken or beef
           1 cup corn meal   stock
           2 cups wheat germ   1 beaten egg and a little
           ½ cup powdered nonfat   milk, combined
              dry milk

HOW TO: Combine all dry ingredients. Add stock gradually, mix-
         ing thoroughly. Shape into balls and roll out on a floured
         board. Cut out cookies using a cookie cutter in the shape
         of a dog bone. Brush tops with the egg and milk mixture.
         Bake 40–45 minutes at 300°. Cool and store in airtight
         container. These cookies may be frozen.
         To make a dog-bone cookie cutter, draw a bone on stiff
         cardboard, then cut it out. Place the pattern gently on the
         rolled-out dough, and cut around it with a knife.

HINT: This recipe makes a lot of cookies. Plan to give some to
       your dog's best friend.

Stories To Tell—
Collections and Single Tales

A good story to tell never becomes dated, so you can search the library shelves for new and old stories. There are hundreds of folklore and story collections to choose from, and I have listed my favorites for you. I have not included annotations since you will have to read through the stories in order to find one that suits your particular temperament and style. I have, however, indicated if a book contains just a single tale (S), and if the story or stories might be considered advanced (A). An advanced story is often a literary tale that is an authored selection that should be memorized. Stories that should be told using an accent or that are written in dialect may also be more suitable for advanced storytellers.

Andersen, Hans Christian. *Tales and Stories by Hans Christian Andersen.* tr. by Patricia L. Conroy and Sven H. Rossel. University of Washington Press, 1980. (A)

Alexander, Lloyd. *The Town Cats and Other Tales.* il. by Laszlo Kubinyi. Dutton, 1977.

Asbjørnsen, Peter C. and Jorgen E. Moe. *East o' the Sun and West o' the Moon.* tr. by George Webbe Dasent. il. by Erik Werenskiold. Dover, 1970.

Babbitt, Natalie. *The Devil's Storybook.* il. by author. Farrar, Straus, 1974.

Bang, Molly, comp. *The Goblin's Giggle and Other Stories.* il. by author. Scribner, 1973.

Bleecker, Mary Noel, comp. *Big Music, or, Twenty Merry Tales To Tell.* il. by Louis S. Glanzman. Viking, 1946.

Brenner, Anita. *The Boy Who Could Do Anything & Other Mexican Folk Tales.* il. by Jean Charlot. W. R. Scott, 1942.

Bryan, Ashley. *Beat the Story-Drum, Pum-Pum.* il. by author. Atheneum, 1980.

Carlson, Natalie Savage. *King of the Cats and Other Tales.* il. by David Frampton. Doubleday, 1980. See also *The Talking Cat and Other Stories of French Canada.* il. by Roger Duvoisin. Harper, 1952.

Chambers, Aidan. *Funny Folk: A Book of Comic Tales.* il. by Trevor Stubley. Heinemann, 1976.

31

Chase, Richard, ed. *Jack Tales.* il. by Berkeley Williams, Jr. Houghton, 1971. See also *Grandfather Tales: American-English Folk Tales.* il. by Berkeley Williams, Jr. Houghton, 1948. (A)

Child Study Association of America. *Castles and Dragons; Read-to-Yourself Fairy Tales for Boys and Girls.* il. by William Pène Du Bois. Crowell, 1958.

Colwell, Eileen. *A Storyteller's Choice; A Selection of Stories, with Notes on How to Tell Them.* il. by Carol Barker. Walck, 1964. See also *A Second Storyteller's Choice; A Selection of Stories, with Notes on How to Tell Them.* il. by Prudence Seward. Walck, 1964. (A)

Courlander, Harold, and Wolf Leslau. *The Fire on the Mountain and Other Ethiopian Stories.* il. by Robert W. Kane. Holt, 1950. See also *The Hat-shaking Dance and Other Tales from the Gold Coast.* il. by Enrico Arno. Harcourt, 1957.

Corrin, Sara and Stephen. *Stories for Eight-Year-Olds and Other Young Readers.* il. by Shirley Hughes. Prentice-Hall, 1973.

Craig, M. Jean. *The Donkey Prince.* il. by Barbara Cooney. Doubleday, 1977. (S)

Curtis, Edward S. *The Girl Who Married A Ghost, and Other Tales From the North American Indian.* Collected and with photographs by Edward S. Curtis. ed. by John Bierhorst. Four Winds, 1978.

De Paola, Tomie. *Fin McCoul: The Giant of Knockmany Hill.* il. by author. Holiday, 1981. (S)

Fenner, Phyllis, comp. *Fools and Funny Fellows; More "Time to Laugh" Tales.* il. by Henry C. Pitz. Knopf, 1961. See also *Ghosts, Ghosts, Ghosts; Stories of Spooks and Spirits, Haunts and Hobgoblins, Werewolves and Will-o'-the-Wisps.* il. by Manning de V. Lee. Watts, 1958.

Fillmore, Parker. *The Shepherd's Nosegay: Stories from Finland and Czechoslovakia.* ed. by Katherine Love. il. by Enrico Arno. Harcourt, 1958.

Gág, Wanda. *Millions of Cats.* il. by author. Coward-McCann, 1928. (S)

Gág, Wanda. *Tales from Grimm.* tr. and il. by Wanda Gág. Coward-McCann, 1936. See also *More Tales from Grimm.* Coward-McCann, 1947.

Galdone, Paul. *King of the Cats: A Ghost Story by Joseph Jacobs.* il. by author. Houghton, 1980. (S)

Hatch, Mary C. *13 Danish Tales.* il. by Edgun. Harcourt, 1947.

Haviland, Virginia, ed. *North American Legends.* il. by Ann Strugnell. Collins [distributed by Philomel Bks.], 1979.

Hoke, Helen, ed. *Devils, Devils, Devils.* il. by Carol Barker. Watts, 1976. See also *Dragons, Dragons, Dragons.* il. by Carol Barker. Watts, 1972.

Housman, Laurence. *The Rat-Catcher's Daughter: A Collection of Stories.* ed. by Ellin Greene. il. by Julia Noonan. Atheneum Pubs. 1974. (A)

Hughes, Richard. *The Wonder Dog: The Collected Children's Stories of Richard Hughes.* il. by Anthony Maitland. Greenwillow Bks. 1977. (A)

Jacobs, Joseph. *English Fairy Tales.* il. by John D. Batten. Dover, 1967.

Jaquith, Priscilla. *Bo Rabbit Smart for True: Folk Tales from the Gullah.* il. by Ed Young. Philomel, 1981. (A)

Kelsey, Alice Geer. *Once the Hodja.* il. by Frank Dobias. Longmans, 1943.

Kendall, Carol and Yao-wen Li. *Sweet and Sour; Tales from China.* il. by Shirley Felts. Seabury [distributed by Houghton], 1979.

Kennedy. *The Parrot and the Thief.* il. by Marcia Sewall. Little, 1974. (S) See also *Come Again in the Spring* il. by Marcia Sewall. Harper, 1976. (A) (S)

Laurin, Anne. *Little Things.* il. by Marcia Sewall. Atheneum Pubs., 1978. (S) See also *Perfect Crane.* il. by Charles Mikolaycak. Harper, 1981. (S)

Nic Leodhas, Sorche. *Heather and Broom: Tales of the Scottish Highlands.* il. by Consuelo Joerns. Holt, 1960. (A)

Lester, Julius. *The Knee-High Man and Other Tales.* il. by Ralph Pinto. Dial Press, 1972.

Phelps, Ethel Johnston. *The Maid of the North; Feminist Folk Tales from Around the World.* il. by Lloyd Bloom. Holt, 1981. See also *Tatterhood and Other Tales; Stories of Magic and Adventure.* il. by Pamela Baldwin Ford. Feminist Press, 1978.

Rettich, Margret. *The Silver Touch and Other Family Christmas Stories.* il. by Rolf Rettich. Morrow, 1978.

Ross, Eulalie Steinmetz, ed. *The Buried Treasure, and Other Picture Tales.* il. by Josef Cellini. Lippincott, 1958. See also

33

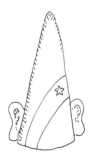

The Lost Half-Hour: A Collection of Stories. il. by Enrico Arno. Harcourt, 1963.

Saunders, Susan. *Wales' Tale.* il. by Marilyn Hirsh. Viking, 1980. (S)

Scribner, Charles. *The Devil's Bridge.* il. by Evaline Ness. Scribner, 1978. (S)

Singer, Isaac Bashevis. *Zlateh the Goat, and Other Stories.* tr. by author and Elizabeth Shub. il. by Maurice Sendak. Harper, 1966.

Tashjian, Virginia A., comp. *Juba This and Juba That; Story Hour Stretches for Large or Small Groups.* il. by Victoria de Larrea. Little, 1969.

Uchida, Yoshiko. *The Magic Listening Cap: More Folk Tales From Japan.* il. by author. Harcourt, 1955. See also *The Sea of Gold.* Scribner, 1965.

Wales, Katie, ed. *A Book of Elephants.* il. by David McKee. Parents Mag. Press, 1977.

Wilde, Oscar. *The Selfish Giant.* il. by Joanna Isles. McGraw, 1979. (A) (S)

Williams, Margery. *The Velveteen Rabbit; or, How Toys Become Real.* il. by William Nicholson. Doubleday, 1926. (A) (S)

Wolkstein, Diane. *The Magic Orange Tree and Other Haitian Folktales.* il. by Elsa Henriquez. Knopf, 1978.

Yolen, Jane. *Dream Weaver.* il. by Michael Hague. Collins, 1979. (A)

Storytelling for Volunteers— A Minicourse

Anyone can tell a story. I'm absolutely convinced that if you can talk you can learn to tell a story. Obviously there are those wonderfully talented people who can hold you in a story spell with the simplest of folktales, but even ordinary everyday people can present a story with verve and enthusiasm.

It would be especially wonderful if more students were taught to tell stories so that they, in turn, could present stories to their peers and to younger and older students, and perhaps turn them on to books. In this country, there have been several successful "read-aloud" programs, in which middle-grade children have been scheduled by primary teachers to come and present picture books to their classes (an outline of a program is given on pages 143–6).

A slightly more ambitious undertaking would entail training storytellers in a more structured program. Presented as a minicourse, it would probably be run as an elective, an after-school activity or a vacation club project, so I've kept the sessions short. You can adjust the schedule according to your needs.

The same schedule can be followed to introduce adult volunteers and club groups to the art of storytelling. The ultimate aim of the training 35

sessions is for students to be able to present stories effectively to audiences. The stories will introduce children to literature and the delights of reading as well as the heritage of folk stories.

Telling stories can also afford children an opportunity for oral performance in front of an audience, which helps develop public speaking skills. For those children interested in drama, storytelling is the perfect vehicle, for they can perform without needing sets, lighting, costuming, or a cast of thousands.

Here is an outline schedule for teaching and introducing a group to traditional storytelling. A half-hour or 40-minute class session will be adequate if you are able to limit your group to ten or twelve enthusiastic students.

SESSION I—DEMONSTRATION

The purpose of this session is to show your potential students what storytelling is all about. This can be an informal demonstration with you or a guest telling stories, or a more formal presentation that doubles as a program and recruitment session.

If you are the only storyteller, you run the risk of having your group emulate your style exclusively simply because they are unaware that there are other ways to tell stories. You might, therefore, recruit guest storytellers from local libraries, the school system, or theater groups. After you've given one minicourse, you will also be able to recruit former students as demonstration storytellers. Try to arrange to have a varied program. Ideally, the storytellers will each have a distinct style and will give students an interesting range of possibilities by telling folktales, literary fairy tales, and short stories. I always like to invite at least one good storyteller who gets the story across without being overwhelming, so that everyone in the room gets an "I can do that" feeling.

Assignment for students: Collect riddles and jokes to share.

SESSION II—GETTING ACQUAINTED THROUGH JOKES, RIDDLES AND PERSONAL STORIES

It is extremely important that your group feel as relaxed with each other as they would sitting around someone's kitchen chatting. In fact, if you can meet in a less formal atmosphere than a traditional classroom you will achieve this aim more quickly. If you are in a classroom, arrange the chairs in a circle so everyone can easily see and relate to each other.

Start this session by letting people introduce themselves and tell about their interests. Try not to have the participants simply go around in a circle one right after the other, but encourage them to ask questions about what the others are saying. "Have you been skiing for a long time? Does anyone else ski?" Don't rush these introductions. They are very important to relax the group.

You have asked the group to bring riddles and jokes with them to exchange. Make sure that you have brought some source material to share on the spot. Let the students read from the books if they feel shy about participating without a book as a crutch. There is usually one person in the group who loves to tell jokes and can break a strained atmosphere, but if you do have trouble getting the group going, fall back on the personal introductions and try to get each person to tell a personal anecdote. Some will be more articulate and vocal than others, but usually you will be able to point out after this initial exchange that all the members of the group have been telling stories for years in general conversation and that they have just told stories during this session.

Assignment for students: Prepare a familiar folktale to tell to the group. If you use a book, to refresh your memory, read the story through only once so that you will be telling the story in your own words.

SESSION III—TELLING A SIMPLE FOLKTALE

In this session the students tell familiar folktales, such as "The Three Billy Goats Gruff," "Little Red Riding Hood," and "The Three Bears," or camp stories. It is better if the participants don't follow a written text too closely because the primary objective of this session is to build confidence. However, I have found that students, particularly adult students, have forgotten the nursery tales and are a bit hazy as to who did what when. So now I suggest that students refer to a book, but that they read through the text only once to establish the order of events in their minds. Then they should use their own words to tell the story.

This session is interesting if a variety of tales are told, but if the same story is told by four people it is also interesting, because you will immediately see stylistic variations emerging. Ask at the beginning of the ses- 37 sion which stories will be told so that you can space out retellings of the same story during the session. Be encouraging. Find something nice to say to each person.

Assignment for students: Learn a poem by heart.

Assignment for group leader: If you can, collect various poetry books for circulation among the group. If you are familiar with the books, give a short oral annotation for some of the books to make selection easier (see the bibliography on pages 257–66).

SESSION IV—POETRY

Each participant recites a poem to the group. In my college classes, this was the first assignment that I gave. This was to emphasize that poetry is difficult to learn because it must be learned word for word. The students recited their poems to the rest of the class while they were being videotaped. The idea was to make the experience a little bit uncomfortable so that subsequent assignments seemed incredibly easy and a whole lot less threatening. Since this was the first formal assignment, I took the opportunity to critique the class as a whole. In *every* class, for thirteen years, the same mistakes were made, so I always had examples that everyone could relate to. For instance, in every class there was someone who spoke too quickly or too slowly. There was almost always at least one person who went blank or forgot part of a poem, and someone who spoke too softly or who mispronounced a word. I mentioned these common faults and always tried to sound easygoing and nonthreatening, as though they were everyday occurrences, which they were. As the participants recited, I took brief notes, and if there was some glaring correctible fault that related to one particular person's delivery I tried to discuss it with the student privately.

The practice of videotaping the class was really worthwhile because students got to see everyone's presentation twice—during and after the general critique—*and* they got to see themselves, which was very beneficial to the learning procedure.

Assignment for students: Bring a collection of stories to class and be ready to discuss them.

SESSIONS V AND VI—EXPLORING SOURCES FOR LONGER STORIES

These two sessions are for learning about possible sources of storytelling materials. A lecture can be given by the leader or reports by the students. When I first started to teach storytelling I had my students each choose a country, region, or folklore collector and do an oral report to the class with an accompanying bibliography. This worked beautifully and each student was then well versed in the folklore of one country and had a general impression of other regions. However, after a few years I decided that the time the students spent researching their projects would have been better spent learning a story to add to their repertoires. I then did the lecturing myself simply to familiarize the students with possible sources.

It seems to me that a compromise between these two methods might be the best, particularly if you, the teacher, are not an expert on the literature yourself. Bring to Session V a variety of story collections and assign one book to each student to discuss in the sixth class. Allow time during Sessions V and VI for students to browse through the collections for a story to learn. Looking for the perfect story is the best way to familiarize yourself with the literature. Some students might be lucky enough to find a suitable story almost immediately, but most will have to search and read several books to find a story they want to learn. Emphasize that each person will be attracted to a different story. A reserved person might enjoy telling a romantic myth, whereas a vivacious student might prefer learning a rollicking noodle-head story. When you are presenting a book to the group, try to point out some of its storytelling features. For instance, a well-written literary tale might need to be memorized, but a folktale might need only the characters' names and order of incidents memorized.

After everyone has chosen a story to tell, you might give hints on learning the story. Children currently in school will not need your ideas on learning since they have probably developed their own techniques for learning material. Adults, however, may need reassurance that they can attempt a story at all, since they may have been out of the memorization business since they left school. Learning stories takes practice.

Assignment for students: Learn a story.

39

SESSION VII—PRESENTATION OF STORIES

This is a working session. There should be no audience except other members of the class. Each student presents a story to the class. When everyone has told a story, you can critique some of the major faults to bring the individual deliveries up to performance level. Some teachers let the students discuss each other's performance; I prefer class comments to be of a general nature, since I strongly believe that self-confidence is the key to good storytelling.

During this presentation session I try to encourage a performance feeling by turning the lights low, using a storytelling candle, and encouraging the students to treat this session with respect.

If you have a good group, you might want to plan a public performance in place of the next meeting, or you might want to send the students home to practice and perform for each other one last time.

Assignment: Meet with your storytelling group and practice.

SESSIONS VIII AND IX—PERFORMANCE

Arrange to break the group up into twos or threes, depending on the lengths of the stories and performance levels. It may be that not every student has reached an adequate performance level and you or they may not want them to go out to another group to perform. If you feel that everyone should get a chance to perform, have the less accomplished member introduce the performers and perhaps recite a poem. Arrange to have storytellers give a program of stories and poems to younger children, adult groups, or classmates.

A Storytelling Contest

Once you have taught children the techniques of storytelling, why not hold a contest? When librarians in Long Island, N.Y., decided to do this, they established a joint committee representing libraries in Nassau and Suffolk counties. The public libraries acted as coordinating units and the schools cooperated. Two levels of competition were offered: Level I for grades 3 and 4, and Level II for grades 5 and 6.

Contest promotion began late in the fall; in December and January children were registered and librarians helped them select and practice their stories. The first competitions were held in February, at town libraries. Regional and county runoffs followed, and in May the winners performed at the annual Storytelling Institute, at the Palmer Graduate Library School (C. W. Post Center, Long Island University). They received engraved trophies, donated by Citibank.

Nassau County judges and winners, 1980 (from left): Carolyn Butler, librarian, West Hempstead Public Library; Sylvia Carter, "Kidsday" Editor, *Newsday*; Jill Edmondson, Uniondale—Level II winner; Kathleen Sheehan, Children's Services Consultant, Suffolk Cooperative Library System; Marian Sanito, Lynbrook—Level I winner; Rosalie Zacharias, librarian, Hempstead Public Library; Esther Hautzig, author; M. B. Goffstein, author/illustrator. (Tri-County Photo Service, Inc.)

The following guidelines were sent to librarians:

Librarians in participating libraries will have the responsibility for helping children select, learn, and practice their stories under supervision. They will need to be sure that the stories selected are appropriate and worth the time the children will be putting in to learning them. Books containing stories suitable for learning should be prominently displayed. Librarians will want to discuss with the children the proper techniques of storytelling, including: eye to eye contact, voice control, timing, memorization, pronunciation and enunciation. Differences between storytelling and dramatization should be carefully explained.

Librarians are encouraged to work with local school librarians to the greatest extent possible. For some, this may include joint planning and conducting of the contest. It may include schools running initial contests, with winners competing in a local run-off at the public library. At the very least, school librarians should be notified of the contest, their help enlisted in promoting it, and their ideas incorporated to whatever extent possible. Librarians may wish to initiate registration with school visits that include storytelling demonstrations.

Librarians will be responsible for selecting judges at the local level. It is recommended that six judges be selected, three for each category of competition, and that these judges come from outside your community; preferably they will be librarians, teachers, authors, or other professionals in the field. Prior to the contest, librarians should discuss with the judges contest guidelines, criteria and the evaluation form.

The purposes of the storytelling contest were to introduce children to literature and the art of storytelling; encourage their interest in reading; broaden their knowledge of folklore; assist in the development of their public speaking skills and provide an outlet for practice of these skills; and promote the library and its resources to children and their parents.

Thousands of children participated through twenty-seven Nassau County and twenty-two Suffolk County libraries, and the contest was hailed as a big success. The organizers, exhausted but triumphant, said, "We'll do it again, but . . . let's wait a year."

Multimedia Storytelling Packets

Once upon a time, my friend Mary Norman and I started exchanging story and program ideas. Whenever she got an idea she would call me, and whenever I tried something new I called her. Since neither of us sews or is outstandingly artistic, we started scouring the city for craftspeople who could carry out our ideas. When lending and borrowing materials back and forth became too cumbersome ("Help, my car won't start, I can't bring you the carrot") or impossible ("Sorry, I'm using the anteater puppet in Florida this week") we decided to buy two of everything. Our husbands suffered ("You can't possibly fit another stuffed animal in that cupboard"), and our food allowance got smaller and smaller as our puppet and prop bills got larger and larger.

We thought that many other librarians must have the same problems: lack of money, time, expertise, or even ideas for book programs. We yearned for a central place from which to borrow materials. With an LSCA (Library Services and Construction Act) grant our dream became a reality. A pilot project in Washington and Clackamas counties in Oregon enabled us to hire a children's consultant and have enough money to produce twenty-two multimedia storytelling packets to circulate in the two counties.

You can see the proof of the success of the project by visiting the county libraries, which store the packets, in July, when all the packets are checked out, including the Christmas and Halloween boxes.

Since librarians and teachers around the country have expressed interest in our project, I will tell you a little about how we accomplished our goal. Incidentally, I introduced our packet idea in workshops in Saudi Arabia and Australia, and now American children in Dhahran, Saudi Arabia, and Australian children in Queensland, Australia, are enjoying the same storytelling programs that children appreciate in Lake Oswego, Oregon.

You will need volunteer help and some money. In Australia two women wrote a grant proposal for this packet idea and were turned down with the suggestion that they resubmit with a larger budget. They did and then received $2,500 to fulfill their goal of making 44 storytelling packets. Don't

43

let that sum frighten you. You can begin modestly, and your success may enable you to get more funding.

These packets are made up with large storage boxes, purchased from the local stationery store. On the lid of each box is pasted a typed label showing the title of the packet, its theme, and a list of the contents of the box. Inside each box are specially ordered new copies of the featured picture books and at least one storytelling item. Mary and I decided in advance what each theme was to be, what major item was to go into the box, and then commissioned a person to make that object.

We then held four all-day college credit workshops for school and public children's librarians and some parents. At the workshops we demonstrated storytelling techniques with the media objects and described in detail what we thought a well-rounded storytelling program might entail. We invited guests to demonstrate some of their story-related activities. Then we asked the 75 attendees to divide themselves into groups of three and four people. Each group was handed a media object that we had ordered and the accompanying theme books. They were to take the packets home and add to them in any way they wished. We suggested that they look for poems, fingerplays, or songs. Or perhaps they could make another media story for their packet, add craft or recipe suggestions, or maybe create ways to publicize their packets. Some groups opted to do their own packets from scratch. We anticipated heavy holiday use of the packets, so we had several duplicates of the Halloween, Thanksgiving, and Christmas packets. Each group made two of everything since we wanted to house the packets in each county office.

I think the involvement of the workshop participants not only improved the initial packets but also made the people feel much more a part of the creative side. Their enthusiasm was the best publicity for the packets. They learned how to put additional packets together themselves and intimately knew the contents of at least one packet. Putting the names of all the contributors on the packets added to a competitive spirit that made each group strive to make their packets as imaginative and as professional as they could. We gave the workshop people a liberal period of several months to complete their tasks and then we met for a packet party. At this all-day event (it should have been several days to allow ample time) each group showed the larger audience what was contained in each packet, familiarizing everyone with each and every packet. Groups were asked to write introduction ideas for their programs. These directions, along with a list of the contents of each box, were collected and printed in a booklet that was distributed to each member library. This booklet serves as a catalog from which to order the packets and also enables even neophyte storytellers to give a program after only minimal preparation.

The individual groups had splendid ideas for the packets. Some groups were so creative and industrious that they added two or three media story ideas to the packets, as well as games, exhibits, and cassettes. Such a variety of materials has made some of the packets useful for several different story sessions. Some participants were inspired to create their own story boxes, and some also made minipackets containing books and just one storytelling object, with room for additions. The boxes created in this workshop are meant to be used with the preschool and primary grades, but I hope that, someday, this idea will be adopted for middle and upper grades.

Perhaps you will be inspired by our experience to make your own original packets, but I will list a few of the books and materials in the boxes to give you a general idea of what we did, and include sections of some of the booklets. My only real hints for producing packets are to have (1) a 45 good administrator, like Donna Selle, who can find and get money, (2) an enthusiastic and creative group of "packet packers," and (3) a packet director, like my friend Mary Norman, to prod those who are sluggish in getting their packets ready and to pull the whole project together.

Following are some representative ideas from the booklet that accompanied our storytelling packets, *Happy Storytelling; a Guide to the Multimedia Packets* (By Mary Norman, Director, Multimedia Packets, and Caroline Feller Bauer, Children's Consultant. Published under the auspices of an LSCA grant, Clackamas/Washington Counties Children's Consultant Grant. P.O. Box 5129, Aloha, Oregon 97005, 1978).

Note: The storytelling boxes were meant to supply beginning and experienced storytime presenters with a prepared set of materials. Please remember that at the core of each box filled with puppetry, felt board, and posters were the BOOKS themselves.

46

NAUGHTINESS

(Program by Cathy Mann, Sally Johnston, and Karen McCune)

BOOKS

De Paola, Tomie. *Strega Nona.* il. by author. Prentice-Hall, 1975.

Harper, Wilhelmina. *The Gunniwolf.* il. by William Wiesner. Dutton, 1967.

McCloskey, Robert. *Blueberries for Sal.* il. by author, Viking, 1948.

Mosel, Arlene. *Tikki Tikki Tembo.* il. by Blair Lent, Holt, 1968.

STORYTELLING MATERIALS

Tin pail and "blueberries" for use with *Blueberries for Sal.* (Artificial grapes are used as blueberries.) Used to demonstrate the sound "plink, plank, plunk" of the blueberries in the story.

Three knitted finger puppets to use when telling *The Gunniwolf.*

A small cauldron and "spaghetti" to use with *Strega Nona.* (Surgical tubing available from a medical supply house is used for spaghetti.) Samples of pasta. Children are familiar with spaghetti but need to be shown other types of pasta (macaroni, noodles) to learn what *pasta* means.

Posterboard figures for use on a Velcro board when telling *Tikki Tikki Tembo.*

Copies of poems with a naughtiness theme.

INTRODUCTION IDEAS

Give children one blueberry each to use as a ticket to the story hour, then proceed with a brief introduction about blueberries, picking them, eating them, etc. Follow the introduction by sharing *Blueberries for Sal.*

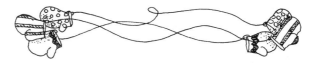

Use a poem or nursery rhyme to introduce the theme of naughtiness, such as, "Three Blind Mice" or "Three Little Kittens."

47

ACTIVITY IDEAS FOR EACH STORY

Blueberries for Sal

Go on a blueberry hunt with the children. Have blueberries hidden throughout the storytelling area and give each child a small pail or sack in which to collect the berries.

Creative dramatics: Have children pretend they are the bear or Sal and have them act out what they would do if they were lost from their mothers.

Pass out the berries, and each time the storyteller says "ker-plunk" the children can pass the pail and drop in their berries.

As the storyteller is telling the story, she can drop the berries in the pail at the appropriate times in the story. Have the children listen for the "ker-plunk" sound and then the sound the berries make when they are dropped in a full pail.

The Gunniwolf

Divide the group of children into Wolves and Little Girls. Have them participate in the storytelling by having the Wolves repeat with storyteller, "Why for you move" and "Hunkercha." Little Girls repeat, "I no move" and "Pit-pat, pit-pat" and "Kum-kwa."

Have flowers scattered throughout the storytelling room, then have children "pick" the flowers after the story to take home with them.

Pass out Wolf bookmarks for children to take home with them. (A sample was enclosed in the packet.)

Strega Nona

Creative dramatics: Pretend to stir a pot and slowly pull rubber noodles out of the pot at the appropriate time.

Give each child a balloon after the story. Have the children blow up the balloons and then stuff them under their shirts and pretend they are as full as Big Anthony.

Give each child different kinds of noodles to take home.

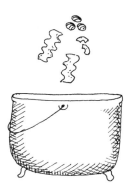

Feel the difference between textures of various starchy foods, such as pastas, rices, and potatoes. You could have an example of cooked and uncooked food for more contrast.

Tikki Tikki Tembo

Ask the children their names and write them on the chalkboard under *Tikki Tikki Tembo,* etc. Compare the number of letters and the different lengths of each name to show how long Tikki's name actually is.

Some possible artifacts for the children to take home with them:

A miniature well and ladder from a novelty store.

Cards with each child's name and Tikki's entire name on it.

STORY-TABLE DISPLAY IDEAS

Blueberries for Sal—berry display, fresh if in season or plastic berries from the dime store (blueberries, strawberries, boysenberries, etc.).

The Gunniwolf—a vase of orange, pink, and white flowers.

Strega Nona—pasta display, e.g., lasagna noodles, seashell macaroni, elbow macaroni, egg noodles, spinach noodles, corkscrew macaroni, and spaghetti.

Tikki Tikki Tembo—Chinese doll display. You will probably have to find someone to lend you dolls, unless you want to start your own collection.

TREATS

Blueberries for Sal—fresh or frozen blueberries, blueberry tarts, blueberry pie, or different types of berries.

Strega None—spaghetti, if you are game to make it.

Tikki Tikki Tembo—fortune cookies or almond cookies.

CRAFTS

Mittens for the Three Little Kittens (pattern enclosed in packet)

49

Felt bookmarks—Sample in packet. To be made from scratch or finished by children.

Flowers for *The Gunniwolf:* Kleenex, tissue-paper, or paper flowers. (For instructions on how to fold-and-cut paper flowers, see *Handbook for Storytellers,* Caroline Feller Bauer, American Library Association, 1977, p. 306)

MONSTERS

Program by Francis Brady, Janis McGraw, Helen Parent, and Peggy Sharp)

BOOKS

Crowe, Robert L. *Clyde Monster.* il. by Kay Chorao. Dutton, 1976.

Mayer, Mercer. *There's a Nightmare In My Closet.* il. by author. Dial Press, 1968.

Prelutsky, Jack. *The Snopp on the Sidewalk, and Other Poems.* il. by Bryon Barton. Greenwillow Bks, 1977.

Sendak, Maurice. *Where the Wild Things Are.* il. by author. Harper, 1963.

Stone, Jon. *The Monster at the End of This Book.* il. by Mike Smollin. Western Pub. Co., 1977.

Zemach, Harve. *The Judge: An Untrue Tale.* il. by Margot Zemach. Farrar Straus, 1969.

STORYTELLING MATERIALS

Large fake-fur monster hand puppet

Small felt monster finger puppet

Magnetic board figures for use with *There's A Nightmare In My Closet*

Ditto master; mix and match monsters

Poster: Monsters from Greek myths

Jack-in-the-box for use with the poem "The Lurpp on the Loose"

Paper and felt masks to use as examples for craft activity

Cassette of music to use with *Where the Wild Things Are*

SAMPLE PROGRAM

What does a monster look like? Ask the children to tell you what a monster looks like. Have each child give one characteristic of a monster. Draw the features with col-

ored chalk on a piece of paper or on a blackboard as the children suggest them.

Say that you have a friend who is an expert on monsters who would like to take a look at the monster the children have described. Show the large monster puppet. After examining the picture, the puppet gives his approval and says that all monsters certainly do not look alike. He says that he has a friend he would like the children to meet who looks different from any other monster they've seen.

Read *The Judge* aloud. After hearing the story, the monster puppet says that not all monsters have to be big. He's heard of one that isn't very big at all but certainly causes his share of trouble.

Using the finger puppet, recite "The Gibble," from *The Snopp on the Sidewalk.* After the poem, the monster puppet says that some of his friends show up in strange places.

Present the poem "The Lurpp Is On The Loose," from *The Snopp on the Sidewalk.* Open the jack-in-the-box as you say the last line of this poem. (See page 203 for the text of the poem.)

The monster puppet asks the children if they know where the monsters live. Of course they live *Where the Wild Things Are.* Read this aloud.

Activity: After the children have heard this story they make wild-thing masks using paper bags or felt and fabric scraps and then dance to recorded music. (The packet contained examples of masks that were easy to make in order to help the reader plan for this activity.)

The monster puppet says that he hopes the children have enjoyed meeting some of his friends. He is sure that his friends have enjoyed meeting the children. He then asks, "What do you do with a green monster?" Answer: "Wait until it ripens."

TREAT

Monster Cookies. For a recipe, see *Handbook for Storytellers,* by Caroline Feller Bauer. American Library Association, 1977, p. 344.

CRAFT

Add-a-monster. Divide the children into groups of five. Have a scrap box of collage materials for each group. Give each child a piece of paper. Give the children two minutes to start to make a monster by gluing materials on a piece of paper. At the end of two minutes, the children

51

pass their monsters to the next child and spend two more minutes working on another monster. Each monster is finished after all five children have worked on it for two minutes each.

ACTIVITIES

Dragons and Other Animals, A Walters Art Gallery Coloring Book. Have children color the pictures for a contest. Find poems that best accompany each picture. Have the children write their own poem or story about one of the monsters. Enlarge the pictures on an overhead projector for a special project.

DISPLAY

Monsters of the Greek myths poster. Exhibit monster books. Bibliography is included in packet.

SOUVENIR

Monster stickers from Educational Supply House.

BACKGROUND MUSIC

The In Sound From Way Out by Perrey/Kingsley, Vanguard Records, VSD-79222.

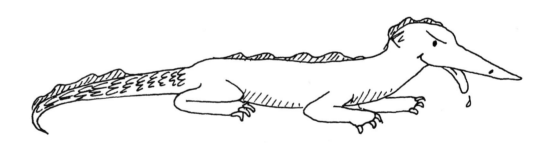

Several more storytelling boxes and their contents are listed to give you some inspiration, but you might find it more advantageous to start your own boxes from scratch. Use your own favorite books and ideas for story presentation.

CATS

(Program by Linda Denney and Wendy Swanson)

BOOKS

Gág, Wanda. *Millions of Cats.* il. by author. Coward, 1928.

Gantos, Jack. *Rotten Ralph.* il. by Nicole Rubel. Houghton, 1976.

Ipcar, Dahlov. *The Cat Came Back.* il. by author. Knopf, 1971.

Kent, Jack. *The Fat Cat; a Danish Folktale.* il. by author. Parents Mag. Press, 1971.

STORYTELLING MATERIALS

Two pom-pom cats.

Pussywillows for display.

Pictures to use on magnetic board with *The Fat Cat.*

Cat poems laminated on poster board.

Five knitted finger puppets to use with *Millions of Cats.* Each puppet will represent a number in the refrain "hundreds of cats, thousands of cats, millions and billions and trillions of cats."

DIRECTIONS for finger puppets, by Linda Herkhof.
Use size 3 knitting needles (other size knitting needles may be used and puppet size can be adapted to finger).
BODY: Cast on 12 stitches (or adapt to finger diameter) in 4-ply yarn. Work 25 rows in garter stitch. *Do not* cast off, but thread yarn in blunt needle and pass through stitches as you remove them from knitting needles. Pull tight. With wrong side out, stitch top and back seam. Turn right side out. Stuff top with Fiberfill. Run a thread around neck and pull tight. Knot or stitch securely.

EARS: Cast on 3 stitches. Decrease to 2 stitches, then decrease to 1. *Do not* cast off, but run blunt needle through last stitch and attach to head.

LEGS: Cast on 3 stitches, decrease to 2. Stitch 5 rows. *Do not* cast off. Run threaded blunt needle through last row and attach to body. Make 2 legs.

TAIL: Cast on 1 stitch. Knit 15 rows. *Do not* cast off. Run blunt needle through last row and attach to body.

FEATURES: Separate 4-ply yarn into single strands. Using blunt needle, embroider eyes. Embroider nose and mouth

53

with black yarn. For whiskers, take short strand of 4-ply yarn and run through face on either side of nose. Separate plys and stiffen with white glue. When glue dries, trim whiskers.

Make 5 cats: grey, white, black; yellow and brown tiger cat and black and white spotted cat.

TIGER CAT: Alternate 2 rows yellow and brown yarn throughout body. Make 26 rows long. Make appendages and ears yellow.

SPOTTED CAT: Knit white cat. Embroider black spots on body using 1 strand from 4-ply yarn and blunt needle. Make one arm and ear black and one arm and ear white.

JAM SESSION

(This was just one of three packets dealing with music and noise. Program by Carol Ginzburg and Joanne O'Brien.)

BOOKS AND STORIES

"The China Spaniel," in Richard Hughes, *The Spider's Palace and Other Stories*. il. by George Charlton. Looking Glass Library, 1960.

Kraus, Robert. *Ludwig. The Dog Who Snored Symphonies.* il. by Vip. Dutton, 1973.

McGovern, Ann. *Too Much Noise.* il. by Simms Taback. Houghton, 1967.

Spier, Peter. *Gobble, Growl, Grunt.* il. by author. Doubleday, 1971

STORYTELLING MATERIALS

Handmade rhythm instruments. For instructions on how to make them, see *Handbook for Storytellers*, by Caroline Feller Bauer (American Library Association, 1977, p. 260).

Wooden slot drum.

Magnetic board figures for use with *Too Much Noise*.

Bag of "pink and green silver paper toffee" to exhibit with "The China Spaniel."

STONES AND ROCKS

(Program by Phoebe Cannill, Anne Nolte, and Carole Schneider)

BOOKS

Baylor, Byrd. *Everybody Needs a Rock.* il. by Peter Parnall. Scribner, 1974.

Brown, Marcia. *Stone Soup: An Old Tale.* il. by author. Scribner, 1947.

Lionni, Leo. *Alexander and the Wind-up Mouse.* il. by author. Pantheon Bks., 1969.

Steig, William. *Sylvester and the Magic Pebble.* il. by author. Windmill Bks., 1969.

STORYTELLING MATERIALS

A box with a purple pebble inside to use for introducing *Alexander and the Windup Mouse.*

Paperback book pictures cut from *Sylvester and the Magic Pebble* for use on magnetic board.

A green velvet box with a pebble inside to display when you tell *Sylvester and the Magic Pebble.*

PEOPLE PACKETS

(Compiled by committees of children's librarians for the Public Library of Columbus and Franklin County)

CONTENTS OF PACKETS

DOCTOR: *Medical Kit*

Stethoscope	Cotton balls
Bathroom Scale	Nurse puppets
Bandaids, bandages	White coat
Tongue depressors or popsicle-sticks	Doctor bag

Books

Rockwell, Harlow. *My Doctor.* (Macmillan Pub. Co., 1973)
Scarry, Richard. *Nicky Goes to the Doctor.* (Western Pub. Co., 1978)
Watson, Jane Werner. *My Friend the Doctor.* (Western Pub. Co., 1972)
Wolde, Gunilla. *Betsy and the Doctor.* (Random House, 1978)

55

FARMER: *Farmer Kit*

Wood dairy barn   Straw hat
Toy farm animals   Neckerchief
Tractor

Books

Duvoisin, Roger. *Petunia.* (Knopf, 1950)
Farmer in the Dell. (Little, 1978)
Hewett, Anita. *Mrs. Mopple's Washing Line.* (McGraw, 1966)
Holl, Adelaide. *Rain Puddle.* (Lothrop, 1965)
Nakatani, Chiyoko. *My Day on the Farm.* (Crowell, 1975)
Stiles, Norman. *Farmer Grover.* (Western Pub. Co., 1977)
Tresselt, Alvin. *Wake Up, Farm.* (Lothrop, 1955)
Zalben, Jane. *Basil and Hillary.* (Macmillan Pub. Co., 1975)

FIREFIGHTER: *Firefighter Kit*

Firefighters' hats   Child's rubber raincoat
Flashlight   Child's rubber boots
Small bucket   Toy fire truck
Rope   Finger play

Books

Barr, Jene. *Fire Snorkel Number 7.* (Whitman, 1965)
Brown, Margaret Wise. *The Little Fireman.* (Addison-Wesley, 1952)
Gergely, Tibor. *Great Big Fire Engine Book.* (Western Pub. Co., 1950)
Trivers, James. *The Red Fire Book.* (Prentice-Hall, 1974)

DENTIST: *Dentist Kit*

Large toothbrush
Large teeth
Coloring pages from *ABC's of Dental Care* (American Dental Association)
Dental aprons
"Fishing for Healthy Teeth" game, including a fishing pole and paper teeth
White coat

Books

Barnett, Naomi. *I Know a Dentist.* (Putnam, 1978)
Bate, Lucy. *Little Rabbit's Loose Tooth.* (Crown, 1975)
Kessler, Ethel. *Our Tooth Story.* (Dodd, 1972)
Rockwell, Harlow. *My Dentist.* (Greenwillow Bks., Morrow, 1975)
Schaleben-Lewis, Joy. *The Dentist and Me.* (Raintree Pubs., 1977)

Babysitting Boxes

Adapting the idea of multimedia packets, pack some boxes for teenage or adult babysitters to take with them on the job. Use these ideas as springboards for your own boxes.

PIGS
(for children 5–7 years old)

BOOKS TO SHARE

Getz, Arthur. *Humphrey, the Dancing Pig.* il. by author. Dial, 1980.
In clear, bright watercolors, Humphrey dances to lose weight.

Hauptmann, Tatjana. *A Day in the Life of Petronella Pig.* il. by author. Sunflower, 1978.
Large-size picture book with cut-out pages showing a charming pig.

Lobel, Arnold. *A Treeful of Pigs.* il. by Anita Lobel. Morrow, 1979.
A lazy farmer is fooled by his wife into jointly caring for their pigs.

McPhail, David. *Pig Pig Grows Up.* il. by author. Dutton, 1980
Pig Pig tries to remain a baby.

Rayner, Mary. *Mr. & Mrs. Pig's Evening Out.* il. by author. Atheneum, 1976.

Stevens, Carla. *Pig and the Blue Flag.* il. by Rainey Bennett. Seabury, 1977.
Pig is not good at sports but learns that "capture the flag" can be fun.

For the babysitter:

"Perfection of Orchard View," by Walter D. Edmonds, in *The Night Raider and Other Stories.* Little, 1980.

GAMES TO PLAY

HIDE THE PIG

Provide a miniature pig in the box. "It" starts the game by hiding the pig in plain sight (on a picture frame, next to a lamp) while the other players leave the room. As each player spots the pig, he or she sits down. The first player to find the pig is "It" the next time. This can be played with two or more players.

CAPTURE THE FLAG

Directions for this game are given in *Pig and the Blue Flag*. You need at least three players.

RHYME A PIG

Ask the children to think of words that rhyme with *pig*. The babysitter takes a turn, too.

> Pig in a wig.
> Pig doing a jig.
> Pig riding a rig.

ACTIVITY

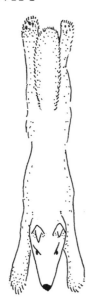

PUT ON A PLAY

Three ways to present "The Three Little Pigs"

1. Use finger puppets—knitted ones from the babysitting box or paper ones, made with the child's help.

2. Use your bare fingers to represent the pigs and your hands for the successive houses.

3. Utilizing the techniques of creative dramatics, act out the story without props.

The babysitting box should contain a copy of the story or the book. Here are two of my favorite versions:
Three Little Pigs. il. by Paul Galdone. Seabury, 1970.
The Three Little Pigs. il. by Erik Blegvad. Atheneum, 1980.

FRIENDS
(for children 5–7 years old)

BOOKS TO SHARE

Sharmat, Marjorie Weinman. *The 329th Friend.* il. by Cyndy Szekeres. Four Winds, 1979.
Emery finds out that he is his own best friend.

Gantos, Jack and Nicole Rubel. *The Perfect Pal.* Houghton, 1979.
Vanessa is looking for just the right pet and finds one in Wendell, the pet store salesman.

Baylor, Byrd. *Guess Who My Favorite Person Is.* il. by Robert Andrew Parker. Scribners, 1977.
An adult and a child verbally explore their favorite things.

BOOKS FOR THE CHILDREN TO READ

Here are two books that have short chapters that could be read aloud or by the children alone, and returned to the babysitter's box at the end of the play.

Child Study Children's Book Committee at Bank Street. *Friends Are Like That!* il. by Leigh Grant. Crowell, 1979.
Short stories on friendship for beginning readers.

Fremlin, Robert. *Three Friends.* il. by Wallace Tripp. Little, 1975.
Cat, Squirrel, and Pig are friends despite their faults.

ACTIVITIES

1. FRIENDSHIP LIST

   Use the above five books to help the children make up these lists:

   List all the things you like about yourself.
   List the things you like about a good friend.
   List animals that would make good pets and tell why.
   List your favorite color, place to live, plaything, etc. and tell why it is your favorite.

2. DRAW A FRIEND

   The child draws a picture of an inanimate object (for instance, a tree, a teapot, or a toy) and then dictates how the object can be considered a friend. You write what the child says under the picture.

II PROGRAMS

In this section, I have given outlines for putting programs together on specific themes. I have included a variety of subjects to show the great range of themes that can be used to introduce books. With the information provided you should be able to duplicate the programs, adapt them to your needs, or use them as springboards for developing your own programs.

This collection comprises holiday programs, single programs inspired by one theme or author, and continuing programs. I have included celebrations for both legal and fanciful holidays, to show how you can use special occasions to promote books. The single programs take from twenty minutes to an hour to present and are to be used as one-time presentations to a group in a library, classroom, or clubhouse setting. Continuing or series programs are those activities that are presented not in a single session, but rather over a period of weeks or even months.

While the primary objective of these programs is to introduce a group to literature, each program also offers an opportunity to improve listening skills, art experiences, or subject awareness.

The Audience and Types of Programs

A program can be as simple as a father reading to his child in a corner of the library or as complex as a highly publicized community Fourth of July celebration. Each activity, no matter how simple, requires some sort of planning. The purpose of the programs that appear in this book is to introduce children, young adults, and adults to the joy and wonder of books. Programs, in the broadest sense, enable us to combine the reading of books with some of our daily activities. Not everyone would agree that everything we do should revolve around books, but few would doubt that a love of books can enhance the enjoyment of life. These programs suggest ways to present books by playing games, telling stories, reading aloud, doing arts and crafts, and engaging in creative dramatics.

ADULTS

Children are usually introduced to books and reading by adults. Therefore, it is imperative that adults, particularly parents, become aware of the resources in our libraries and of the variety of information and fun available through books. One way to make parents more aware of books and libraries is to give programs that are book oriented. This does not mean that every program has to be about books, but rather that every program should include some sort of discussion about related books.

Adults can have book clubs just as children do. In addition, other clubs and organizations—church, PTA, sorority, or service—have meetings in which time is devoted to book discussion. A suitable presentation at one of these meetings might be anything from a formal booktalk on the latest books to a program on a particular theme, such as gardening.

As an interested speaker, you will in many cases have to take the initiative of offering your services to an adult group simply because they are unaware of your expertise and because they haven't thought of having a book program. Here is a list of contacts that you might consider:

PTAs
Religious groups
Civic groups
Veterans' organizations
Public libraries
Volunteer bureaus
Friends-of-the-library groups
Retirement homes and communities, senior citizen groups
Special interest groups—boat clubs, motorcycle clubs, dog breeders, garden clubs, art associations, bridge clubs, theater groups, athletic clubs, exercise groups
Hospitals—staff and patients

Resort hotels
Bookstores
College libraries
Company picnics
Museums

Any adults who work with children. In addition to teachers and librarians, who can be addressed at "in-service" meetings, don't forget: Head Start workers, Scout leaders, zoo workers, museum guides, lifeguards, day-care workers, parents in babysitting co-ops, staff at institutions for orphaned or delinquent children

61

CHILDREN

Children can be reached through day-care centers, schools, playgrounds, special interest groups, and service organizations such as 4-H or the Camp Fire Girls. You might want to plan a book program for a particular group much as you would for adults. Or you might want to form your own group for book activities on a continuing or series basis. This group might be involved in only one program activity, such as listening to stories or participating in creative dramatics. Some children might enjoy membership in a book club that involves itself in a single activity, such as "book discussion." Others might want a club that includes varied activities, for instance, storytelling, puppetry, games, and booktalks—all related to books. The crafts and booktalk sections in this book will give you ideas to use in such a club.

YOUNG ADULTS

Junior high and high school students are also receptive to programs. Just as with children and adults, their particular interests must be taken into account. The interests of the young adults are ever-changing, and the adult planning the programs must be aware of the specific needs and interests of the group. New methods of introducing books, such as the use of videotape, are particularly effective with many young adults.

MIXED AGE GROUPS

Sometimes a program, particularly one open to the public, will attract a mixed age group. A Chinese shadow show, for instance, might draw an audience of adults interested in an art form, young adults interested in Eastern culture, and children interested in a good story. You may welcome such a diverse audience for some programs. However, if you want to limit a group by age or interest, make sure to specify in your promotional material to whom the program is geared.

FAMILIES

Many of the programs in this book can be easily adapted for home use. As a mother, father, or friend of a family, you might plan an at-home program for one family, or you might want to plan an evening in a library for a group of families.

SPECIAL PROGRAMS

Occasionally you will want to plan a special program to attract new patrons to your library or organization and reinforce its presence in the community.

Some examples of special programs are a Mexican fiesta, a circus day, and a book week celebration. Programs can also center on holidays, ranging from one-day celebrations, such as Washington's birthday, to longer and more extravagant celebrations of holiday seasons, such as Christmas. Changes in seasons might also inspire programs. In the summer, when many peoples' attention is directed to outdoor activities, you might present a program focusing on summer readings that relate to those activities. Book clubs and book parties might take on a special character for vacations.

FIELD TRIPS

The term *field trip* is used whenever a group leaves its usual meeting place—the classroom, library, or clubhouse—to visit another location. Field trips often involve extra planning. Arrangements need to be made for transportation, as well as chaperones, money for entrance fees, and sack lunches. Those of you who are already connected with an organization are probably well aware of the extra problems involved in taking a field trip. You probably also know the excitement and satisfaction of being on the spot to make firsthand observations. In fact, if you reflect back to your own school days, you will find that the field trips often stand out as the most memorable times.

Parents, too, can take their children on field trips, although they would call them outings or visits. Try to plan to share a relevant book before or after the trips. Visiting the zoo? Read an animal book. Going to the circus? There are many books about the "big top." In fact, there are good books about almost any place you might go.

I once worked for a boarding school that took a week each spring to explore the Four Corners area in the Southwest. On the eve of the trip, a faculty member read from a pioneer's account of that same journey made over a hundred years before. The next day we viewed the area with renewed interest and a greater appreciation of our forebears.

A hooked rug shows *The Very Hungry Caterpillar*
(Norman, OK, community project).

CRAFT PROGRAMS

A craft activity can be an effective means of demonstrating the worth of how-to-do-it books to a group. I urge you not to turn your book club into an arts and crafts class unless the crafts are book related. It is my feeling that craft activities should relate to books. For example, bulletin boards should promote a book or books, clay models should represent book characters, and puzzles should have a book theme.

If you are demonstrating a craft, be prepared to show various stages of the process: the materials needed, the steps in making it, and the finished product. If your group is going to make something together, make sure you have provided enough tools and materials for everyone.

Program Planning

After you have made a reading game, decorated a kleenex box with decoupage, or read a few books on one topic, you might want to undertake the more ambitious task of putting together an entire program integrating activities and books. As the group leader, you are like the producer-director thinking in terms of an entire theatrical production. Perhaps

A bag of stuffed toys for *Millions of Cats*.

you will start by reading aloud from a book and then have your audience participate in an art project. The next time you may want to tell the story rather than read it aloud. Begin to add flavor to your programs. Show a film, put on a play, give out favors. Maybe you have a favorite recipe for a snack that would be appropriate to prepare. Can you think of any music to complement the theme of the book program or to play in the background? Maybe you could decorate the program room in advance. Posters, exhibits, or a personal collection might add to the occasion.

If you are out shopping, at a flea market, or attending a carnival or concert, and you see a figurine, a craft item, a demonstration, or a lecture, and you think to yourself, "That would make a good program item," you are becoming a convert. But don't forget the books. They should always be the focus of your program.

As a program planner, you must acquaint yourself with hundreds of new books each year in order to keep informed. In addition to these, you will undoubtedly find older worthwhile titles you haven't read. Now that you are planning book programs, you have another reason for reading books besides just "keeping up." New books may give you a program idea, but you shouldn't forget the older books that have proved successful over the years.

Your first programs should treat subjects with which you are familiar. Do you collect stamps? Press flowers? Attend horse shows? Almost any activity you engage in is potentially a theme for a book program. Activities that may seem ordinary to you will seem fascinating to an audience if you present your subject in an organized fashion and with enthusiasm. After you have given presentations on your own hobbies, branch out and find new interests, using library resources to help you.

Can you really give a program on a subject you know only a little about? Why not? The purpose of most programs is to introduce a group to books or to the available resources. There is no reason you can't admit that the information you have comes from books, and that the group can learn as much as you have simply by reading the same books.

One of the aims of this book is to show you ways of presenting or introducing books to groups. Combining your knowledge of books with effective techniques of presentation should give you a good start toward getting people and books together.

First, decide on a theme—for instance, dogs, spring, happiness, the circus, or war. Create a program around the theme using books and possibly other media, as well. Look over the following suggestions when you plan a program to see if you have considered all of the possibilities in order to have the most successful program possible.

BEFORE THE PROGRAM—CHECKLIST

AUDIENCE

Decide who the audience will be. Consider the ages of the people in the group, their background, their potential interests, and the size of the group.

EQUIPMENT

Are you going to the group or is the group coming to you? If you are going to them, you will have to ask whether they have or can get the things you may need. There is no use planning a slide exhibition if you're not sure there is a slide projector available.

Elaborate programs should probably be left for your home ground, where you know you can get what you need. If you insist on putting on a three-ring circus in foreign territory, be prepared to adjust your thinking and hold on to your sense of humor. It is possible to avoid some failures by taking backup equipment, such as your own projector and screen. Or at least take along an extension cord, a long cord for a remote control (so you can stand in front of the audience), an extra lens that will zoom or adjust to any distance from the screen, and an extra bulb.

If you need exhibit space, tables, or bulletin boards, you should arrange for them. Also keep in mind that, if the group is large, you will need extra exhibit space for showing any small items, unless you plan on passing them around (which is sometimes awkward with a large audience). Plan for enough chairs, proper lights, and a microphone if you need one.

PUBLICITY

There is no point in having a program without an audience. This doesn't mean that there has to be a mob. Ten to twenty attentive people make a better audience than three hundred uninterested people. Often you will have a built-in audience in the form of a club or class. Even though the audience is a captive one, publicity is still valuable because it keeps the rest of the community aware of your activities and makes the event more special for those involved. Promotion can range from a simple oral announcement in a classroom to a full-scale campaign.

THE PROGRAM ITSELF—CHECKLIST

The main portion of the program may consist of one or more of the following:

PANEL

Three to five people can be assigned to give brief introductions on the same subject. They might even be asked to respond to each other's remarks. Be sure to limit their speaking time, so the program does not become too long.

BOOKTALK

Present a talk on one or more books. This is rather like an oral book review.

POETRY

There is almost always room for a poem or two in a program. Take the time to memorize your poem so that you can recite it rather than read it.

SLIDES

Using slides to illustrate a lecture is becoming more common—and for good reason. You can take your audience out of the lecture hall to a foreign country, show them a close-up of something small or rare, and let them actually see what you are talking about. Slides are available commerically, but usually you will want to take your own, or copy pictures from books or prints.

TRANSPARENCIES

There are advantages to using an overhead projector instead of a slide projector. It can be used with the lights on. You can show homemade or commercial transparencies, you can write or draw on them with a grease pencil, and you can add overlays.

FILM

Some programs consist entirely of a film showing. Others include a film as one portion of a balanced program. If, however, you advertise that a major film will be shown, you can't expect the audience to be too fascinated with a lecture before or after unless you've specified a film and lecture.

VIDEOTAPE

Television is being used more often in group presentations. It is especially useful for showing small objects that can't otherwise readily be seen by a large group, or large or fragile objects that would be difficult or impossible to transport into a classroom or library. In addition, a guest can "visit" the group over and over without appearing in person, or an event that took place in the past can be shown now. Don't use television unless there are enough monitors (at least one for every twenty-five people) that are mounted high enough so that everyone in the group can see well.

DEMONSTRATION

Part or all of your program might center on some sort of demonstration, such as cooking. Make sure the audience can see everything you do. If the entire process would take too long to show, prepare parts in advance. It is sometimes effective to show the finished article first and then proceed with the demonstration.

CRAFTS

Working with crafts can take the form of either a demonstration or an audience participation program in which the audience learns how to make something. (A fee covering the cost of materials can be charged to participants.)

GUEST PRESENTATION

A guest may be the main attraction of your program. The guest might use any one of these program ideas as part of a presentation.

LECTURE

A prepared lecture or an extemporaneous speech revolving around a particular subject can be all or part of a program.

STORYTELLING

A story should be memorized or learned well enough in advance to be told without the use of notes. It might be told with the use of props or such equipment as a slide projector.

READING ALOUD

A passage or an entire story or chapter might be read aloud in the course of a booktalk or speech. Reading aloud, rather than storytelling, is usually reserved for those passages that must be quoted exactly or that are too long to recite without using notes.

PUPPETRY

A puppet or a puppet show can be used with children or adults to entertain or inform.

DRAMA

A formally-prepared skit or play might highlight a program or, in fact, constitute the entire program.

CREATIVE DRAMATICS

Informal skits or a play can be performed. Role playing (acting out real-life situations) can also be used.

MUSIC AND DANCE

Live or recorded music might be used to open or close a session, or as part of the formal program. The special feature of a program may be a dance performance.

DISCUSSION

A discussion is effective only if the group is small—fifteen or fewer. The ideal group is one in which people know each other or have similar interests. A large group can sometimes be broken up into several small groups for the purpose of the discussion. Set up an agenda and find someone to report comments from the small groups to the larger one. An agenda can consist of nothing more than a few specific questions for discussion or response. As the leader, be prepared to make a few preliminary remarks to focus the group's attention.

QUESTION-AND-ANSWER PERIOD

This usually comes after a prepared speech, but an entire program can be presented in the form of a question-and-answer session. If the subject is a sensitive or complex one, the questions can be written out and presented to the speaker, who then reads them and responds. When questions come orally from the audience, the lecturer should notice if and when they cannot be heard by everyone and repeat them. Often no one seems to want to ask the first question. You could plant a question. (Tell one of your friends to ask something to start things going.) If my father were speaking and heard no questions after a certain time, he would turn to the side and ask himself a question: "Mr. Feller, I have a question." Everyone would laugh and feel more relaxed about participating.

GET-TOGETHER

Before or after a formal program, it is nice to provide some time for the members of the audience to talk with each other, to talk informally with the speaker, or to look at displays and books. Food or drink might be offered at this time.

70

EXHIBITS—CHECKLIST

Almost all programs can be improved by an exhibit, which can be viewed by the audience before, during, or after the main event. Exhibits can include one or more of the following.

BULLETIN BOARDS

These can be propped up on easels or attached to the wall.

OBJECTS

These can be large or small—models, curios, machines, specimens of nature, or handmade objects. You may want to have an assortment of items and/or a central object, such as a computer or combustion engine. Care should be taken to protect any valuable or breakable objects from theft or damage. Be sure you provide for any insurance needed on borrowed exhibits.

ANIMALS

Live animals make fascinating exhibits, but only if there are adequate space, equipment, and personnel to take care of them.

ART

Paintings, drawings, or sculpture can be valuable additions to an exhibit. Again, make sure that items are properly insured.

BOOKS

Books should always be exhibited. If the program does not take place in a library, borrow books from the library or a personal collection. You could also hold a book sale. Invite a local bookstore owner or jobber to bring books to sell before or after the program.

THINGS TO GIVE AWAY OR TO SERVE—CHECKLIST

PROGRAM SOUVENIRS

An outline of your program, similar to a playbill, can serve as a free souvenir of the event.

BIBLIOGRAPHIES

Bibliographies listing discussed or recommended books, articles, or 71 media can be distributed. Booklists are more effective if they are annotated.

PAMPHLETS

Subject-related pamphlets to give away can often be obtained without cost from organizations and government agencies.

FAVORS

Small gifts such as bookmarks or flower seeds, provided by an institution or an organization, such as a chamber of commerce, can be a part of the program.

TREATS

The custom of offering "tea and cookies" or some other food is appreciated. Donations for the food and service are sometimes acceptable. Food appropriate to the theme of the program can link the presentation to the social hour.

SPEAKING AND LECTURING IN PROGRAMS

My favorite quote about speaking comes from Walter Brooks' *Freddy Goes to Florida* (Knopf): "There wasn't anything left to say, but he was fond of making speeches and spoke so beautifully that everyone liked to hear him, although when they got home they could never remember anything he had said."

I'm not suggesting, of course, that the content of your program be meaningless, merely that even material of high interest can be enhanced by a good presentation.

Unless your talk is to be handed out to the press beforehand or will be published word-for-word in a journal, I suggest you not read your speech from a prepared manuscript. Very few people, unless they have had a lot of practice (such as television newscasting), can read aloud well to an audience of any size. Eye contact, as well as freedom to gesture or demonstrate, is inhibited if you are tied to a script.

Most of us, however, need some sort of notes or visual cues to remind us of what we want to say and the order in which we want to say it. You can use note cards, as some speakers do, but be careful not to overdo them. It can be tempting to write down so much that you are forced to actually read the cards instead of being able to use them as springboards for major points.

You might find it useful to prepare cards just to organize your thoughts, whether or not you end up referring to them during your presentation. They can also be helpful reminders if you plan to repeat the program at a later date.

Sometimes we are so sure of our material that we can talk without notes, but more often we need the reminders. My method of using notes has been successful for me with audiences, and it might help you. I often make a list of topics, give copies of it to members of the audience and keep one for myself. On my copy, I may make additional notes, such as a reminder to show an object or a quotation that I want to use at a particular point. The audience's copy not only tells them the order of the program, but often serves as a teaching device. I include information that would ordinarily be written on a chalkboard, such as proper spellings of titles and authors' names and directions for a craft item made during the program. The group can add their own notes to the sheet or use it to doodle on if they get a little bored.

You can also use props to help organize your talk. If you are showing a series of things to your group, such as a collection of shells or porcelain dolls, you can arrange the objects in the order in which you will show them. If you are familiar enough with your material, the objects will give you visual cues as to what to say next. This method works especially well in demonstrations of how to make things.

Transparencies or slides can work in the same way. I have a tendency to get sidetracked from the points I want to make, but if I have a series of visuals arranged in a set order, I know I must get through them by the end of the program, so they keep me to the point.

HINTS FOR SPEAKING

My personal rules for speaking can be summed up in a few sentences:

1. Never *tell about* something when you can *show* or *demonstrate* it.
2. Be enthusiastic. Impart only information you sincerely want to share with others.
3. Don't say in five sentences what can be said in two. Most talks are too long. It's quality, not quantity, that you want to give.
4. Be personal, but not too personal. Your audience might like to know how you came to visit Afghanistan or about your own experiences at a dog show. They might appreciate a glimpse of your family in a slide lecture, but they are probably not interested in your Aunt Matilda. You need to reach a balance between impersonality and autobiography.

74 Johanna Hurwitz leads a parade (see page 118).

Holiday Programs

Any holiday, real or imaginary, lends itself to a celebration with books. This section contains programs for all seasons of the year. The focus of each program is on books, storytelling, and reading. The suggestions given here are meant to stimulate your imagination and provide you with ideas for holding your own holiday celebrations.

FAIRY TALE DAY

JANUARY 4 OR JANUARY 12

January 4, 1785, is the birthdate of Jacob Grimm, who, with his brother William, collected the fairy tales known as Grimm's Fairy Tales. January 12, 1628, is the birthdate of Charles Perrault, who collected the stories Little Red Riding Hood, Cinderella, Puss in Boots, and Tom Thumb in France.

Celebrate a day in January as Fairy Tale Day. This is a good time to show middle- or upper-grade students that they can enjoy fairy tales that have been transformed into novels.

BOOKS TO SHARE

Exhibit or share the picture-book versions of one of the following fairy tales and then discuss the retellings.

BEAUTY AND THE BEAST

PICTURE BOOKS: *Beauty and the Beast.* Translated from the French of Madame de Beaumont and il. by Diane Goode. Bradbury Press, 1978.

Beauty and the Beast. Retold by Phillippa Pearce. il. by Alan Barrett. Crowell, 1972.

75

Beauty and the Beast. Retold by Rosemary Harris. il. by Errol Le Cain. Doubleday, 1980.

Beauty and the Beast. Retold by Marianna Mayer. il. by Mercer Mayer. Four Winds, 1978.

NOVELS: **McKinley, Robin.** *Beauty: A Retelling of the Story of Beauty and the Beast.* Harper, 1978.

CINDERELLA

PICTURE BOOKS: *Cinderella: Or The Little Glass Slipper.* A free translation from the French of Charles Perrault. il. by Marcia Brown. Scribner, 1954.

Cinderella. tr. by John Fowles. il. by Sheilah Beckett. Little, 1976.

NOVELS: **Farjeon, Eleanor.** *The Glass Slipper.* il. by Ernest H. Sheperd. Oxford Univ. Press, 1955.

Murphy, Shirley Rousseau. *Silver Woven in My Hair.* il. by Alan Tiegreen. Atheneum Pubs., 1977.

THE PIED PIPER OF HAMELIN

PICTURE BOOKS: **Baumann, Kurt.** *The Pied Piper of Hamelin.* il. by Jean Claverie. Methuen, 1978.

Browning, Robert. *Pied Piper of Hamelin.* il. by Kate Greenaway. Warne, 1889.

Browning, Robert. *Pied Piper of Hamelin.* il. by C. Walter Hodges. Coward McCann & Geoghegan, 1971.

NOVELS: **Huddy, Delia.** *Time Piper.* Greenwillow Bks., 1979.

Skurzynski, Gloria. *What Happened in Hamelin.* Four Winds, 1979.

SLEEPING BEAUTY

PICTURE BOOKS: *The Sleeping Beauty.* il. by Trina Schart Hyman. Little, 1977.

The Sleeping Beauty. Retold and il. by Warwick Hutton. Atheneum Pubs., 1979.

Sleeping Beauty. Told by G. S. Evans. il. by Arthur Rackham. Dover, 1971.

The Sleeping Beauty. tr. and il. by David Walker. Crowell, 1977.

COMMENTARY: **Travers, P. L.** *About the Sleeping Beauty.* il. by Charles Keeping. McGraw, 1975.

ACTIVITY   Plan a storytelling contest and you'll have fairy tales and folktales all year long. A description of one successful contest is given on pages 41–2.

GEORGE WASHINGTON'S BIRTHDAY

FEBRUARY 22

George Washington was born on February 22, 1732. Tradition tells us that he never told a lie, but I'll bet your children would love to tell a lie, the bigger the better.

Hold a liars' contest in honor of George Washington's birthday. Divide the group of contestants by age, so five-year-olds don't compete with twelve-year-olds. Give ribbons obtained from a trophy store as prizes.

EXHIBIT   Exhibit collections of tall tales and Doris Orgel's *Merry, Merry FIBruary* (il. by Arnold Lobel. Parents Mag. Press, 1977).

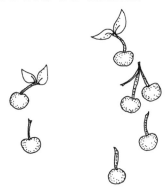

TREAT   CHOCOLATE CHERRIES

YOU NEED: 1 jar of maraschino cherries with stems
5 squares of semisweet chocolate

HOW TO: Melt the chocolate in a double-boiler. Drain the juice from the cherries. Dip the cherries into the melted chocolate. Let the cherries cool on wax paper.

HINT: Give these as gifts, or eat them while you're rereading your favorite book.

BOOKS TO SHARE

Bulla, Clyde Robert. *Washington's Birthday.* il. by Don Bolognese. Crowell, 1967.
A short biography of Washington includes descriptions of celebrations in honor of his birthday.

Fritz, Jean. *George Washington's Breakfast.* il. by Paul Galdone. Coward McCann & Geoghegan, 1969.
A young boy wonders what the first President ate for breakfast . . . and finds out.

77

STORY

LIES

Would you like to hear some lies? If you'll listen, I will tell. One day I saw two roast geese running in the sky. They ran fast, fast, with their feet up, and their backs down. A hammer floated down the river, and a frog sat on an ice floe and ate two wolves. This happened in July. Three peasants wanted to catch a hare. One was blind, the other mute, and the third lame. The blind peasant saw the hare, the mute one told the lame one about it, and the lame one caught it. Last year I traveled to a distant country just across the river where mosquitoes were as large as dogs and rode bareback on cats. The people in that country went sailing on land in ships. They sailed across fields and hills, over rye and corn, till they came to a high mountain, and there they drowned. A turtle chased a mouse, and a cow ran up on the roof and lay down to rest. And now it's time to open the window and let all the lies fly out.

From *Three Rolls and One Doughnut: Fables from Russia.* Retold by Mirra Ginsburg.

NONSENSE DAY

MAY 12

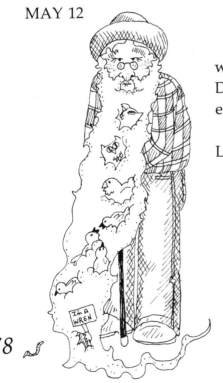

Edward Lear, known for his nonsense verse, was born on May 12, 1812. Celebrate Nonsense Day on his birthday by creating your own limericks and enjoying pure nonsense.

Introduce the group to the works of Edward Lear. Here are two verses:

> There was an Old Man with a beard,
> Who said, "It is just as I feared!
> Two Owls and a Hen,
> Four Larks and a Wren,
> Have all built their nests in my beard!"

> There was an Old Person of Burton,
> Whose answers were rather uncertain;
> When they said, "How d'ye do?"
> He replied, "Who are you?"
> That distressing Old Person of Burton.

NONSENSE TO SHARE

POEMS BY EDWARD LEAR:

Lear, Edward. *Complete Nonsense Book.* ed. by Lady Strachey. Intro. by the Earl of Cromer. Dodd, 1962.
Verses, alphabet poems, and narrative poems, such as "The Owl and the Pussycat."

Lear, Edward. *The Owl and the Pussycat and other nonsense.* il. by Owen Wood. Viking, 1978.
Sophisticated artwork.

Lear, Edward. *The Scroobious Pip.* Completed by Ogden Nash; il. by Nancy Ekholm Burkert. Harper, 1968.
Large-format picture book, delicately illustrated, questions the existence of the Scroobious Pip.

Lear, Edward. *Whizz!* il. by Janina Domanska. Macmillan Pub. Co., 1973.
Six limericks are illustrated in colorful double-spaced drawings.

RECORDING:

Lear, Edward. *Edward Lear's Nonsense Stories and Poems.* Read by Claire Bloom. Caedmon TC 1279 33 rpm stereo or monaural or cassette CDL51279.
A teacher's guide accompanies this vigorous reading of Lear's work.

OTHER NONSENSE VERSE:

Bodecker,N. M. *A Person From Britain Whose Head Was the Shape of a Mitten and Other Limericks.* il. by author. Atheneum Pubs., 1980.
"A person named Briggs whose hair grew like branches and twigs," and "A person of taste in Aruba played a highly unusual tuba," in a collection of absurd limericks. See also other nonsense collections of poems by Bodecker: *Let's Marry Said the Cherry, and Other Nonsense Poems.* (Atheneum Pubs., 1974) and *Hurry, Hurry, Mary Dear! And Other Nonsense Poems.* (Atheneum Pubs., 1976).

Cole, William (comp.) *Oh, Such Foolishness!* il. by Tomie de Paola. Lippincott, 1978.
"The land of the Bumbley Boo," "Jimmy Jupp, who died of over-eating" and "Ode to a Sneeze" are some of the silly titles in this collection.

Farber, Norma. *Never Say Ugh to a Bug.* il. by José Aruego. Greenwillow Bks., 1979.
"Rub-a-dub-dub, make way for the grub . . ." and "Down in the pond, there's a scorpion slim . . ."

Livingston, Myra Cohn. *A Lollygag of Limericks.* il. by Joseph Low. Atheneum Pubs., 1978.
"A three-day old infant in Leek" and "a discerning young lamb of Long Sutton" in a delightful collection.

79

Stokes, Jack. *Looney Limericks From Alabama to Wyoming.* il. by author. Doubleday, 1978.
Each state has at least one limerick about it in this collection.

Tripp, Wallace (comp.) *A Great Big Ugly Man Came Up and Tied His Horse To Me; A Book of Nonsense Verse.* il. by compiler. Little, 1973.
Silly, ridiculous, delightful verses accompanied by colorful, zany cartoons.

Watson, Clyde. *Catch Me & Kiss Me & Say It Again.* il. by Wendy Watson. Collins [distributed by Philomel Bks.], 1978.
Rhymes to play with.

Yolen, Jane. *How Beastly! A Menagerie of Nonsense Poems.* il. by James Marshall. Collins, 1980.
The walrust, the edgehog and the taughtus.

NONSENSE STORIES:

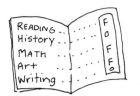

Allard, Harry. *The Stupids Have a Ball.* il. by James Marshall. Houghton, 1978.
The Stupids celebrate their dreadful report cards. See also *The Stupids Step Out* (Houghton, 1974).

Hale, Lucretia. *Stories From the Peterkin Papers.* il. by Lisl Weil. Scholastic Bk. Services, 1964.
These stories about a ridiculously silly family are perfect for telling or reading aloud.

Langstaff, John. *Oh, A-Hunting We Will Go.* il. by Nancy Winslow Parker. Atheneum Pubs., 1974.
The old nonsense song with funny pictures.

Seuss, Dr. *Oh Say Can You Say?.* il. by author. Random House, 1979.
Almost anything written by Dr. Seuss qualifies as grade-A nonsense. This book contains "terrible tongue twisters."

Wilson, Gahan. *The Bang Bang Family.* il. by author. Scribner, 1974.
After you say "bang bang" a few times the children will join in or start laughing, or both.

ACTIVITY

WRITE A LIMERICK
Look at and listen to some limericks to feel their rhythm, then write your own.

A limerick has 5 lines—two long, two short, and then another long one. The first two lines rhyme, the next two lines rhyme, and the fifth line rhymes with the first two. The first line will often contain the name of a place.

See Livingston, Myra Cohn. "Do You Want to Write a Poem?: The Limerick," *Cricket Magazine,* Vol. 6, No. 9, May 1979.

TREAT

SNICKERDOODLES

This is a traditional New England goody with an odd name.

YOU NEED:

1 cup shortening
(part butter or margarine)
1½ cups sugar
2 eggs
2¾ cups flour
2 teaspoons cream of tartar

1 teaspoon baking soda
¼ teaspoon salt
2 tablespoons sugar
2 teaspoons cinnamon

HOW TO: Heat oven to 400 degrees. Mix shortening, sugar, and eggs together thoroughly. Blend flour, cream of tartar, baking soda, and salt. Blend with the shortening mixture. Shape the dough into 1" balls. Roll in mixture of 2 tablespoons of sugar and 2 teaspoons of cinnamon. Place balls 2" apart on an ungreased sheet and bake 8–10 minutes. Makes 6 dozen cookies.

THE LONGEST DAY

ABOUT JUNE 21

At the summer solstice the Northern Hemisphere of our Earth is closer to the sun than on any other day. The result is the longest day of the year, which occurs on June 20, 21, or 22. Celebrate by taking a long time to think up lengthy things to do.

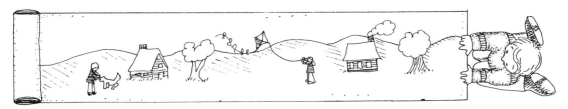

81

ACTIVITIES

1. Draw the longest picture in the world. Use a roll of shelf paper or adding machine tape.

   See "Ramona to the Rescue," in Beverly Cleary's *Ramona and Her Father*. il. by Alan Tiegreen. Morrow, 1977.
   In this chapter, Ramona and her father draw the longest picture in the world.

2. Sing the longest song in the world.

   Try "Ninety-nine bottles of beer on the wall,
   Ninety-nine bottles of beer.
   If one of the bottles happens to fall,
   Ninety-eight bottles of beer on the wall. . . ."

   "Found a Peanut" is long, too. If you don't know the words, ask a fourth-grader to tell you.

3. Start a long book.

   Adams, Richard. *Watership Down*. Macmillan Pub. Co., 1974.
   Wild rabbits search for a better life. (426 pages)

   Alcott, Louisa May. *Little Women*. il. by Jessie Wilcox Smith. Little, 1968.
   Written in 1868, this book follows the fortunes of four girls growing up in America. (444 pages)

   Bond, Nancy. *A String in the Harp*. Atheneum Pubs., 1976.
   An ancient tuning key draws Peter back into the sixth century. (370 pages)

   Grimm Brothers. *The Complete Grimm's Fairy Tales*. il. by Josef Scharl. Pantheon Bks., 1972.
   Everything from Cinderella to Rapunzel. (864 pages)

   Lagerlöf, Selma. *The Wonderful Adventures of Nils*. tr. from the Swedish by Velma Swanston Howard; il. by H. Baumhauer. Pantheon Bks., 1947.
   In this saga, a small boy is miniaturized and tours Sweden on the back of a goose. (539 pages)

4. Play the longest game in the world.

   Try Monopoly. See *After The Goat Man* by Betsy Byars. il. by Ronald Himler. Viking, 1974.
   This book begins, "The game of Monopoly had been going on for a day and a half."

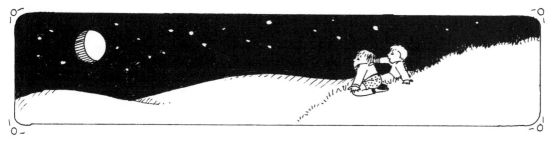

TANABATA FESTIVAL

JULY 7

Tanabata is a Japanese Festival whose origins are based on a Chinese legend. The King of Heaven had a lovely daughter who was a fine weaver. She took her weaving skills seriously and passed the days at her loom. One day, she looked out her window and instantly fell in love with a handsome young man whom she saw tending cattle in the field.

When the weaving maiden begged her father for permission to marry the cowherd, he consented. But when the pair were married, the cattle roamed unattended over the hills and the maiden's looms were idle because the couple spent all their time together.

The king became furious and banished the two lovers to opposite sides of the Heavenly River, which we call the Milky Way. You can see the cowherd and the weaving maiden if you look at the summer-night sky for the two brightest stars on either side of the Milky Way.

The lovers are allowed to meet one night in the year. If the sky is clear on the seventh day of the seventh month, the birds form a bridge across the Heavenly River so that the two lovers can meet. If the sky is not clear, the birds cannot make their bridge and they must wait to meet until the following year. The lovers are very patient and remain eternally young.

ACTIVITIES

1. Decorate the room with thin paper streamers of green, yellow, red, white, and purple. These are the five colors that shine from the stars.

2. In your best handwriting, print poems in the form of wishes on paper strips hung from branches. Traditionally, poems for good harvests are addressed to the cowherd, and poems or prayers to the weaving maiden ask for skill in the arts of weaving, sewing, and handwriting. The wish branches should be floated on a river, lake, or ocean after the conclusion of the festival. Since all the waters of the world eventually end up flowing to the Heavenly River in the sky, it is said that a wish you make will be read by the two lovers.

83

TREAT

Offer seasonal fruit, such as melons, peaches, and pears, to the stars and then eat it in celebration of Tanabata.

BOOKLIST

Here is a way to mix and match books for your celebrations. Using Tanabata as your central theme, you can introduce books about Japan, books that feature a wish theme (see page 117), books on papercraft or origami, and books that tell about the stars or astronomy.

Here is a list of books to use if you are emphasizing Tanabata as a star festival:

 NONFICTION:

Asimov, Isaac. *Galaxies.* Paintings by Alex Ebel and Denny McMains. Follett, 1968. Full color photographs and paintings illustrate our galaxy.

Branley, Franklyn M. *A Book of the Milky Way Galaxy for You.* il. by Leonard Kessler. Crowell, 1965.
An introduction to the family of stars known as the Milky Way.

Branley, Franklyn M. *Sun Dogs and Shooting Stars; A Sky-watcher's Calendar.* il. by True Kelley. Houghton, 1980.
Facts and fantasy in the night sky.

Gallant, Roy A. *The Constellations; How They Come To Be.* Four Winds, 1979.
Fifty myths and legends associated with the stars, including the Tanabata story.

Simon, Seymour. *The Long View Into Space.* Crown, 1979.
Five regions of space are explored with clear photographs.

Simon Seymour. *Look To The Night Sky: An Introduction To Star Watching.* Viking, 1977.
Practical suggestions for star gazing.

STORIES TO SHARE:

Hearn, Lafcadio. *The Romance Of The Milky Way and Other Studies And Stories.* Tuttle, 1974.
The first section of this book includes the story of Tanabata and various ways of celebrating it.

Lurie, Alison. *The Heavenly Zoo: Legends and Tales of the Stars.* il. by Monika Beisner. Farrar, Straus, 1979.
Short legends of the star creatures.

Radley, Gail. *The Night Stella Hid The Stars.* il. by John Wallner. Crown, 1978.
Stella rebels against her job as star-keeper in a full-color picture book.

"The Spinning Maid and the Cowherd" *in* Frances Carpenter. *Tales Of A Chinese Grandmother.* il. by Malthé Hasselriis. Tuttle, 1973.
First published in 1937, this is the Chinese version of the Tanabata story.

BALLOON DAY

AUGUST 17

Balloonists have tried to cross the Atlantic Ocean since 1873. Finally, on August 17, 1978, Maxie Anderson, Larry Newman, and Ben Abruzzo completed the first successful crossing. They left Maine on August 11, and on August 17 they landed near Paris in their balloon, *Double Eagle II.*

ACTIVITY

Balloon Day can be the culmination of a summer reading program. On that day, release helium-filled balloons, each containing the name of a program participant and the address of your library.

The May 1981 issue of *American Libraries* magazine reported that the Sauk School in Richton Park, Illinois, tried this idea during Children's Book Week and that one of their balloons landed in Madras, India.

You may want to have participants agree to read a number of books or pages to qualify for a balloon. Or, you may want to eliminate competition and just make Balloon Day a celebration of books.

The publicity for this program should not be limited to children. Open up your celebration to the whole community.

PROGRAM SIGN UP:

The _____ Library will sponsor a celebration of Summer Reading on August 17. If you would like to participate in this event, please fill out the coupon below and bring it to the library by July 1 [about six weeks before the celebration].

Name _____ Age _____

Address _____

I will try to read 5 books between now and August 17.

_____
signature

This event is open to the whole family, but each person who will send up a balloon must read five books or have them read to him or her.

To keep interest high during the six weeks, each time a book is read write its title and the reader's name on a paper balloon and affix it to a bulletin board or wall.

Each child or adult who reads five or more books receives a balloon certificate:

Fly High With Books

I earned a balloon for reading the following books:

_____

_____

_____

_____

_____

Name _____

Balloons for Balloon Day can be imprinted with:

Library Name

Date

Fly High With Books (or another slogan)

Print flyers to go inside the balloons:

I read books to earn a balloon.
If you find this bookmark, please
send it back to me, _____, at
(name and address of library). P.S. Read a book!

Imprinted balloons and helium are available from novelty supply houses. Look in the Yellow Pages under "advertising specialties."

On Balloon Day all children and adults meet in the library parking lot, park, or shopping mall to send up their balloons. (Hope for sunshine and a slight breeze.)

Suggest that participants return to the library from time to time to see if their bookmarks have been returned . . . and to take out books!

BOOKLIST

PICTURE BOOKS:

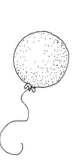

Calhoun, Mary. *Hot-Air Henry.* il. by Erick Ingraham. Morrow, 1981.
A Siamese cat stows away in a hot-air balloon.

Chase, Catherine. *My Balloon.* il. by Gail Gibbons. Dandelion Press, 1979.
Only forty-six words tell the story of a boy blowing up a balloon and the inevitable POP!

Coerr, Eleanor. *The Big Balloon Race.* il. by Carolyn Croll. Harper, 1981.
Easy-to-read story based on the life of a real ballooning family of the 1800s.

Fenton, Edward. *The Big Yellow Balloon.* il. by Ib Ohlsson. Doubleday, 1967.
Roger and his balloon are followed by a cat who wants to kill the balloon, a dog who wants the cat, etc. Roger ends up with a medal.

Goodall, John S. *The Ballooning Adventures of Paddy Pork.* il. by author. Harcourt, 1969.
Wordless picture book with unevenly cut pages that make following the story fun.

Lamorisse, Albert. *The Red Balloon.* il. with photographs. Doubleday, 1957.
Pascal makes friends with a balloon in Paris.

Hughes, Shirley. *Up and Up.* il. by author. Prentice-Hall, 1979.
A small girl wants to fly in this wordless picture book.

Park, Ruth. *The Gigantic Balloon.* il. by Kilmeny and Deborah Niland. Parents Mag. Press, 1976.
Peter and his faithful dog Belle pilot a gigantic balloon against fearsome odds.

READ ALOUD **Du Bois, William Pène.** *The Twenty-one Balloons.* il. by author. Viking, 1947.
The story of how Professor Sherman starts out with one balloon and ends up with twenty-one makes a delightful award winning fantasy.

NONFICTION: **Wells, Barry and Paul Stumpf.** *Hot Air Ballooning.* Harvey House, 1980.
History and structure of balloons and directions for operating them.

ADULT REFERENCE: **McCarry, Charles.** *Double Eagle: Ben Abruzzo, Maxie Anderson, Larry Newman.* il. with photographs. Little, 1979.
An account of the successful Atlantic Ocean balloon crossing in 1978.

JOHNNY APPLESEED'S BIRTHDAY

SEPTEMBER 26

John Chapman, known as Johnny Appleseed, spent much of his life walking around the Midwest planting apple seeds and giving away saplings to pioneers heading west.

Chapman walked nearly 100,000 miles as he planted and preached the gospel. "Apples are God's food," said Chapman. Chapman, who is believed to have been born on September 26, 1774, is commemorated in Leominster, Massachusetts, with an annual Appleseed Civic Day, and the community of Ashland, Ohio, has built a monument to him. A three-day Johnny Appleseed Festival is celebrated in Lisbon, Ohio, near the time of his birthday.

Create your own Apple Festival by reading books that feature apples, making apple dolls, and eating apples in a new delicious fashion.

TO MAKE

APPLE DOLL

Apple dolls were made by the Iroquois Indians. American pioneers learned to make them from the Iroquois. Save your apple dolls to use in the celebration of other American holidays as well. The withered apples often turn out to look like the faces of old pioneers, so you also could exhibit them with books about the Old West.

YOU NEED (for the head): a firm apple (Delicious and Rome Beauty apples make good doll heads)
a paring knife
cloves or craft beads
yarn
glue

HOW TO: Peel the apple. Carve large features. The apple will shrink to a quarter of its size, so don't take too much away. Stick in cloves or craft beads for eyes. Leave it on a plate in your kitchen or in the library, away from drafts so that it does not mildew. Check it periodically.

It takes about four weeks for the apple to shrink and harden. Since the apple will become quite distorted, you won't know what it will look like for a month. It may look like a clown, a pirate, a pioneer, or Struwwelpeter when it has dried completely. When it is dry, glue on yarn for hair.

YOU NEED (for the body): 4 cups unsifted flour
1 cup salt
1½ cups water
felt-tip pen, or acrylic or enamel paint

clear varnish or acrylic polymer medium
wire hanger

89

HOW TO: Mix flour, salt, and water together thoroughly and knead for five minutes. Shape clay into a body. You can use water to hold pieces together.
Insert a short piece of wire to make a neck.
Place on cookie sheet covered with aluminum foil and bake at 350 degrees for one hour.
When cool, decorate the clay with a felt-tip pen or paint. Finish with varnish or other finish to prevent crumbling. Stick neck into apple head.

HINT: The body can also be made from a stick or from cloth stuffed with cotton.

TREAT

APPLESAUCE FRUIT LEATHER—to eat while reading about apples.

YOU NEED: aluminum foil
applesauce

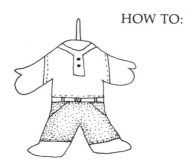

HOW TO: Spread the aluminum foil smoothly over a cookie sheet. Spread the applesauce evenly and thinly on the foil. Put the sheet in the oven on the center rack. Prop the door slightly open with a stick, a pencil, or a piece of rolled tinfoil. Set the oven on the lowest possible temperature—105–150 degrees.
When all the moisture has evaporated (after 7 to 10 hours), you will be able to peel the "leather" away from the foil. Roll the leather up in a fresh piece of wax paper or plastic wrap and it's ready for your snacking pleasure.

BOOKLIST

Aliki. *The Story of Johnny Appleseed.* il. by author. Prentice-Hall, 1963.
Story of John Chapman's pioneer tree-planting expedition.

Barrett, Judi. *An Apple a Day.* il. by Tim Lewis. Atheneum Pubs., 1973.
Jeremy hides his "apple a day" in his room until it is overflowing.

Blair, Walter. "Johnny Appleseed," in *North American Legends.* ed. by Virginia Haviland. il. by Ann Strugnell. Collins [distributed by Philomel Bks.], 1979.
A folksy tale about Johnny Appleseed that is perfect for storytelling.

Hogrogian, Nonny. *Apples.* il. by author. Macmillan Pub. Co., 1972.
Wordless picture book shows apple from seed to tree to eating.

Kohn, Bernice. *Apples: A Bushel of Fun and Facts.* il. by Roland Rodegast. Parents Mag. Press, 1976.
Myths, recipes, history, and botanical facts.

McMillan, Bruce. *Apples: How They Grow.* Photographs by author. Houghton, 1979.
Close-up photographs chart the growth of an apple from blossom to fruit. Nonfiction.

Orbach, Ruth. *Apple Pigs.* il. by author. Collins & World, 1977.
How a little girl and her family cope with an overabundance of apples.

Rothman, Joel. *A Moment in Time.* il. by Don Leake. Scroll Press, 1973.
An apple falls from a tree.

Scheer, Julian. *Rain Makes Applesauce.* il. by Marvin Bileck. Holiday House, 1964.
Nonsense rhyme. Inset shows the growth and harvesting of apples, and the making of applesauce.

HALLOWEEN
OCTOBER 31
STORIES TO TELL

Bang, Betsy. *The Old Woman and the Red Pumpkin: A Bengali Folk Tale.* il. by Molly Garrett Bang. Macmillan Pub. Co., 1975.
A rhythmic Bengali folktale, in which an old woman outwits a group of animals. Good for creative dramatics.

Bang, Molly. *The Goblins Giggle and Other Stories.* il. by author. Scribner, 1973.
Five scary tales from Japan, Ireland, Germany, France, and China.

Credle, Ellis. "The Perambulatin' Pumpkin," in *Clever Cooks; A Concoction of Stories, Charms, Recipes and Riddles,* ed. by Ellin Greene. il. by Trina Schart Hyman. Lothrop, 1973.

91

Finger, Charles G. "The Hungry Old Witch," in *Witches, Witches, Witches,* comp. by Helen Hoke. il. by W. R. Lohse. Watts, 1958.
"She was a witch, she was very old, and she was always hungry . . ."

Gorey, Edward, ed. *The Haunted Looking Glass,* il. by editor. Random House, 1959.
Twelve ghost stories.

Hardendorff, Jeanne B. *The Bed Just So.* il. by Lisl Weil. Four Winds, 1975.
Finding a satisfactory bed for a hudgin is not easy. This is a small picture book and the story should be told rather than read. Easy to learn.

Hardendorff, Jeanne B. *Witches, Wit and a Werewolf.* il. by Laszlo Kubinyi. Lippincott, 1971.
Stories of ghosts, ghouls, and murderers.

Hoke, Helen, ed. *Spooks, Spooks, Spooks.* il. by W. R. Lohse. Watts, 1966.
Spook stories collected by a well-known anthologist.

Kahn, Joan, ed. *Some Things Strange and Sinister.* Harper, 1973.
Fourteen stories of the supernatural.

Wilkins, Mary E. *The Pumpkin Giant.* retold by Ellin Greene. il. by Trina Schart Hyman. Lothrop, 1970.
A long amusing story tells the origin of pumpkin pie.

READ ALOUD: **Godden, Rumer.** *Mr. McFadden's Hallowe'en.* Viking, 1975.
Delightful story of a young girl who befriends a cantankerous but kindly old man. Eight chapters. Make sure you practice your reading; there is a Scottish accent but the book is worth it.

ACTIVITIES

1. Have a pumpkin-carving contest:
   Ask each child to bring an adult. This is a family activity. Ask the adults to bring a carving knife and a big spoon. Provide the pumpkins or sell them at cost. Be sure to have plenty of paper towels for clean-up. Tell a story or two before or after the carving begins. Give lots of ribbons for the most original, most artistic, prettiest, largest, smallest, etc. (Ribbons are available from trophy supply shops.)

2. Decorate trick-or-treat bags with original pictures based on the stories heard. Use large grocery bags saved from shopping.

3. Have a Halloween Poetry Read-in. (See page 254.)

4. Tell "The Old House":

THE OLD HOUSE

Ringo Raffin was hiking across the mountain on the way into town. It was a cold, windy night. Ringo was sure he was lost, but at last, twinkling through the trees, he saw the lights of an old house. "I'll stop and ask directions," thought Ringo. No one answered Ringo's knock, but he noticed the front door was slightly ajar. Ringo Raffin pushed the door open and called, "Is anyone home?" A sound came from the second story: "Rap, Rap, Rap," came the sound from above. Ringo started up the stairs and the sound became louder and steadier. "RAP, RAP, RAP." At the top of the stairs there was a door; Ringo pushed it open and the sound was louder. "RAP, RAP, RAP!" Ringo shivered in the empty room. The sound came from behind a door. "RAP, RAP, RAP!" Ringo tried it and found an empty closet. On the shelf in the closet was a box. The RAP, RAP, RAP came from the box. Ringo slowly lifted it down and slowly opened the box . . .

and found

wrapping paper.

Presentation (idea from Gregg Smotts): On the last line of the story, pick up a box, slowly open it, and pull out crumpled wrapping paper.

5. Trick or treat in the library. Using painted refrigerator cartons the Portage County District Library in Hiram, Ohio, held a trick or treat session in a model village. Each carton was decorated with poster paint to look like a village building. Puppets gave out small treats from Brunhilde's Gingerbread House, Max Monster's Mansion, Harry Hermit's Cottage, and the Adams' Family Restaurant. Storyteller Dave Titus reports that the village was moved to various libraries in the area, the children were ecstatic, and the staff survived. (See photo on page 94.)

93

TREATS

1. TOASTED PUMPKIN SEEDS. Let the children take home the seeds from their pumpkins and suggest that they try this recipe:

YOU NEED: 2 cups of seeds
1½ tablespoons of melted butter or oil
1¼ teaspoons salt or garlic salt

HOW TO: Separate the fiber from the unwashed pumpkin seeds. Mix oil and salt with seeds. Bake them in a slow oven (200–250°) until crisp and brown. Stir them around from time to time.

2. PUMPKIN BREAD—easy to make and good to eat:

YOU NEED: 5 cups flour
4 cups sugar
1 cup oil
1 cup raisins
1 cup nuts
1 teaspoon cinnamon
½ teaspoon ground cloves
1 teaspoon mace
1 teaspoon salt
4 teaspoons baking soda
1 large can pumpkin (about 3½ cups)

HOW TO: Combine all ingredients. Grease and flour loaf pans. Bake for eighty minutes at 350°. Makes three loaves.

94

Photo by Gus Chan, *Record Courier*, Ravenna, Kent, Ohio.

POPCORN DAY

Pick a fine fall day to celebrate popcorn.

STORIES TO TELL

Asch, Frank. *Popcorn.* il. by author. Parents Mag. Press, 1979.
The guests at Bear's party make too much popcorn and have to eat their way out of the living room.

Greene, Ellin. "Princess Rosetta and the Popcorn Man," From *The Pot of Gold,* by Mary E. Wilkins. il. by Trina Schart Hyman. Lothrop, 1971.
A kidnapped princess is freed with popcorn.

Preston, Edna M. *Pop Corn and Ma Goodness.* il. by Robert Andrew Parker. Viking, 1969.
Nonsense musical story.

Sandburg, Carl. "The Huckabuck Family and How They Raised Popcorn in Nebraska, in *The Sandburg Treasury: Prose and Poetry for Young People.* il. by Paul Bacon. Harcourt, 1970.

BOOKS TO SHARE OR EXHIBIT

De Paola, Tomie. *The Popcorn Book.* il. by author. Holiday House, 1978.
Nonfiction picture book about popcorn.

Fleischman, Sid. *McBroom's Ear.* il. by Kurt Werth. Norton, 1969.
The McBrooms grow an ear of corn that is not only higher than an elephant's eye, but twice as large as an elephant.

Fritz, Jean. *George Washington's Breakfast.* il. by Paul Galdone. Coward, McCann, & Geoghegan, 1969.
What did George like best for breakfast?

Kusche, Larry. *Popcorn Cookery.* H.P. Books, 1977.
Two hundred ways to enjoy popcorn.

Selsam, Millicent E. *Popcorn.* Photographs by Jerome Wexler. Morrow, 1976.
Picture study of the life cycle of the popcorn plant.

Williams, Barbara. *Cornzapoppin! Popcorn Recipes and Party Ideas For All Occasions.* Photographs by Royce L. Bair. Holt, 1976.
Popcorn recipes for every month of the year.

Woodside, Dave. *What Makes Popcorn Pop!* il. by Kay Woon. Atheneum Pubs., 1980.
History, recipes, crafts.

TO MAKE POPCORN COLLAGES

YOU NEED: construction paper   popcorn
glue   crayons

HOW TO: Draw with crayons on construction paper. Spread glue and afix popcorn onto drawing.

HINT: Eat as you create!

TREATS

1. POPCORN (of course!). It's easy to make and especially fun if you can pop it with the group. Borrow an electric corn popper.

2. OLD-FASHIONED MOLASSES POPCORN BALLS. Ask parents to volunteer to make this treat. Perhaps a local grocery store would donate the ingredients.

YOU NEED: 3 quarts freshly popped corn   1 cup light corn syrup
½ teaspoon salt   1 tablespoon vinegar
1 cup molasses   3 tablespoons butter

HOW TO: Put molasses, syrup, and vinegar in a large (so mixture doesn't boil over), heavy (so mixture doesn't burn) saucepan. Boil until hard-boil stage (270° on candy thermometer). Remove from heat and stir in butter (just enough to blend). Pour syrup mixture over salted popcorn and mix to coat. Butter hands and form into balls. Yield: about 30 two-inch balls. Obviously, this would be fun for children to make. Are you lucky enough to have a kitchen, or a hot plate? Could several homes in your area invite children to make popcorn balls?

THANKSGIVING

FOURTH THURSDAY IN NOVEMBER

THE BEST THIRD GRADE TEACHER IN THE WORLD: MISS JONES

BULLETIN BOARD

THE SUNNY DAY ON MY BIRTHDAY

MY NEW BABY BROTHER

Easy! Simple! Fast!

Write "Thank you for . . ." on the board. Have 3" x 5" cards and pins nearby. Invite children to write about things for which they are thankful. Start things going by putting up your own thank-you's. Keep it light.

Other Dates to Celebrate

JANUARY

  9 First Successful Balloon Flight in the United States
15 Martin Luther King's Birthday
16 National Nothing Day
24 California Gold Rush

FEBRUARY

  2 Groundhog Day
  8 Boy Scout Day (February is Boy Scout Month)
14 Valentine's Day
Second Monday—Lincoln's Birthday

MARCH

12 Girl Scout Day (Girl Scout Week begins on Sunday of the week including March 12)
17 St. Patrick's Day
21 First Day of Spring (during National Wildlife Week)
Dates vary—Easter; Purim

APRIL

  1 April Fool's Day
  2 International Children's Book Day; Barnum and Bailey's Circus opened at Madison Square Garden, 1896
18 Paul Revere's Ride
Last Friday—Arbor Day
Last full week—National Library Week
Dates vary—Be Kind to Animals Week

MAY

  1 May Day
  5 First American in space, 1961
Second Sunday—Mother's Day
Last Monday—Memorial Day

JUNE

10 Children's Day
18 Susan B. Anthony Day
Third Sunday—Father's Day

JULY

  1 Canada's Birthday
  4 Independence Day
14 Bastille Day

AUGUST

17 Davy Crockett's Birthday

SEPTEMBER

First Monday—Labor Day
17 Citizenship Day
24 American Indian Day

OCTOBER

12 Columbus Day
24 United Nations Day
31 Halloween
(Also death of Harry Houdini, 1926; good day for a magic show.)

NOVEMBER

  5 Guy Fawkes Day
  9 Sadie Hawkins day
Second Week—Children's Book Week

DECEMBER

13 Feast of Santa Lucia
25 Christmas
Date varies—Hanukkah

Any time you would like to celebrate, proclaim a day, such as:

Dog Day	Giant Day
Circus Day	Frontier Day
Pet Day	Sports Day

To find more holidays, see:

Amazing Days by Randy Harelson. Workman, 1979.
The American Book of Days. ed. by Jane M. Hatch. H. W. Wilson, 1978.
Light the Candles! Beat the Drums! A Book of Holidays by Jane Sarnoff and Reynold Ruffins. Scribner, 1979.
Special Days: The Book of Anniversaries and Holidays. by Ruth W. Gregory. Citadel, 1978.

Chases' Calendar of Annual Events. comp. William D. Chase. Apple Tree Press. (Box 1012, Flint, Mich. 48501).
Anniversaries and Holidays, by Ruth W. Gregory. A.L.A., 1975.
Celebrations: The Complete Book of American Holidays, by Robert J. Meyers. Doubleday, 1972.
Festivals Sourcebook: A Reference Guide to Fairs, Festivals, and Celebrations, by Paul Wasserman. Gale, 1977.

Author's Day

Authors are people. The best way to prove that to a child is to have a real live author come and visit the school or library. Three public schools in Portland, Oregon, celebrated the visit of authors with cake and parades.

Above: Ezra Jack Keats

Right: Beverly Cleary

A parader in costume.

Betty Fry, librarian at the Sabin school, was the inspiration behind the visit of author and illustrator Ezra Jack Keats. Three schools joined forces to raise the needed money by having bake sales, film showings, and adult storyhours featuring a local college professor. Keats's honorarium was raised by the children. Other expenses, including air fare, were paid by the author's publisher. The author visited each of the schools at an assembly, but the big event was the parade. Each school was assigned three book titles and made banners ten feet by three feet. The children dressed like book characters and marched behind the banners. Ezra Jack Keats rode in a white Volkswagen convertible surrounded by red balloons. A teacher designed a bookplate so that Keats could sign the books for sale without spending hours at autographing sessions.

The following year in another section of the city a third grade teacher, Ramona Alsman, applied for and received a grant to bring an author to the Maplewood School. Johanna Hurwitz arrived from New York, spoke to the school and was grand marshal of a parade of children. Many dressed as their favorite book characters. The day honored the author and the children who had written and illustrated their own books. Cake was served to the entire school. The next year Beverly Cleary was the honored guest.

Authors' Birthday Parties

Everybody loves a birthday party. Johanna Hurwitz at the Great Neck Public Library in New York found that birthday party programs couldn't fail to be popular library offerings.

Each month her library has a birthday party for an author. About thirty children attend each party and costs are kept to a minimum.

A short talk about the author, a reading or story from the author's work, and a simple activity precede the eating of a birthday cake complete with birthday candles. Johanna says that when she's feeling ambitious, she bakes the cake herself, but that the children, who are not gourmets, devour a store-bought cake with equal relish.

A. A. MILNE'S BIRTHDAY
BIRTH DATE, JANUARY 18, 1882

TO READ

Read or recite poems from these books by A. A. Milne:
Now We Are Six; il. by Ernest H. Shepard. Dutton, 1961.
When We Were Very Young; il. by Ernest H. Shepard. Dutton, 1961.

Read or tell a story from:
Winnie-the-Pooh; il. by Ernest H. Shepard, colored by Hilda Scott. Dutton, 1974
The House at Pooh Corner; il. by Ernest H. Shepard. Dutton, 1961.
Particularly recommended is the birthday story "In Which Eeyore Has a Birthday and Gets Two Presents," in *Winnie the Pooh.* Eeyore, the donkey, gets a burst balloon and an empty honey pot and finds them useful. At the library party, Johanna read "In Which We Are Introduced to Winnie-the-Pooh and Some Bees, and the Stories Begin," from *Winnie the Pooh.* Pooh attempts to fool some bees by disguising himself as a cloud under a blue balloon. A story that relates to the following activity is "In Which Eeyore Loses a Tail and Pooh Finds One," also in *Winnie the Pooh.*

ACTIVITY   PIN THE TAIL ON EEYORE

YOU NEED: An outline drawing of Eeyore, the donkey, on a large
              sheet of drawing paper.
              Yarn tails
              Pins
              Blindfold

HOW TO: Each child, blindfolded, takes a turn trying to pin the tail
              on Eeyore.

FAVOR   blue balloon, red balloon (not burst!), or the yarn tails.

JUDY BLUME'S BIRTHDAY
BIRTH DATE: FEBRUARY 12, 1938

Johanna says, "Judy Blume didn't need the publicity that my party gave
her, but her name gave *my* parties a publicity boost."

TO READ   *Tales of a Fourth Grade Nothing,* (il. by Roy Doty. Dutton,
                  1972).
                  Try "The Birthday Bash" if you don't have another favor-
                  ite chapter. The birthday party of a younger brother is
                  attended by "an eater, a biter, and a crier."

101

TO MAKE

1. TURTLE FAVORS

YOU NEED: walnut shells (use the nut meat in the birthday cake)
felt scraps cut in the shapes of heads, feet, and tails (children can cut their own if you have enough scissors)
white glue

HOW TO: Children glue the head and feet onto the shells.

2. FRECKLE JUICE

YOU NEED: A large can of fruit juice relabeled.
The label for "Freckle Juice" says that it contains:

grape juice	mayonnaise	ketchup
vinegar	juice from one lemon	olive oil
mustard	pepper, salt	speck of onion

HOW TO: All the children are asked to try the Freckle Juice and are promised that freckles will appear as a result. "That's impossible," a 10-year-old boy once exclaimed. "Nothing is impossible," said the librarian, and she pulled out an eyebrow pencil and everyone got freckles.

DR. SEUSS'S BIRTHDAY

BIRTH DATE: MARCH 2, 1904

Show books by Theodore Geisel and explain that Dr. Seuss created his own name but that he got an honorary doctorate from a college and then called himself "Dr. Dr. Seuss."

TO READ

McElligot's Pool. il. by author. Random House, 1947.
The 500 Hats of Bartholomew Cubbins. il. by author. Vanguard, 1938.
In an effort to remove his hat for the king, Bartholomew removes 500 hats!

TO MAKE

1. FISH
Make fish that might be caught in McElligot's pool.

YOU NEED: fresh carrots or potatoes
map pins
felt scraps

HOW TO: Design exotic fish by cutting the vegetables and attaching felt scraps with pins. Johanna says, ''While I was reading *McElligot's Pool,* one boy said, 'That fish looks just like a carrot' ''; the perfect comment to lead into the activity.

2. HATS
Make exotic hats to go with *The 500 Hats of Bartholomew Cubbins.*

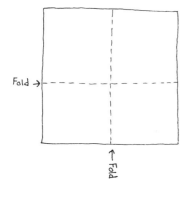

YOU NEED: 9" x 12" sheets of construction paper
scissors
white glue or staples

HOW TO: Fold a 9" x 12" sheet of construction paper into fourths.
Make an L-shaped cut. (Do not cut through the folded edges.)
Make additional cuts as your imagination dictates.
Open up. Join A to A and B to B at *right angles.*
Fold out and curl the inside parts to give a festive air to your hat.

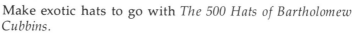

Fold →

↑ Fold

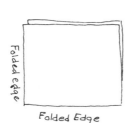

Folded edge

Folded Edge

Cut out

103

JOHANNA HURWITZ

BIRTH DATE: OCTOBER 9, 1937

TO READ

"The Birthday Party," in Hurwitz, Johanna. *Aldo Applesauce.* il. by John Wallner. Morrow, 1979.
Aldo, a vegetarian, has a hard time at a birthday party where hot dogs and hamburgers are on the menu.

"An Invitation for Teddy," in *Superduper Teddy.* il. by Susan Jeschke. Morrow, 1980.
Teddy goes to the wrong party.

"Ice Cream on Wheels," in *Aldo Ice Cream.* il. by John Wallner. Morrow, 1981.
DeDe finally gets her ice-cream machine.

ACTIVITIES

1. Have a bubble-blowing contest and refer to "Gum Day" in Johanna Hurwitz's *New Neighbors for Nora* (il. by Susan Jeschke, Morrow, 1979).
   Hint: gum can be removed from hair with a small pinch of butter or margarine.

2. Have a sculpture contest. This may sound offensive, but I remember the practice with great affection from summer camp in Maine circa 1947. On rainy days we all met in the social hall and were awarded the privilege of chewing a piece of gum. To make sure, no doubt, that the gum was discarded at the end of the afternoon, a contest was held. Each camper received a small piece of paper and a toothpick and was asked to fashion something out of the gum. Even after 30 years I remember the flowers, flags, and animals the girls made. Once I won a prize by forgetting about the toothpick and using my hands to model a tiny dog.

TO MAKE

DEDE'S MUSTACHE

YOU NEED: black construction paper
scissors

HOW TO: Everyone cuts out a mustache and wears it by putting it between the nose and upper lip.

TREAT

Serve applesauce cake as the birthday cake in honor of Aldo Applesauce. Serve chocolate ice cream (since DeDe is afraid to try any other flavor) to accompany the cake.

PAM'S APPLESAUCE CAKE

½ cup butter, at room temperature
¾ cup white sugar
1 egg
2 cups flour
½ teaspoon baking soda
1 teaspoon baking powder
½ teaspoon salt
3 teaspoons cinnamon
½ tsp. allspice
¼ tsp. ground cloves
1¼ cups applesauce
½ cup raisins (optional)
¾ cup finely chopped nuts

Cream butter and sugar. Beat in egg. Mix in applesauce. Add dry ingredients.
Put into greased and floured 9" x 9" x 2" pan. Bake at 350° for 30–40 minutes. Yield: About 12 large pieces.
Serve with ice cream or whipped cream.

BIRTH DATES OF SOME AUTHORS AND ILLUSTRATORS

Find your own favorites in:

Something About the Author. Anne Commini, ed. Gale Research. Series.

Fourth Book of Junior Authors and Illustrators. Doris de Montreville and Elizabeth D. Crawford, eds. H.W. Wilson. 1978. A volume in the Junior Authors Series.

Below are listed birth dates of some well-known authors and illustrators.

January 12, 1728. Charles Perrault. *Cinderella.*

January 14, 1886. Hugh Lofting. *Dr. Doolittle.*

January 21, 1832. Lewis Carroll. *Alice in Wonderland.*

February 7, 1867. Laura Ingalls Wilder. Little House Books.

February 13, 1881. Eleanor Farjeon. Stories and poetry.

March 5, 1853. Howard Pyle. *Robin Hood.*

March 8, 1859. Kenneth Grahame. *The Wind in the Willows.*

March 12, 1933. Virginia Hamilton. *Zeely, M.C. Higgins the Great.*

March 17, 1846. Kate Greenaway, illustrator.

March 22, 1846. Randolph Caldecott, illustrator. "Father of the picture book."

105

April 2, 1805. Hans Christian Andersen. *The Ugly Duck-ling*, *The Emperor's New Clothes*, and other fairy tales.

April 12, 1916. Beverly Cleary. *The Mouse and the Motor-cycle*. Ramona books.

April 25, 1873. Walter de la Mare. Poetry, plays.

May 9, 1860. James Barrie. *Peter Pan*, plays.

May 12, 1812. Edward Lear. *The Owl and the Pussycat*, other nonsense verse, limericks.

May 22, 1859. Arthur Conan Doyle. *Sherlock Holmes*.

May 23, 1935. Susan Cooper. *The Grey King*.

June 10, 1928. Maurice Sendak. *Where the Wild Things Are*.

June 24, 1916. John Ciardi. Poetry.

June 25, 1929. Eric Carle. *The Very Hungry Caterpillar*.

June 29, 1900. Antoine de Saint-Exupery. *The Little Prince*.

July 11, 1899. E. B. White. *Charlotte's Web, Stuart Little*.

July 11, 1936. Helen Cresswell. The Bagthorpe series. *The Winter of the Birds*.

July 16, 1935. Arnold Adoff. *Ma nDa La, Tornado*.

July 28, 1932. Natalie Babbitt. *The Devil's Storybook, Tuck Everlasting*.

July 28, 1866. Beatrix Potter. *The Tale of Peter Rabbit*.

August 6, 1946. Frank Asch. *Monkey Face, Moon Bear*.

August 9, 1932. José Aruego, illustrator. *Leo the Late Bloomer, Look What I Can Do*.

September 8, 1940. Jack Prelutsky. *Nightmares*. Poetry.

September 13, 1916. Roald Dahl. *Charlie and the Chocolate Factory*.

September 14, 1950. John Steptoe. *Stevie, My Special Best Words*.

October 18, 1930. Nancy Winslow Parker. *Poofy Loves Company*.

October 27, 1924. Constance C. Greene. *A Girl Called Al*.

November 13, 1850. Robert Louis Stevenson. *Treasure Is-land*.

November 20, 1919. William Cole, compiler of poetry col-lections *Oh, What Nonsense!* and *Oh, That's Ridiculous!*

November 30, 1835. Mark Twain. *Tom Sawyer*.

December 18, 1927. Marilyn Sachs. *The Bear's House*.

December 30, 1865. Rudyard Kipling. *Just So Stories*.

Programs Inspired by a Single Theme

HATS

Collect many hats from your family and friends:* "You all wear hats. You wear different hats for different occasions. Can you guess who would wear these hats?" Show your hat collection:

cowboy hat	tennis visor
firefighter's hat	crown
police officer's hat	baseball cap
armed services cap	rain hat
ski cap	chef's hat
party hat	witch's hat

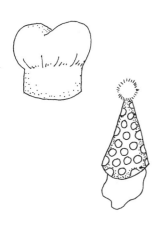

Tell the children that book characters wear hats, too. Paddington Bear always wears his hat (show a toy Paddington if you or a friend has one), and Bartholomew Cubbins tried to take off his hat to the king and he took off 500 hats before he was finished. You can use your hat collection to throw out into the audience; or perform the appearing-hats magic trick mentioned below. End your hat-collection show with a magician's hat and begin your magic tricks.

MAGIC TRICKS

*APPEARING HATS: These hats fold up into a 6" circle and spring open spectacularly at a touch to the hat band. They come packaged in sets of two. The more you show, the more impressive the trick will be, but one is enough to surprise the audience.

Appearing Hats to introduce Dr. Seuss's *The 500 Hats of Bartholomew Cubbins* are available from the following suppliers.

---

*I presented a program using the starred items to 200 children in grades K-5. They loved everything. My only addition was the telling of Ron and Judi Barrett's *Cloudy With a Chance of Meatballs* (Atheneum, 1978), using my hat with soft-sculpture food attached to it (see page 108).

Magic Room
P.O. Box 3803
Centerdale, RI 02911

Hollywood Hats & Tie Co.
17 Lane 3 Chang Chun Road
Taipei, Taiwan

*PAPER HAT TEAR: This is a paper tear. A piece of tissue paper, 10" x 5", is shown to the audience. The tissue paper is torn into shreds by the magician and a helper from the audience. After a few magic words are spoken, the shreds of tissue become a paper hat, which is given to a spectator.

Paper Hat Tear is available from:

Suds
3203½ West Ball Road
Anaheim, CA 92804

GIANT HAT: In this trick, a small paper hat is unfolded many times until it becomes a giant hat that reveals a monster mask.

Ali Bongo's Giant Hat available from:

Supreme Magic, Inc.
64 High Street
Bideford, Devon, England

Left: To tell *Cloudy With a Chance of Meatballs*, I use a big straw hat laden with soft-sculpture food. As the story progresses, I let pieces of "food" rain down—the pieces are attached to the hat with fish line. Milliner: Bev Sokol.

STORIES

"The Magic Listening Cap," *in* Yoshiko Uchida, *The Magic Listening Cap: More Folk Tales from Japan.* il. by author. Harcourt, 1955.
An old man is given a red cap that enables him to hear crows talking and trees thinking.

"The Magic Cap," by Johan Hart *in* Helen R. Smith (ed.), *Laughing Matter*. il. by Kurt Wiese. Scribner's, 1949.
In this Dutch story, a farmer tricks three rogues into thinking his cap is magic.

"Hats to Disappear With" by Tanya Lee *in* I. K. Junne (comp.), *Floating Clouds, Floating Dreams: Favorite Asian Folktales*. Doubleday, 1974.
A Korean story in which a thief steals a goblin's hat to make himself invisible.

*"The Hat-shaking Dance," *in* Harold Courlander, *The Hat-shaking Dance, and Other Tales From The Gold Coast*. il. by Enrico Arno. Harcourt, 1957.
An African Anansi story. Lots of action for the storyteller.

"New Year's Hats for the Statues," *in* Yoshiko Uchida, *The Sea of Gold, and Other Tales from Japan*. il. by Marianni Yamaguchi. Scribner, 1965.
A Japanese farmer puts his reed hats on statues and is rewarded.

"The Irishman's Hat," *in* Aidan Chambers, *Funny Folk: A Book of Comic Tales*. il. by Trevor Stubley. Collins, 1976.
Similar to "The Magic Listening Cap," this English story is more sophisticated.

"Holding Down the Hat," *in* Maria Leach, *Noodles, Nitwits, and Numskulls*, il. by Kurt Werth. Collins [distributed by Philomel], 1961.
Short trickster story.

POEMS

*HELP!

Can anybody tell me, please,
a bit about the thing
with seven legs and furry knees,
four noses and a wing?

Oh what has prickles on its chin,
what's yellow, green, blue,
and what has soft and slimy skin?
Oh tell me, tell me, do.

And tell me, what has polka dots
on every other ear,
what ties its tail in twenty knots,
what weeps a purple tear?

Oh what is growling long and low
and please, has it been fed?
I think I'd really better know. . .
it's sitting on my head.

by Jack Prelutsky

Presentation: On the last line, put a creature fitting the description on your head.

Hint: Any wild critter will probably work.

*CHIC CHAPEAU

In former years a well dressed man
was always seen in spats.
The lady sometimes wore white gloves
But always, always hats—
a feather here, a blossom there,
perhaps a perky bow,
but never was milady seen
without her chic chapeau.

by Nonie Borba

Presentation: While reciting the poem, decorate a plain hat with feathers, bows, and flowers. Show the audience the hat on the last line.

*CAPS 'N HATS

Paul Revere wore one they say
As he galloped from town to town
Some people wear them with a brim
Turned smartly up or down
The Mexican ladies wear them with veils
They're worn by brave Vaqueros
We call them caps, fedoras or hats
In Mexico, they're called sombreros
No matter what we call them
They're classified as hats.
Are you watching what I'm doing?
Well, I'll show you: That's a hat!

by Nonie Borba

Presentation: Use this poem while tearing the tissue paper for the paper hat tear trick or while glueing and cutting the king's hat.

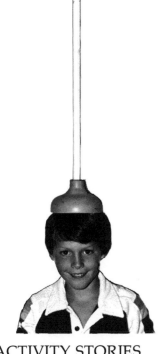

OTHER POEMS TO USE:
"A Man and His Hat," by Letitia Parr *in* Michael Dugan, *Stuff & Nonsense.* il. by Deborah Niland. Collins & World, 1977.

*"Hat," *in* Shel Silverstein, *Where the Sidewalk Ends.* il. by author. Harper, 1974.
On the last line put a toilet plunger on your head.

"Tight Hat," *in* Shel Silverstein, *Where the Sidewalk Ends.* il. by author. Harper, 1974.

"Mr. Spats," by Shel Silverstein, *in* William Cole, *Oh, What Nonsense!* il by Tomi Ungerer. Viking, 1966.

ACTIVITY STORIES

"The Rainhat," *in* Nancy Schimmel, *Just Enough To Make A Story: A Sourcebook For Storytelling.* 2nd printing, slightly rev. Sister's Choice Press (2027 Parker Street, Berkeley, CA. 94704), 1979 1978.
Also in Chesler, Bernice. *Do a Zoom Do.* Little, 1975.
A cut and fold story.

Keats, Ezra Jack. *Jennie's Hat.* il. by author. Harper, 1966. Jennie tries on various household items as hats. The birds decorate her hat with easily available items. Use the actual objects to tell the story.

ACTIVITY

Children wear hats representing book characters or make hats decorated with book characters.

SOUVENIRS

Make a king's hat, following the directions given on page 103 (HATS).

Alternative souvenirs:
    hats from novelty companies
    petits-fours paper cups ("elf hats"). Tell the children to keep the elf hats by their beds at home; tell them that if they wake up early and are very quiet, they may see an elf trying on the hat.
      Petits-fours cups are available from:
    Amscan, Inc.
    South Road
    Harrison, New York 10528

*RIDDLE

Use drawings on poster board to present this riddle:

If you throw a green hat into the Red Sea, what will it become?
Wet.

SONG

Teach this short song and sing as a group. This is a hat song that my husband learned as a child in Austria. It's the *only* song he knows by heart and it does stay in your head . . . forever.

MEIN HUT, DER HAT DREI ECKEN

My hat it has three corners;
Three corners has my hat;
And had it not three corners,
It would not be my hat.

Mein hut er hat drei Ecken;
Drei Ecken hat mein Hut;
Und hat er nicht drei Ecken;
Denn das ist nicht mein Hut.

Motions—(1) On "my" point to self. (2) On "hat" touch top of head. (3) On "three" raise 3 fingers. (4) On "corners" touch elbow of left arm.

PICTURE BOOKS

Show these picture books during your program and leave them on exhibit afterwards.

Corney, Estelle. *Pa's Top Hat.* il. by Hilary Abrahams. Deutsch, 1980.
Pa's top hat is used to dress a scarecrow and save a New Zealand family from a cold winter.

Drawson, Blair. *I Like Hats!* il. by author. Scholastic-TAB, 1977.
Many different hats are celebrated.

Goodall, John S. *Paddy's New Hat*. il. by author. Atheneum Pubs., 1980.
"The Hat," in Arnold Lobel, *Days with Frog and Toad*. il. by author. Harper, 1979.

Lear, Edward. *The Pelican Chorus & The Quangle Wangle's Hat*. il. by Kevin W. Maddison. Viking, 1981.

Munari, Bruno. *Jimmy Has Lost His Cap, Where Can It Be?* il. by author. World, 1959.
Jimmy finds his hat . . . on his head.

Nödset, Joan L. *Who Took the Farmer's Hat?* il. by Fritz Siebel. Harper, 1963.

Seuss, Dr. *The 500 Hats of Bartholomew Cubbins*. il. by author. Vanguard, 1938.

Ungerer, Tomi. *The Hat*. il. by author. Parents Mag. Press, 1970.

ADULT REFERENCE

Couldridge, Alan. *The Hat Book*. il. by author. Prentice-Hall, 1980
Techniques for making all kinds of hats, from scarves to turbans.

113

TEETH

POEM

TOOTH TROUBLE

When I see the dentist
I take him all my teeth:
Some of me's above them,
But most of me's beneath.
And one is in my pocket,
Because it grew so loose
That I could fit a string to it
And tighten up the noose.
I'll grow another, dentist says,
And shall not need to noose it.
Another still to drill and fill?
Not me! I won't produce it.

by David McCord

RIDDLE

What is the best thing to put into apple pie?

Your teeth.

BOOKS TO SHARE

Bate, Lucy. *Little Rabbit's Loose Tooth.* il. by Diane de Groat. Crown, 1975.
The tooth fairy visits Little Rabbit.

De Groat, Diane. *Alligator's Toothache.* il. by author. Crown, 1977.
In a wordless picture book, Alligator refuses to go to the dentist until his friends trick him. Show the pictures slowly to a musical accompaniment. Movie themes make good backgrounds for wordless stories.

Pomerantz, Charlotte. *The Mango Tooth.* il. by Marylin Hafner. Greenwillow Bks., 1977.
Each tooth is named for the way it is loosened, ending with an "elephant tooth." Tell the story, then show selected pictures from the book.

Weiss, Leatie. *Heather's Feathers.* il. by Ellen Weiss. Watts, 1976.
Heather loses feathers instead of teeth. This story makes a good puppet show, or let the children act out the story with paper bag masks.

Williams, Barbara. *Albert's Toothache.* il. by Kay Chorao. Dutton, 1974.
"Turtles don't have toothaches." This book is available as a paperback. Buy two copies. Mount the pictures on posterboard and tell the story using the "flip" cards to present it.

SOUVENIR

Feathers as a souvenir of Heather's Feathers. Check at your local craft supplier.

TREAT

Animal crackers to remember The Mango Tooth.

EXHIBIT

On a bulletin board, display snapshots of the class showing their toothless smiles.

ACTIVITY: TOOTH FAIRY POCKETS

Provide envelopes to decorate; or felt scraps, large needles and yarn, and notions so the children can make their own tooth-fairy pockets.
Copy this poem to put on or in the pockets:

Dear Tooth Fairy,

In this pocket you will find
A teeny tiny tooth of mine
So while I sleep where dreams are made
Let's see if you can make a trade.

RESOURCE PERSON

Do you know an articulate children's dentist or dental hygienist to invite to the story hour?

WISHING

POEM

I KEEP THREE WISHES READY

I keep three wishes ready,
Lest I should chance to meet,
Any day a fairy
Coming down the street.
I'd hate to have to stammer,
Or have to think them out,
For it's very hard to think things up
When a fairy is about.
And I'd hate to lose my wishes,
For fairies fly away,
And perhaps I'd never have a chance
On any other day.
So I keep three wishes ready,
Lest I should chance to meet,
Any day a fairy
Coming down the street.

by Annette Wynne

A selection of poems by children about wishes appears on pages 66–86 in *Wishes, Lies and Dreams,* comp. by Kenneth Koch. (Random House, 1970).

STORIES TO SHARE

This story is a classic wishing story. It is also easy to learn, and delightful to tell.

THE THREE WISHES *

Once a poor woodcutter was working in the woods when he met a fairy. Yes, a real fairy who grants wishes. She told him that he could wish for any three wishes, but of course he had to choose the wishes carefully.

On the way home he thought of all the wonderful things he could wish for: a new house, children, jewels, new clothes. When he got home he excitedly told his wife about the fairy and they started to discuss what three wishes they would make, but they couldn't agree on the wishes. The woodcutter wanted a new car, a ranch-style house, and five children. His wife wanted a motorboat, a colonial style house, and six children. As they argued, it got later and later and they decided to have dinner, which, as usual, was bread and cheese. "Oh," sighed the man,

116

"I wish there were a sausage for dinner." Instantly a fat, juicy sausage appeared on his plate. "Look what you've done!" screamed his wife. "You've used up one of the wishes!" She ranted and raved and screamed and yelled until the woodcutter said with disgust, "Oh, I wish that sausage were at the end of your nose." Instantly the sausage flew from the plate to the woman's nose, where it stuck fast. "Oh," she cried, "Now look what you've done. You've used up another wish *and* I am disfigured for life." She carried on in such a temper that finally the man sighed, "I wish that sausage would fall off your nose," and it did. They had used up all three wishes so . . . they didn't have a new house, jewels, a new car, a motorboat, children, or new clothes. But . . . they did have sausage for dinner.

A LONGER STORY: "The Three Wishes," by Barbara Leonie Picard, *in* Child Study Association of America, *Castles and Dragons: Read-to-Yourself Fairy Tales for Boys and Girls.* il. by William Pène du Bois. Crowell, 1958.
A young man gets all of his wishes without ever having to actually make them.

SHORTER STORIES: "Wishes," *in* Natalie Babbitt, *The Devil's Storybook.* il. by author. Farrar Straus, 1974.
A search for the perfect wish.

"If You Had a Wish," by Charles J. Finger, *in* Association for Childhood Education International, *Told Under the Magic Umbrella.* il. by Elizabeth Orton Jones. Macmillan, 1967.
A variant of "The Three Wishes."

"Did the Tailor Have a Nightmare?" *in* Blanche Serwer, *Let's Steal the Moon: Jewish Tales, Ancient and Recent.* il. by Trina Schart Hyman. Little, 1970.
Napoleon grants a poor tailor three wishes.

PICTURE BOOKS: (not necessarily only for preschoolers!)

Brothers Grimm. *The Fisherman and His Wife.* il. by Margot Zemach. tr. by Randall Jarrell. Farrar Straus, 1980.
A gloriously graphic interpretation of the Grimms' story in which a woman doesn't know when it's time to stop wishing.

---

*If the contemporary additions of a car or motorboat offend your traditionalism, create your own version. That's how folktales evolve.

Williams, Jay. *One Big Wish*. il. by John O'Brien. Macmillan Pub. Co., 1980.

Farmer Fred Butterspoon, granted one wish, decides to make it a BIG one, with hilarious results.

SONG

"I Wish I Was a Mole in the Ground," *in* Virginia A. Tashjian, *Juba This and Juba That; Story Hour Stretches for Large or Small Groups.* Little, 1969.

Once you have learned the rhythm and pattern of this song, you and the children can make up new verses.

TREAT

Cookies cut into star shapes to go with:

> Star light, star bright
> the first star I see tonight.
> I wish I may, I wish I might
> Have the wish I wish tonight.

SOUVENIR

A WISHING CANDLE

Let everyone make a wish on a lighted (supervision, please!) birthday candle. The candles are take-home souvenirs.

ACTIVITIES

WISH BOOK

Each child can make a wish book with a title such as:

I wish I had one ————————————

I wish there really were ————————————

I wish I could go to————————————

I wish I could hear————————————

I wish I had a toy that ————————————

I wish I had enough money to ————————————

I wish everyone loved————————————

I wish trees could ————————————

What would the wish look like? Have the children draw their wishes.

Place the completed wish books on the bulletin board.

WISH SUPERSTITIONS

Discuss wish superstitions, such as wishing on:

a star
a new moon
the first fruit of the season
a wishbone
an eyelash
a dandelion gone to seed
a ladybug

Or follow the Japanese custom of writing your wish on a paper streamer (adding-machine tape?) and tying it to a tree (see Tanabata celebration, p. 83).

BOOK EXHIBIT

On a table place a selection of your favorite titles with a sign that says I WISH YOU WOULD READ THESE BOOKS.

Photos on pages 118, 119, 128, and 129 by Hoda Bakhshandag.

119

TEDDY BEARS

Sometimes you can use just one object to present several stories (see also the puppet routine, p. 228). For instance, use a teddy bear to tell a group of bear stories such as these.

Asch, Frank. *Sand Cake.* il. by author. Parents Mag. Press, 1979.
Papa Bear draws designs in the sand for Baby Bear.
Presentation: Reproduce the drawings in the story in a sandbox or on a chalkboard.

Freeman, Don. *Corduroy.* il. by author. Viking, 1968, and *A Pocket for Corduroy.* Viking, 1978.
In *Corduroy,* a stuffed bear loses a button and finds a home. In *A Pocket for Corduroy,* the same bear needs a pocket and finally gets one.
Presentation: Use the same teddy bear, for both stories. You will also need a pair of green trousers, velcro, a button, and a pocket. Attach the button and pocket to the trousers with velcro so that you can start the stories without the button and pocket and put them on later.

Freeman, Don. *Beady Bear.* il. by author. Viking, 1954.
A windup stuffed bear is afraid of the dark.
Presentation: Besides a teddy bear, you will need a flashlight, a pillow, and a book. Narrate the story while you manipulate the bear and the props.

Minarik, Else Holmelund. *Little Bear.* il. by Maurice Sendak. Harper, 1957.
Presentation: Use a snowsuit and hat to dress a bear for a cold day, and then undress him to reveal his fur coat.

Murphy, Jill. *Peace at Last.* il. by author. Dial Press, 1980.
Mr. Bear is kept awake by various night noises: snores, birds, clock, refrigerator.
Presentation: Have the teddy bear lie down and then sit up each time he is unable to sleep as you narrate the story. Children will enjoy participating by making the various noises.

Watanabe, Shigeo. *How Do I Put It On? Getting Dressed.* il. by Yasuo Ohtomo. Collins [distributed by Philomel Bks.], 1979.
A little bear, getting dressed, at first puts everything on in the wrong place (shoes on his ears, cap on his foot). Finally he gets dressed correctly all by himself.
Presentation: Use a stuffed bear, and a cap, shirt, pants, and shoes. You will need a bear with long arms and legs so that the clothes fit.

Hint: I bought clothes to fit my bear at a baby shop. A much less expensive way to acquire baby clothes is to wait until a friend's baby grows out of them.

MORE BEAR STORIES: There are many wonderful bear books. These are a few to balance with the object stories above. The books listed work particularly well with a group.

Ginsburg, Mirra. *Two Greedy Bears.* il. by Jose Aruego and Ariane Dewey. Macmillan Pub. Co., 1976.
Two bears show off to each other. Clear pictures for presentation.

Jeschke, Susan. *Angela and Bear.* il. by author. Holt, 1979.
A little girl draws a bear that becomes alive and steps out of the page.

McCloskey, Robert. *Blueberries for Sal.* il. by author. Viking, 1948.
A mother bear and her cub are blueberrying in the same area as a little girl and her mother.

Mack, Stan. *10 Bears in My Bed: A Goodnight Countdown.* il. by author. Pantheon Bks., 1974.
Based on an old counting song, "Roll over, roll over." This makes an excellent participation book.

Milne, A. A. *Pooh's Bedtime Book.* il. by Ernest H. Shepard. Dutton, 1980.
A collection of Milne's verse and stories that makes a good introduction to the Winnie the Pooh stories.

Myers, Bernice. *Not This Bear!* il. by author. Four Winds, 1967.
Herman, bundled up for winter, is mistaken for a bear. Tell this story rather than show the pictures.

Turkle, Brinton. *Deep in the Forest.* il. by author. Dutton, 1976.
A little bear explores a log cabin. A wordless variant of "Goldilocks and The Three Bears."

Winter, Paula. *Bear and Fly.* il. by author. Crown, 1976.
A wordless picture book shows a fly bothering a bear.

SOPHISTICATED PICTURE BOOKS:

Asch, Frank. *In the Eye of the Teddy.* il. by author. Harper, 1973.
What it is like to be inside a teddy bear looking out. A wordless floating sensation.

Parker, Nancy Winslow. *The Ordeal of Byron B. Blackbear.* il. by author. Dodd, 1979.
A bear fouls up a scientific experiment.

Steiner, Jörg. *The Bear Who Wanted to Be a Bear.* il. by Jörg Müller. Atheneum Pubs., 1976.
A bear awakens from hibernation and is mistaken for a factory worker. A more sophisticated version of a book originally written by Frank Tashlin. (*The Bear That Wasn't.* Dover, 1962 or Dutton, 1946.)

"Teddy Bear Gets Too Fat for His Jacket," by Margaret Gore, *in* Eileen Colwell (ed.), *More Stories to Tell.* il. by Caroline Sharpe. Penguin, 1979.
Teddy Bear's jacket doesn't fit, so he follows the advice of his friends to jump and run.

Presentation: Use the bear as a puppet following the actions.

Stevenson, James. *The Bear Who Had No Place to Go.* il. by author. Harper, 1972.
Ralph, a bear, is fired from the circus and looks for friends and a job.

ADULT REFERENCES: **Bialosky, Peggy and Alan.** *The Teddy Bear Catalog.* Workman, 1980.
"Prices, care and repair, lore, hundreds of photos."

Hutchings, Margaret. *Teddy Bears and How To Make Them.* il. by author. Dover, 1977.
77 pages of patterns, 77 figures, 12 photographs.

A catalog of stuffed bears, bear totes, books, ceramics, toys, and miniatures is available for $1.00 from:

Bear-in-Mind, Inc.
73 Indian Pipe Lane
Concord, MA 01742

NEWS ITEM PROGRAM

Current events are often excellent sources of program material. In an election year, librarians and teachers can be of great help by making books and articles available on candidates and issues, or they can have fun with an election and run Snoopy or Winnie-the-Pooh for President.

Building a program around a news item has one great advantage: TV and newspaper coverage of the subject will serve as free publicity for your program.

MT. ST. HELENS: A VOLCANO IN THE NEWS

EXHIBIT

I live near Mt. St. Helens, a mountain in southwest Washington. The mountain made national news in 1980, when it suddenly showed its true identity as an active volcano.

Both *Time* and *Newsweek* featured the major eruption in full color on their weekly covers. I used the covers of these magazines (free pictures!) on a bulletin board to promote books. Instead of featuring volcano books (there were not an abundance of these), I used a survival theme for my bulletin board display. A paper pocket on the board contained annotated catalog cards of books in which children combat a natural disaster, for example: a tropical storm in Theodore Taylor's *The Cay* (Doubleday, 1969), a

123

landslide in Veronique Day's *Landslide!* (Coward, 1963), and a blizzard in Marietta Moskin's *Day of the Blizzard* (Coward, 1978). I displayed the books directly below the bulletin board, so they were easily accessible.

ACTIVITY

After several eruptions of ash and steam, everyone in our area went a little volcano-crazy. One school built a huge papier-mâché volcano and then held a contest to see who could come up with an idea for simulating an eruption. In another school, the members of a fifth-grade class built their own volcanos, clay covered and on newspaper bases. The winning eruptions in the first school and in the fifth-grade class were created with a chemical called ammonium dichromate, which is available from chemical suppliers (look under "Chemicals" in the Yellow Pages). The chemical is expensive (about $5 for 4 ounces), but you don't need much to create a lovely volcanic eruption complete with volcanic ash.

Hints: Put newspaper under the volcano to catch the ash. Fill a 2" volcano cavity with about an inch of the chemical. Light with fireplace matches, or stick two or three match heads into the chemical and then light those. (An adult should do the actual lighting.) Turn down the lights, and watch the sparks fly.

STORY OR BOOKTALK   To complete your program, you could briefly talk about disaster books or tell a related story. I found the story below in a book I picked up while taping a television series in Fiji.

WHY THERE IS A VOLCANO ON TANNA

In the long ago days there was a man who was also a volcano. His name was Iahuei, and he was looking for a place to live. On Tanna Island there was a place called Memtahui. Should he settle there? No, it was too near the salt water. It would not do for a volcano.

Iahuei journeyed on. He crossed the sea to Aniwa, which was a flat island. How could a volcano live on a flat island? So he crossed the sea again to Futuna, and climbed up two thousand feet. Would this do? No, the top of the island seemed to be too flat for a volcano because there was a broad plateau there. So Iahuei went back by sea to Tanna. There also was a central plateau which was a sandy waste.

As he walked on across this flat sandy place, Iahuei suddenly saw two women making puddings. They had pounded taro and mixed it with coconut. They had spread it on a big flat leaf and placed it in an earth oven to cook. Soon the puddings were steaming and tender on the hot stones of the earth oven. The women served portions of the pudding on banana leaves for plates. They asked Iahuei if he would like some, and he said he would. The pudding smelt delicious.

Iahuei sat down in the sand. He was tired after all his long journeying. He sat in the sand, working himself into a deep hole. It was very comfortable, so he eased his back two feet down into the sand.

"Bring me more pudding!" he cried.

The women brought him more, which he ate sitting at his ease, leaning on the sand at his back. Again Iahuei called out, "Bring me more pudding!"

Again the women brought it to him, and he ate it.

"Bring me more pudding!" he called a third time.

At this the women lost their tempers. One of them picked up a pointed digging stick. She raised it above her head and brought it down with all her strength. The pointed stick went right through Iahuei's stomach and pinned him to the sand. But Iahuei was a volcano. Out spurted hot ashes, molten lava, steam and jets of boiling water. As this continued the volcano rumbled and shook the ground. And there to this day stands Iahuei, half god-man, half volcano.

From *Folk Tales of the South Pacific*,
comp. by Inez Hames. University of London Press, 1969.

NOW IT'S YOUR TURN

Parents, teachers, librarians, group leaders: the possibilities for your programming are endless. Present the programs in this book, or create your own around one of the following themes.

Science fiction
Sports
Drugs
Ecology
Architecture
Seasons
War
Religion
Sex education
Travel in a foreign country
Folk heroes

The sea	Caves	Card games
Careers	Music	Witchcraft
Politics	Photography	Coin collecting
The United Nations	Dreams	Urban living
Cooking	Ballet	Reindeer
Birds	Toys	Weaving
Elephants	The paperback revolution	Trees
A period of history	Carousels	Books in foreign languages
Poetry	Rivers	Sport cars
Short stories	Dragons	Bicycles
The movies	Organic gardening	Musical instruments
Rare books	Minorities	Houseboats
Airplanes	Diaries in books	Music boxes
Nature	Mountain climbing	Umbrellas
Drama	Insects	Mysteries
Books for reluctant readers	Children and television	Kayaking

For book activities to use with younger children, consult:

Agostino, Peggy. *Amelia Burt and Charlie: Children's Book Activities.* Parkside Press, 2026 Parkside Ct., West Lin, Or. 97068. Also *Friends of Amelia Burt and Charlie* (1981). An excellent collection of creative ideas for activities using picture books.

Polette, Nancy. *E is for Everybody; A Manual for Bringing Fine Picture Books into the Hands and Hearts of Children.* Scarecrow, 1976.
Group activities with picture books.

or, have you an idea of your own?

Continuing Programs

PRESCHOOL PARENT PROGRAM

As a parent group, preschool parents are generally the most visibly concerned with doing something for their children. Often they are new parents who want to learn about parenting. Most preschool children spend most of their time at home, and parents are eager to find activities to help socialize and educate them. Take advantage of this enthusiasm and plan activities for preschoolers and their parents.

This is the outline for a lecture that I have given to numerous groups of parents and teachers on books for very young children. It is a show-and-tell lecture, and I take the magazines and books that I'm discussing. I have also taken slides of these books, as well as of related objects, so I don't have to carry a lot and, also, so a larger group can easily see the books I'm discussing. When I first started working with slides, I resented the time it took to take the pictures, but now that I've seen how much I've used my slide sets, I can honestly recommend making them. It is an efficient method for lecturing, and, if you choose the books wisely, the core of the lecture can remain intact for years. Update the lecture by adding newer titles to the accompanying bibliography and by showing the new books after or in the middle of the slide lecture. Make sure that you speak only about books you have personally seen.

PRESCHOOL LECTURE

INTRODUCTION

People often ask me, "When should I start reading to my child?" My answer is: "as soon as he or she is born." I practice what I preach. When I first saw my daughter, Hilary, the nurses all stood around and watched for my first reaction.

Instinctively I said, "Jack be nimble
           Jack be quick
           Jack jump over the candlestick."

"Isn't that cute?" one of the nurses said to another. "She teaches children's literature, you know." (Actually, recit-

127

ing a nursery rhyme to my three-hour-old daughter was all the conversation I could manage.)

Introducing your child to print doesn't need to be an expensive activity. Start with materials around the house.

SHOW AND TELL

[Briefly discuss items that can be collected from around the house to interest a child in "looking and seeing." Show these items on slides or hold the actual items up to the audience. It is not mandatory that the audience see details of an item, but they should get a general impression of the objects you are discussing.]

Magazines: Give the child practice in turning pages, while identifying such objects as people, food, and furniture. Magazines are expendable, so don't be upset if your child tears the pages. Some experts feel that children should learn to respect any bound volume, but I feel that there is only a brief period in your life when you feel like tearing up a magazine, and you might as well indulge this instinct. In fact, my favorite all-time present to an eight-month-old child is a roll of wax paper to unravel, crinkle, and tear up.

Greeting Cards: Save the best Christmas cards and other greeting cards to give your child an introduction to colors, patterns, and composition. As your child grows older, you can use the greeting card pictures as illustrations for a story you or your child writes.

Store Catalogs: Department stores or mail-order catalogs usually feature simple, clear photographs or drawings of merchandise. Use these for a "see and say" session, or cut the pictures up to make a counting, alphabet, or object scrapbook.

House Decorations: Make a point of showing your child the paintings and drawings on your walls and any special knick-knacks and sculpture in your home. Tell him the story of your art—the name of it, what it represents, where you got it, and why it's special to you.

CLOTH OR CARDBOARD BOOKS

These books printed on cloth or sturdy cardboard are published for young children whose lack of coordination makes it difficult for them to manipulate paper pages . . . and for those children who are tempted to eat their books rather than read them. Most of the publishers of the books leave intervals between printings, so generally you will have to take whatever is available. The following publishers usually have a selection of cloth or "board" books available:

> Albert Whitman & Co.
> Grosset & Dunlap Inc. (Platt & Munk imprint)
> Brimax Books (Cambridge, England)
> Random House Inc.

Although we generally associate fantasy images with children, scrutinize these books to make certain that the illustrations are realistic. For a one- or two-year-old who is just learning to speak, a picture of a bird dressed in slacks and pushing a baby carriage may be confusing. Let the child learn "bird" before learning fantastic or anthropomorphic birds.

PHOTOGRAPH BOOKS

Baby's Scrapbook: Contains the pictures of baby's immediate family, relatives, friends, and house. Include such signs of the times as titles of current bestsellers, grocery prices, and pictures of current fashions for future fun. Make sure that the second and third children get their individual books too.

Commercial Photo Picture Book: Some board books published for very young children show photographs of such familiar objects as a telephone, hat, and table. Platt & Munk's *My Picture Book* is an example.

Mommy's Books: These are the expensive adult books, usually considered "coffee-table" books because they often reside unread on a living-room coffee table. Share these beautiful books with your young child while baby looks on. Art books and travel titles are common. Use them now, because when your baby gets a bit older—to the crawling/destroying stage—you may want to make them a little less available.

RHYMES AND RHYTHMS

Youngsters use the cadence of sound to understand the language around them. Read simple nursery rhymes and lullabies to help develop their ear for language.

Bennett, Jill. *Roger Was a Razor Fish And Other Poems.* il. by Maureen Roffey. Lothrop, 1981.
A short collection of rhythmic poems for the very young.

Brooke, L. Leslie. *Ring O'Roses: A Nursery Rhyme Picture Book.* il. by author, new ed. Warne, 1977.
Familiar Mother Goose rhymes with full-page illustrations.

Grover, Eulalie Osgood, ed. *Mother Goose; the Classic Volland Edition.* il. by Frederick Richardson. Rand McNally, 1971.
One rhyme per page illustrated with large traditional pictures.

Hush Little Baby; a folk lullaby. il. by Aliki. Prentice-Hall, 1968.
An old English folksong is illustrated with an 18th century background. Warmth and humor make this an excellent song to recite or sing . . . even if you are a bit off-key. Another version is *Hush Little Baby,* by Margot Zemach. il. by author. Dutton, 1975.

Hutchins, Pat. *Good-night, Owl!* il. by author. Macmillan Pub. Co., 1972.
An owl tries to sleep while birds and animals are awake and very vocal. Children enjoy imitating the sounds.

John, Timothy, ed. *The Great Song Book.* music edited by Peter Hankey. il. by Tomi Ungerer. Doubleday, 1978.
A visually beautiful songbook containing sixty of the "best loved songs in the English language," including nursery rhymes and songs.

Kessler, Ethel and Leonard. *Do Baby Bears Sit in Chairs?* il. by authors. Doubleday, 1961.
The difference between fantasy and reality in a rhyming "I can do" book.

Memling, Carl. *Hi, All You Rabbits.* il. by Myra McGee. Parents Mag. Press, 1970.
Domestic animals are shown in action with the sounds they make. Repetitive refrains to encourage child participation.

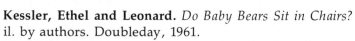

Mitchell, Donald, comp. *Every Child's Book of Nursery Songs.* arranged by Carey Blyton; il. by Alan Howard. Crown, 1968.
A collection of traditional nursery songs accompanied by simple piano music.

Stecher, Miriam B. *Max, the Music-Maker.* Photographs by Alice S. Kandell. Lothrop, 1980.
A young child experiments with objects he finds around the house that make sounds. Black and white photographs.

CONCEPT BOOKS

These books give young children a feel for the world around them. Each child should be introduced to an alphabet book, a counting book, and a color book.

Brown, Margaret Wise. *Goodnight Moon.* il. by Clement Hurd. Harper, 1947.
The ritual of going to bed includes saying "goodnight" to the objects in a bunny's room.

Carle, Eric. *1, 2, 3 to the Zoo.* il. by author. Collins [distributed by Philomel Bks.], 1968.
Count the animals going to the zoo.

Crews, Donald. *Freight Train.* il. by author. Greenwillow Bks., 1978.
Count the colored cars that make up a fast freight train.

Dabcovich, Lydia. *Follow the River.* il. by author. Dutton, 1980.
A simple story and clear pictures follow a river from the mountains to the sea.

Holzenthaler, Jean. *My Feet Do.* Photographs by George Ancona. Dutton, 1979.
Holzenthaler, Jean. *My Hands Can.* il. by Nancy Tafuri. Dutton, 1978.
These two books show the functions of the hands and feet.

Kunhardt, Dorothy. *Pat the Bunny.* il. by author. Western Pub. Co., 1962.
The perfect first book. The child sees himself in a mirror, smells the flowers, feels Daddy's scratchy beard, and waves goodbye.

Lodge, Bernard. *Door to Door.* il. by Maureen Roffey. Lothrop, 1980.
Split pages show the inside of the homes in a neighborhood.

131

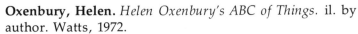

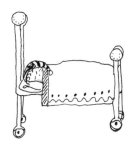

Oxenbury, Helen. *Helen Oxenbury's ABC of Things.* il. by author. Watts, 1972.
Upper and lower case letters. Words sound like they look.

Parish, Peggy. *I Can—Can You?* il. by Marilyn Hafner. Greenwillow Bks., 1980.
Four activity books packaged together are designed to help a child respond to words.

Rice, Eve. *Goodnight, Goodnight.* il. by author. Greenwillow Bks., 1980.
Everyone in town is saying "goodnight."

Rockwell, Harlow. *My Kitchen.* il. by author. Greenwillow, 1980. Everyday kitchen objects for a child to name. See also Anne and Harlow Rockwell's *The Supermarket.* (Macmillan Pub. Co., 1979) and *The Toolbox* (Macmillan Pub. Co., 1971).

Scarry, Richard. *Richard Scarry's Best Word Book Ever.* il. by author. Golden, 1963.
Pictures of everyday objects crowd the pages of this dictionary-like book.

Watanabe, Shigeo. *How Do I Put It On? Getting Dressed.* il. by Yasuo Ohtomo. Collins [distributed by Philomel Bks.], 1979.
First in a series of "I can do it by myself" books. This one shows a bear getting dressed by himself. See also *What a Good Lunch!* Collins, 1980.

STORIES

Now your child is ready to listen to simple stories.

Bright, Robert. *My Red Umbrella.* il. by author. Morrow, 1959.
Animals crowd under a big red umbrella when it starts to rain.

Flack, Marjorie. *Angus and the Cat.* il. by author. Doubleday, 1931.
A Scottie finds out that a cat can be a nuisance . . . and fun.

Gág, Wanda. *Millions of Cats.* il. by author. Coward-McCann, 1928.
"Hundreds of cats, thousands of cats, millions and billions and trillions of cats."

Galdone, Paul. *The Three Billy Goats Gruff.* il. by author. Seabury [distributed by Houghton], 1973.
A beloved Norwegian folktale in which three billy goats outwit a troll.

Ginsburg, Mirra. *Good Morning, Chick.* il. by Byron Barton. Greenwillow Bks., 1980.
Bold, bright pictures show the early days of a chick.

Hill, Eric. *Where's Spot?* il. by author. Putnam, 1980.
A mother dog searches for her puppy in a book with peek-a-boo flip-ups.

Massie, Diane Redfield. *The Baby Beebee Bird.* il. by author. Harper, 1963.
A lively bird keeps the zoo animals awake.

Petersham, Maud and Miska. *The Box with Red Wheels.* Macmillan Pub. Co., 1949.
Farm animals visit a baby.

The Three Little Pigs. il. by Erik Blegvad. Atheneum Pubs., 1980.
A wicked wolf chases three house-building pigs.

TOYS

[Although this lecture emphasizes books in a child's life, it is worthwhile mentioning the existence of toy libraries in the United States and Canada.]

The toys in these libraries are carefully selected for their educational and entertainment value and, of course, to help parents save money to buy such necessities as food . . . and books.

REFERENCES: Canadian Association of Toy Libraries. *Toy Libraries: How To Start a Toy Library in Your Community.* Canadian Association of Toy Libraries (50 Quebec Avenue, Suite 1207, Toronto, Ontario M6P4B4 Canada), 1980. See also *Toy Libraries 2: The Many Uses of Toy Lending,* edited by Joanna von Levetzou. Canadian Assoc. of Toy Libraries, 1980.

American Library Association. *"Toys to Go"—A Guide to the Use of Realia in Public Libraries.* Prepared by the Connecticut State Library Realia Committee. American Library Association (50 Huron, Chicago, Illinois, 60611), 1975.

Surrey Place Toy Library. *Toy Library Handbook.* Surrey Place Toy Library (Ministry of Community and Social Services, 2 Surrey Place, Toronto, Ontario M5S2C2), 1978.

ACTIVITIES: AT HOME PLAY

1. A Word a Day: Hang a chalkboard in your child's room. Each day, ask him to suggest a word he likes. Print it on the board and leave it there until tomorrow.

133

2. Watch Sesame Street on TV with your child so that you know which letters were used that day.

3. Ask your child to dictate a letter to an out-of-town relative or friend so that he knows what words can do.

4. Read aloud to your child at least once a day. Assure him that this practice won't stop when he learns to read.

5. Let your child copy simple words; begin with his name.

6. Read yourself, so your child sees you enjoying it.

7. Write his name on his belongings and show him how it looks.

TREAT

[Demonstrate making alphabet cheese. Show how easy it is.]

Cut American cheese slices into the first letter of his or her name. For snack time.

TO MAKE

1. CHILD'S OWN BOOK
Make a personalized alphabet book for your child.

YOU NEED: A notebook with blank pages.

A set of capital letters. Cut the letters from felt, fabric scraps, sandpaper, poster board, or construction paper.

A set of stick-on letters or a letter stencil.

Photographs and pictures. As children grow up, most families take snapshots of birthday parties, holidays, and trips. After the best pictures have been sent to Grandma, there are still a lot left over. Now is the time to use these. You can also cut pictures from magazines and greeting cards.

Glue.

HOW TO: Make a page for each letter of the alphabet. Use a capital letter and then write a phrase with the stencil or with stick-on letters. Now go through the collection of photographs, greeting cards, etc., and find an appropriate picture to represent each heading.

Here are some examples of page headings:

A is for Aunt (the child's aunt)
B is for Baby (child as a baby)
C is for Cake (birthday)
D is for Dog (the family pet)
E is for Eat (your child eating)
F is for Friend (the girl next door)

HINT: You can cut out large numbers and make a personalized counting book in the same way.

134

2. GRANDMA'S TRUNK

Cut pictures from magazines or draw your own to go into grandma's trunk (for beginning readers).

"I packed my grandma's trunk and in it I put . . ." (each object begins with the succeeding letter of the alphabet). Mount the pictures on cards and print the names of the objects on the back. Use a box for a trunk.

3. PERCEPTION PLAQUES

This is a reading readiness game.

YOU NEED: Two sets of identical pictures.

One source of pictures is material given away at automobile shows or other industry exhibits. Each manufacturer prints a colorful brochure showing the new model cars. The pictures show parts of cars (engines, steering wheels, fenders), as well as front and side views. Take two of each and you will have the ingredients for a perception game for your preschooler. Wallpaper, greeting cards, wrapping paper, and carpet samples can be used the same way.

HOW TO: Mount one set of pictures on a large piece of posterboard, the other set individually on cards.

The object is for the child to match the object on the card with the same picture on the board.

4. FELT SHAPE BOARD

This item can be made by each of the people in your class if you order supplies in advance.

The shape board can be used to teach a child numerals and shapes. The adult places a number on the felt board and asks the child to find "two rectangles" or "one circle" to place next to the number.

YOU NEED:
cardboard or poster board	vinyl tape
felt, 8" x 10"	glue
felt, 5" x 9"	scissors
felt scraps	

HOW TO: Glue the 8" x 10" piece of felt to the cardboard. Turn the board over and make a pocket with the second piece of felt to hold the shape cutouts. Cut out felt numbers from 1 to 5 from the scraps. Cut out felt shapes from the scraps, including:

one square   four triangles
two circles   five hearts
three rectangles

The object of this exercise is for the child to match the shapes with the numerals and at the same time to learn the names of the shapes and numbers.

HINT: Don't forget to use contrasting colors so that the shapes will stand out.

BOOKS ABOUT SHAPES: **Wildsmith, Brian.** *Animal Shapes.* il. by author. Oxford Univ. Press, 1980.
This picture book shows a realistically painted animal and then on a facing page the same animal in bold, colorful shapes. An interesting introduction to the real and the imaginary world.

Youldon, Gillian. *Shapes.* il. by author. Watts, 1979.
Vibrant primary colors and peek-a-boo pages make finding shapes a game.

BOOKLIST: BOOKS FOR PRESCHOOLERS UP TO 5 YEARS

I used to give this assignment in my children's literature class: "If you could buy ten picture books for a child, excluding an alphabet or Mother Goose book, which ten would you choose?"

I dropped the assignment when one of my students challenged me to tell what my ten choices would be and I couldn't decide. Ten books for whom? In what kind of family? A city or country child? A boy, a girl? (Would it matter?) The only ten a child has, or does she have access to other titles? My favorite ten today? Or tomorrow, when a new title is published?

For those of you who have been asked the same question, I offer you this bibliography (of more than ten) that I would recommend that any family purchase. Add your own titles and leave room for the newly published.

After agonizing over this list, I was interested to find that many of the books were first published before 1960. Although there are excellent titles published after this date, most of them have not made it into my classic list of "warm family stories every child should know."

Aardema, Verna. *Why Mosquitoes Buzz in People's Ears; a West African Tale Retold.* il. by Leo and Diane Dillon. Dial Press, 1975.
The story first, later an understanding of the glorious graphics. A book to grow into.

Barrett, Judi. *Animals Should Definitely Not Wear Clothing.* il. by Ron Barrett. Atheneum Pubs., 1971.
Funny pictures showing animals wearing people clothing.

Bemelmans, Ludwig. *Madeleine.* il. by author. Viking Press, 1939.
A first visit to a hospital and a visit to Paris.

Brooke, L. Leslie. *Johnny Crow's Garden.* il. by author. Warne, 1903.
Classic nonsense rhyme illustrated with witty paintings.

Brown, Margaret Wise. *Goodnight Moon.* il. by Clement Hurd. Harper, 1947.
A "must have" in every home library. It is the best goodnight book of them all.

Bruna, Dick. *First Pictures.* il. by author. Otto Maier Ravensburg/Creative Playthings, 1969.
A board book showing brilliantly colored everyday objects for the very young.

Burton, Virginia Lee. *The Little House.* il. by author. Houghton, 1942.
This story shows the growth of the city around a country house. The house has its own personality and feelings. A timeless story.

Carle, Eric. *The Very Hungry Caterpillar.* il. by author. Collins [distributed by Philomel Bks.] 1970.
A voracious caterpillar eats his way through a week's food. Science with fantasy.

Crews, Donald. *Freight Train.* il. by author. Greenwillow Bks., 1978.
A freight train speeds by. Splendid brilliant colors.

Daugherty, James. *Andy and the Lion.* il by author. Viking, 1938.
"A tale of kindness remembered." A picture-book version of Androcles and the Lion for preschoolers and the whole family.

De Brunhoff, Jean. *The Story of Babar, the Little Elephant.* il. by author. Random House. 1937.
This has every ingredient for the "perfect" picture book: adventure, sadness, happiness, and animals.

De Paola, Tomie. *Strega Nona; an old tale.* il. by author. Prentice-Hall, 1975.
A pasta pot that won't stop bubbling gets Big Anthony into trouble.

Gág, Wanda. *Millions of Cats.* il. by author. Coward, 1928.
A really good story with the added attraction of an introduction to the concepts of millions, billions, and trillions.

Keats, Ezra Jack. *The Snowy Day.* Viking, 1962.
A boy's first experience with snow. For children who have or have not seen snow.

Kent, Jack. *The Fat Cat; a Danish folktale.* Parents Mag. Press, 1971.
Repetition creates a folktale rhythm to be enjoyed by children and adult readers.

Kunhardt, Dorothy. *Pat the Bunny.* il. by author. Golden, 1940.
Baby's first picture book with bunnies to touch and flowers to smell.

Lionni, Leo. *Frederick.* il. by author. Pantheon Bks., 1967.
The artist's place in society is introduced through a family of mice.

Lobel, Arnold. *Frog and Toad All Year.* il. by author. Harper, 1976.
One of a series of easy readers that make good family reading too.

McCloskey, Robert. *Make Way for Ducklings.* il. by author. Viking, 1941.
A family of ducks finds a home in Boston.

Mayer, Mercer. *There's a Nightmare in My Closet.* il. by author. Dial Press, 1968.
This book makes having a bad dream fun.

Potter, Beatrix. *The Tale of Peter Rabbit.* il. by author. Warne, 1903.
Still the classic picture story. Naughtiness as an adventure accompanied by full-color paintings in a small format.

Sendak, Maurice. *Nutshell Library.* il. by author. Harper, 1962.
Four tiny picture books: an almanac with poems, a counting book, an alphabet book, and a storybook. A complete library in a slipcase.

Seuss, Dr. *The Cat in the Hat.* il. by author. Random House. 1957.
The beginning reader that changed American easy-to-read books by making learning to read fun.

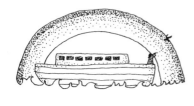

Spier, Peter. *Noah's Ark.* il. by author. Doubleday, 1977.
The detailed drawings make this a book to enjoy alone or as a family. For me it is the most intriguing of the Bible stories.

Steig, William. *Sylvester and the Magic Pebble.* il. by author. Simon & Schuster, 1969.
A really good story. Magic, the seasons, family love, and happy pictures.

Yashima, Taro. *Umbrella.* il. by author. Viking, 1958.
A little girl receives an umbrella as a present and can't wait to use it.

Zion, Gene. *Harry the Dirty Dog.* il. by Margaret Bloy Graham. Harper, 1956.
A dog who does not like taking baths finds out in a delightful way why they are needed.

139

SUMMER READING INCENTIVE PROGRAMS

For years, as each summer approached, there were variations of a cartoon in *The New Yorker* showing a woman settling down into her beach chair and saying to her husband, "This year I'm going to finish *Moby Dick.*" Vacations and summer have traditionally been a time of relaxation when, supposedly, we have more time to read. Since children are out of school and often without organized activities, it would seem that they should also have more time for leisure reading. In an attempt to organize this time into a profitable activity, libraries and schools sometimes offer a summer reading program. There is no reason for parents not to guide a child's reading too. The objective of a family reading program or a library program should not be to see how many books a child can read in an allotted time, but rather to encourage the reading of quality literature. Try not to set up competition between children, but rather give them a feeling of accomplishment after they have read a variety of books—all chosen for their particular enjoyment.

BASIC SUMMER READING KIT

YOU NEED:

access to books
a discrete block of time
  (2 weeks, 6 weeks)

a theme
publicity
an exhibit

components of reading kits:
  bookmarks
  buttons (available from advertising specialty
    companies)
  reading games   membership cards
  reading certificates   prizes
  booklists   a puppet or costumed barker

HOW TO: Start in April to design and collect the components of the reading kits.
Advertise the program to prospective members.
Emphasize how much fun it will be to belong to the club or to take part in the program. The incentives to join might be a button, a membership card, and prizes.
To introduce the program, you might use a puppet.
After the summer has begun, give a book program for members, or have a party so that the readers maintain their enthusiasm.
You'll probably want to assign a certain number of books to read in the allotted time period. Set realistic goals for the children.

Do not encourage competition or give penalties for failure to complete goals.

If you are conducting the program by mail, enclose riddles and booklists to keep up interest.

Be sure you follow through with prizes and congratulatory letters for those who finish, and thank-you letters to those who tried but didn't finish all the books.

HINTS: To choose a theme, have a contest among prospective club members.

To print bookmarks, certificates, or membership cards, try to get donations from local merchants.

To buy printed buttons or balloons, look in the phone book under "Advertising specialties." If you do not have access to a local supplier, write I. Irving Weissler Co., 383 Pearl St., Brooklyn, NY 11201.

The Children's Book Council (67 Irving Pl., New York, NY 10003), publishes certificates for reading programs each year.

Left: A summer party ends with a watermelon-seed contest.
Right: Feathers on the Rare Bird indicate books read (Clark County Library District, Las Vegas, Nevada).

IDEAS FOR SUMMER READING PROGRAMS

PASSPORT TO BOOKS

Provide each child with a World Passport made from posterboard and blank paper. Each page represents a trip with one book. Marked visas on the top of the pages enable the children to write the authors and titles of the books they have read. You can provide a second notebook entitled "Trip Diary" for comments about each book, or the children can write comments on the visa pages. When they come to "passport control" (the librarian, teacher, or parent), their visas should be marked "admitted," with the date. If this is to be a continuous activity or one involving many children, you might want to obtain a rubber stamp made up to look like an official visa stamp.

As a passport official you might ask the children:

Where they went (setting)
Whom they met (characterization)
What they did (plot)
If it was a happy or sad trip (theme)

AIRLINE TICKET

The same idea for reading a number of books can be done using an airline ticket. Make the return trip "open" so that you or the child can fill in the itinerary as each book is completed.

An 8″ × 3″ sheet of paper folded in half encloses the ticket. Make a new sheet for each book read.

CASSETTE RECORDING

Let the children record their reading experiences (giving the author, title, and brief comments) on a cassette.

BULLETIN BOARD EXHIBIT

Let each child add an apple to a tree, a section to a bookworm, a car to a train, or a star to the ceiling for each book read in a collective effort to decorate a room.

If competition is not likely to get out of hand (at home, for instance), children can have their own book bulletin boards on which to record comments, put up drawings about books, and a miniature book made of construction paper for each book read.

BOOK CHARACTER THEME

Choose a popular book character (for instance, Winnie-the-Pooh, Harriet the Spy, Curious George, or Wilbur the pig), and create your summer reading program around the character.

Winnie-the-Pooh's search for a Heffalump can be a search for good books read and enjoyed.

Harriet the Spy's notebook can be a place to record titles of books read and enjoyed.

Curious George's medal can be the "prize" at the end of the summer for those who have participated in the program.

Wilbur's pigpen can be large enough to hold lots of little spiders, each representing a book read.

Choose a book character you love, or let the children vote for the character they want to represent their program.

READING RECORDS

Occasionally I begin a reading record of books I've read, but I never remember to keep it up. Maybe the trick is to begin early enough so that it becomes a habit. Blank books are available at stationery stores. Encourage your children to set aside a page for each book read. Suggest that they write a comment about the book or copy a passage they particularly liked. It might also be fun for them to illustrate the page with a drawing of an incident from the book. Avid readers might want a looseleaf notebook so that they can eventually categorize their reading under "Sports Stories," "Science," "Adventure," "Poetry," etc. To illustrate each category, they could draw or cut and paste a picture.

READ ALOUD SERVICE

A presentation describing how to conduct a read aloud service was given by Gail Dickson at a Nevada Right-To-Read Conference. This adaption of her outline should be useful in setting up your own service.

MECHANICS

1. Advertise your service to the teachers in your school. You will conduct a program using student volunteers to read to children in other classes.

2. Distribute coupons to subscribing teachers to complete, asking the titles of books they want read, and the dates and times they wish a reader.

3. Record the titles of books read to each class in order to eliminate repetition.

4. Give reading assignments to readers on Friday for the following week. Tape a reminder slip on the reader's desk showing the date, time, and class of the Read Aloud. If a student is absent on his Read Aloud day, assign a substitute.

TEACHER'S ROLE IN PREPARING STUDENT READERS

1. Explain the program to the students and enlist their support.

2. Discuss the kinds of books that are suitable for the program and explain where they can be found in the library. Estimate the length of time it will take to read the book out loud. (Our subscribers like about 15- to 20-minute books, and student readers should not be too long away from their own classes.)

3. Discuss and demonstrate the essentials of reading aloud:

   Voice
   Pronunciation
   Knowing all the words
   Showing the pictures
   Reading with feeling
   Behavior in the classroom
   Tell the students that the reader should:
       introduce himself immediately after entering the room and then state his business
       wait for instructions from the teacher
       thank the children and leave when story is finished
       return immediately to his own classroom

4. Always ask the reader, at the first possible chance, how it went and if the children enjoyed it. Then thank the reader for taking part in the service.

READER'S RESPONSIBILITIES

1. Select a book from the library.

2. Check with the head of the service to see if it is appropriate.

3. Check to see if the title is listed on the teacher's list of books to read.

4. Practice reading the book out loud. Be sure you know all the words. Time yourself to see how long it takes to read it. Practice showing pictures and reading with expression.

5. Be sure to be on time for the Read Aloud. Follow rules of classroom conduct.

6. If you forget to go to the assignment, you should see the teacher later, apologize, and set up another time if the teacher wishes.

7. Preplan any activities you may wish to have with the teacher.

8. Leave your own classroom quietly and return quietly.

9. You are responsible for any work missed during the Read Aloud.

QUESTIONS YOU MIGHT ASK

1. *Does everyone have to take part?* I don't recommend that they do, but with encouragement and with time, everyone does. Some read more often than others, naturally.

2. *Do you do this all year?* I have, but find that it works better if it is done for one semester, and I like to do it during the second half of the year.

3. *Can every child take part?* Yes, even the child reading at the lowest level can "read" a picture book or a book with very simple words.

OBSERVATIONS

1. Positive feedback from the subscribing teacher is very valuable in making the reader feel successful.

2. Children like to read to the classes of former teachers, and classes in which they have brothers, sisters, or neighborhood friends.

3. Teachers enjoy seeing their former students.

4. Teachers ask each year if we will have the service again. This is proof that it is successful.

5. I've seen the confidence of poor readers increased when they have been successful in this project.

And just for fun: Read Betty Miles' *Maudie and Me and the Dirty Book* (Knopf, 1980).

This is a book for middle-grade readers (and adults who sponsor a Read Aloud Service). In the story, a censorship case develops after two girls read aloud a book to a younger class about the birth of puppies.

READ ALOUD AT A FAIR

The Enoch Pratt Free Library in Baltimore, Maryland, reports this successful idea. Take a portable microphone sound system to outdoor fairs. Set up a box for children to stand on. Use a music stand to hold read-aloud selections. Fix your sound system to a "narrow cast" range. Selections of poems, riddles, pages, or excerpts from books (photocopied or cut from discarded books) can be mounted on colored posterboard and color-keyed for age appeal and reading skill. Children and adults can volunteer to read aloud from the poems and books.

Think of how exciting it would be for young readers to use a real microphone and have a built-in audience.

How about using the same idea with a videotape machine at indoor gym fairs?

146

III BOOKTALKS

I'm always looking for really good "airplane reads." They must be engrossing, slightly junky paperbacks and, preferably, long enough to last for a whole trip. How do I find books that qualify? It's not an easy task. I read reviews, but they don't always help. The taste of some book reviewers is too refined for this particular quest. Also, many books are only reviewed in hardcover, and by the time they appear in paper I have forgotten whether they sounded good or not.

I read cover blurbs while browsing through bookstores, and I stare long and hard at every title in airport shops. I talk to a lot of people while I'm staring. Sometimes I simply pick up a book I've really enjoyed and say to the person next to me, "This one was really great," hoping that they'll give me a suggestion back.

Hearing an individual's recommendation of a book is the most personal and arresting way to get information towards good reading. Naturally, it all works better if you know and respect the reading tastes of the person recommending the title. As a teacher, librarian, or parent you are in the perfect position to help children find something enjoyable to read. After all, you've read a lot,* and the children respect your opinion.

Expand your own oral recommendations into a program. Call the program a booktalk and you have the perfect medium for presenting a single title or several books to a group. Your main objective is that the audience learn about books and be inspired to read.

This section gives ideas on how to put together a traditional booktalk. It also offers ideas for introducing books in more original ways.

There is no prescribed format for booktalks. The idea is to get readers for books, and anything goes. You can talk about a book's characters, setting, plot, theme, and style just as you would when you critique a book, *but* try to do it in an enthusiastic, comfortable way that will interest your readers.

---

*If you haven't, start now.

Traditional Booktalks

You can introduce a single book; you can talk about one author's work and introduce all the books by that author; or you can group several titles and introduce them more formally in a scripted talk.

INTRODUCING A SINGLE TITLE

A SAMPLE BOOKTALK

All But My Life, by Gerda Weissmann Klein (Hill & Wang, 1957). I always keep several paperback copies of this book in my house. When someone asks me for a good book to read I hand them one of my copies. It's the true story of Gerda Weissmann, who spent her teenage years in Nazi concentration camps during World War II. Most of her friends and her entire family did not survive, and it is difficult to believe that towards the end of the war 4,000 girls were forced to march over 1,000 miles in the freezing winter across Germany to a small Czech town. No wonder only 200 survived the march. Gerda feels that one of the reasons she survived is that her father insisted that she take her sturdy ski boots with her when she was separated from her family seven years earlier. The reader of her story can understand that ski boots and luck, but mostly Gerda's incredible spirit, made her a survivor.

The story has a fairytale ending. The young American lieutenant who liberated the survivors in Volary, Czechoslovakia, became her husband.

THE PERSONAL APPROACH: A SAMPLE BOOKTALK

One day during my senior year, I came home early from a school visit to the Museum of Modern Art, in New York. My mother and I were going shopping to buy shoes to go with a formal for an upcoming subscription dance.

When I got into our elevator to go up to our apartment on the 12th floor, Ralph, the elevator operator, mumbled something about "Sorry about what happened." Since I didn't know what he was referring to, I smiled vaguely and thought about the new shoes.

As I got off the elevator I heard voices coming from inside our apartment. My stomach turned and I had an unexplained tightening feeling of fright. When I opened the door with my key, a close friend of the family enveloped me in a crying hug and explained gently but tearfully that my father had died.

I wish I had had this book to comfort me [hold up *How It Feels When a Parent Dies* by Jill Krementz, Knopf, 1981] in the months that followed. Jill Krementz interviewed a number of children between the ages of 7 and 19 and asked them to remember the death of their mother or father and to talk about how they felt then and now.

Alletta's story made me feel sad because she tells how the children at her school wouldn't play with her because they were embarrassed because they didn't know what to say. My experience was different. The girls in my school later went out of their way to invite me to parties and plays, but I can remember what it was like at first when no one knew what to say to me.

I like Helen Colon's essay in Jill Krementz's book. She relates how she met a woman named Mary Woodell. A school guidance counselor told her about an organization called Big Brothers. [Read from book.]

> I just called up and before I knew it I had an interview. My mother died in September and I got my new Big Sister in October. I think we got matched up because her mother also died when she was very young. We see each other every weekend and we do things like go to movies and go ice-skating. We just got into roller-skating this year. And we go out to eat a lot. That's something that we both love to do. And we go shopping. I have a big collection of stuffed animals. I guess they represent the childhood I never really had. But the best thing we do is just talk.
>
> Meeting Mary is about the most wonderful thing that ever happened to me. (p. 51)

This book made me remember, but it also made me want to know these people. It's the sort of book you can pick up and browse through when you feel like understanding and feeling a little more deeply than usual.

INTRODUCING AUTHORS

THE PERSONAL APPROACH: A SAMPLE BOOKTALK

One of the best things that can possibly happen to a bibliophile (that's someone who's addicted to reading) is

149

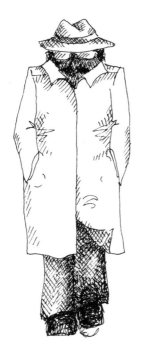

to find an author whose every book is a good read. If you can find two authors who are consistently good, you're set for a summer or winter of reading.

Dick Francis and Ruth Rendell are two mystery writers whose books are guaranteed to give you exciting action, intriguing plots, plenty of gore, and loveable as well as willfully destructive characters.

Dick Francis has considerable expertise in horse racing, and his books nearly always have something to do with horses, race tracks, trainers, or jockeys. *In the Frame,* for instance, features a painter whose major theme is horses. The thing I find most appealing about Francis's books is his characters. They always seem quite ordinary until they are thrust into exciting, often violent, situations. In *Smokescreen* the main character is an actor who plays James Bond–type parts. At home he has a devoted wife and a retarded child. Off the screen and out of the studio he is quiet and reassuring. When he is asked to visit a friend in South Africa he is forced to face situations in real life that he has only encountered in his films.

Dick Francis's books ask the question, If you were put into a dangerous position, could you handle it?

Ruth Rendell's books are deceiving. Her characters always seem to be innocent and gentle, but often they are revealed as pathological killers. All her characters, including the murderers, are realistically, and often charmingly, portrayed. Although I don't usually enjoy reading books that feature detectives, Inspector Wexford and his assistant Burden are interesting enough to make the reader pick up book after book.

Wexford's constant quoting from books makes him particularly attractive. In *One Across, Two Down* the murderer does crossword puzzles in his head. In *A Demon in My View* the multiple murders happen because the killer is an illiterate.

And Ruth Rendell and Dick Francis definitely make murder fun.

To introduce the books mentioned above, I used a personal approach to one of my favorite books and two of my favorite leisure-reading authors. The introductions are brief and general but they have worked. The authors' books are read by all my friends.

Obviously, the best time to enthusiastically introduce a book is immediately after you have read it and have total recall of the characters and themes. Unfortunately, this is not often possible. In time, our memories and excitement fade. It is for this reason that I use exact quotes from the books. Sometimes I don't actually read the paragraphs I've selected but just use them to rekindle my own enthusiasm and memory before I tell about the passage in my own words. Rehearsing is necessary if you plan to read passages aloud. Practice on your family or friends before you meet a group. So often people go through the trouble of finding something excellent to read aloud and then throw it away by rushing the reading or slurring the words. The chosen passages serve, also, as a record of the booktalk to file and keep for future reference so that you can repeat the booktalk.

USING A COMMON THEME

Grouping books by a common theme is a popular way of discussing books. You might find books that have similar themes or that are related only incidentally. Sometimes books that you would like to introduce don't seem at first to fit comfortably into one group, but you may, in fact, be able to find a common link to unite them.

I like to give my booktalks a personal feeling. This is a booktalk I have used with junior high school students. I have chosen specific passages that I read aloud after a brief introduction. I place the actual books on a table so that the audience can see the book jackets and pick up the book and read from the book itself.

A SAMPLE BOOKTALK: "EATS"

People often ask me, "Where do you get ideas for booktalks?" Now I can truthfully say "Anywhere, and anytime." One idea, for instance, came to me when I was out on the tennis court. The score was three all. I was just about to make this perfectly splendid overhead smash when my mind switched from tennis to food. I was hungry. I could hardly wait for lunch. I started thinking about Arnold Adoff's poem from *Eats*:

EATS

    are on my mind from early morning
      to late at night

          in spring
          or winter

151

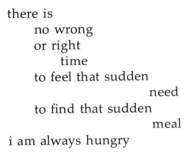

there is
　　no wrong
　　or right
　　　　time
　　to feel that sudden
　　　　　　　need
　　to find that sudden
　　　　　　　meal
i am always hungry

Then I thought that what I'd like to eat was a sardine sandwich. I remember when I wouldn't have even touched a sardine; that was before I had read John Hersey's *The Wall*. I read it years and years ago. It's a long book, five or six hundred pages, about the Jews in the Warsaw Ghetto uprising during World War II. The section that has stayed with me all these years is about one of the men, Slonim, who hasn't had a proper meal in years and has a rendezvous in the Polish sector. While Slonim is trying to keep his mind on directions given by the Pole, he is at first distracted by and then obsessed with an open tin of sardines and a large chunk of bread on a plate. He smells "the heavy fragrance of the sardine oil . . . how smooth the flesh! the little melting bones!" Hersey had made sardines sound so good I could hardly wait to go home to reread the passage. Amazingly, just browsing through the book I almost instantly found the incident, but then I had to reread the entire book.

Other books about people who are hungry began to surface in my mind. I thought of David in *North to Freedom*, by Anne Holm. He's spent practically all his thirteen years in a concentration camp. He's never eaten anything but porridge, bread, and soup; porridge, bread, and soup. After he escapes he realizes that he knows nothing at all about life on the outside. When he finds a round object he saves it in case it is something to eat, but when he bites into the skin it tastes bitter. Eventually he discovers that if he takes off the skin the fruit can be pulled apart and eaten in sections. Imagine not even knowing what it is like to eat an orange!

I thought of Tien Pao in *The House of Sixty Fathers*, by Meindert DeJong. He too was hungry. Separated from his Chinese family during World War II, he finally meets two American soldiers who offer him what he thinks must be candy. He unwraps the double wrapper and tries to chew the candy up but it doesn't get any smaller. Finally, he swallows the chewing gum. The soldiers laugh, but "Tien Pao did not laugh." He was still very hungry.

Think of all the people who could eat well that don't. My own husband and daughter wouldn't think of eating a vegetable, and the whole family eats too many tacos, hamburgers, and milkshakes.

You wonder how you would fare if you had to provide for your own food. I've always been intrigued by Aremis Slake, who at thirteen decides to leave the world as he knows it and goes to live underground in a New York subway station. [This is a long, but effective, passage. Be sure you practice reading it aloud before you perform in front of a group.]

Slake's breakfast consisted of the cubes of sugar which he cadged daily, and the saltines liberally spread with ketchup. This and his luncheonette meal, which was extended to cover his supper, was his total food intake. No one would say it was a balanced diet. But Slake had never been subjected to the benefits of a balanced diet. Scurvy, rickets, iron deficiency anemia, calcium lacks, vitamin and mineral imbalances had always been unimportant compared to the more important objective—filling the void in his middle. And then things became suddenly better.

It was during the Christmas rush. The subway, always teeming, now seemed that it would burst with humanity. The coffee shop was busier than ever. Slake was having his meal of the day when the man who seemed to be in charge spoke to him.

"I see you here every day."

Slake took fright. Did he know the waitress was giving him extras?

"Do you want a job?" Slake looked up. "Tell you what; if you want, you come in after the morning rush and sweep up the floor for me, and I'll give you a good meal. How's that for a business proposition?" Slake nodded. "Good," the man said as he rushed to serve another customer. "I've got just too much to do to do everything."

Slake had entered into his first contract without saying a word or signing his name. Every morning after selling his newspapers, he turned up at the coffee shop and silently took up the broom and swept. He swept like someone planning to learn the art and make it a life work. He got every crumb from under every stool, from every corner. He bent down and pushed the broom under the counter edge and

153

hunted out wadded paper napkins, soda straws, cigarette butts, matches, and all kinds of trash. And he found forty cents in change the very first day.

"What you find, you keep," said the manager. "You sweep good. Real good!"

When had someone said that to Slake before? Sometime. He remembered it; run. Run! That was it. Someone had said, "You run good. Real good." And now he also "swept good." To run, to sweep; what else might he do!

"What'll you eat?" the waitress asked him the first day he worked.

Slake spoke slowly. He was puzzled. He thought she knew his order by now. She never asked him anymore. "Soup and ham sandwich," he said.

She put the soup in front of Slake and then she served a big hamburger on a bun surrounded by french fried potatoes and a tomato. And when Slake thought he was through, she brought him a wedge of apple pie with a lump of vanilla ice cream on it. When Slake started to cut the hamburger in half as he always did to save for his supper, she said, "Don't bother," and she put a wrapped sandwich beside him.

Slake took a long time over lunch. He did not know when he had had so much food. When he got down from the stool, the feeling of fullness was so palpable that he nearly lost his balance.

In his pocket was the extra sandwich, the ketchup packets, the saltines, the sugar. Slake looked at the manager and he struggled for the word and found it. "Thanks," he said, and he nearly looked at the waitress too, so the one word served them both.

From *Slake's Limbo,* by Felice Holman

Slake didn't have much of a choice in his situation; neither did David or Tien Pao, but even if you're not in the midst of a war or living in a subway station you can still feel uncomfortable when you're thrown into a new situation. In Beverly Cleary's *Fifteen,* Buzz takes Jane to a Chinese restaurant. Not only does she not recognize anything that is served but she has to cope with chopsticks for the first time. On her first awkward attempt to use the sticks, a green pepper slides down her blouse into her lap.

Arnold Adoff must have had the same experience. His poem, also from *Eats,* is perfect:

I AM LEARNING

to move my chop
sticks
                through
the
vegetables
                        and
                            meat
and

    through
the
        oriental
                    treat
we
have
tonight

but   in
between
            my
smiles
and
 bites
i
write
a
message
            in
                the
sweet
            and
sour
pork

i
need
a
    fork

My very favorite food excerpt from a book comes from Jacqueline Susann's *Every Night, Josephine!* Susann wrote *Valley of the Dolls* and *The Love Machine,* which some of your parents might be shocked to see you reading, but this book is a love song to the author's pet poodle.

When Jacqueline's mother-in-law comes to visit, Josephine begins to put on weight at an alarming speed. Jacqueline discovers why when one morning she gets up earlier than usual and finds Grandma and Josephine in the kitchen:

As I stumbled drowsily across the living room, I suddenly became aware of all sorts of charming conversation emanating from the kitchen. My mother-in-law was doing the conversing. Josie was answering with exuberant squeals. The conversation went something like this:

"Now finish your oatmeal, Josie, and then I'll give you your soft-boiled eggs. No Josie, you can't have the eggs until all the oatmeal is finished. Here darling, I'll put some more sweet cream on it. Now, isn't that tasty?"

I held on to the door for strength. When I did speak, I croaked, "Good morning, girls."

My mother-in-law was delighted to see me. "How come you're up so early? Sit down. I think there's just enough oatmeal left." She scooped some into a plate for me.

"Mom." I made my voice gentle. "I thought you said you never fed Josie."

She looked at me in genuine surprise. "Would I let a dog die of starvation? I said I never fed her between meals. You're the one who does that, with those sawdust Yummies and coffee at noon."

Slowly I began to get the picture. "And what meals do you feed her?"

"Just the ordinary ones. The hours you and Irving keep aren't right for such a little animal. So I see to it that she has a good breakfast, lunch and dinner. It's the least I can do for you while I stay here."

"What do you give her for lunch?" (It was torture, but I had to know.)

"Well that all depends," she explained. "Sometimes a little boiled chicken and peas and carrots. Sometimes fish. I make sure there's no bones. And sometimes we eat dairy. Sour cream and vegetables—or cheese blintzes. She adores my mushroom and barley soup, but I think soup is a little too gassy."

"And dinner?" I was fascinated with the life of this furry little Henry the Eighth.

"Well, you and Irving always insist that I don't cook dinner and have room service. But who can eat such big portions? So she shares it with me and it works out fine. Don't worry, I see to it that she has a well-rounded diet. Don't forget, I raised Irving and always saw to it that he ate plenty of fruit and vegetables. It was a long time ago, but I haven't forgotten."

She leaned down to pick up the empty egg plate, and I watched with fascinated horror as she poured a mixture of heavy cream, milk, coffee, and sugar into a plate.

"I add just a spoonful of coffee," she apologized. "It's the only way I can get her to drink her quart of milk a day. At lunch I add a little chocolate syrup. Irving hated milk when he was little too. But a quart of milk a day is a must for everyone. You and Irving should drink milk too." Then she said to Josie who was backing away from the half-finished plate, "Finish the milk sweetheart. Do it for Grandma." Grandma! Sweetheart, who knew where her next meal was coming from, obligingly returned to the dish and lapped up the remainder of Grandma's brew.

Grandma beamed and picked her up and cooed, "Good girl. Now kiss Grandma and go play a little." Josie bestowed a wet kiss on her personal chef, and Grandma who was puckered up like a suction pump, received it with maternal pride.

From *Every Night, Josephine!* by Jacqueline Susann.

In the above booktalk I used a personal account of how I created a booktalk as the core of the talk. In the transitions between books I mentioned personal subjects, such as my family, to give the talk a basis in reality. I don't always use this entire booktalk. For instance, I might eliminate or paraphrase the *Slake's Limbo* selection. Too much reading, no matter how well done, can be quite boring. It took all my courage to eliminate some of the wonderful excerpts that would make the booktalk too long. I tried to include books for all levels of reading, and my exhibit relies heavily on picture books with an eating theme to introduce older children to the wonderful world of picture-book art. Other books about food or eating—particularly nonfiction books, cookbooks, or books about 157 survival cooking, such as Laurence Pringle's *Wild Foods*—should be included in the book exhibit.

I have listed the books and the page numbers I used in the booktalk along with alternative selections that could be used for a longer talk, or in case the books mentioned in the original talk are out of the library, or just for a change.

I have to be honest and say that writing out a booktalk as I did above is not the way I usually work. I duplicate the passages from the books to use as file copy but try to read from the actual books. When you pick up the book, you give the audience a chance to see the cover, and the action of picking up a book makes a good transition, particularly from an intense passage to an amusing one or vice versa.

I try to ad-lib between books for a fresher, more natural approach. The Eats booktalk was taped during an actual presentation and then transcribed.

You'll notice that the books I've mentioned are only incidentally about food. I grouped the books around a food theme because they include passages about food, but in reality the books are mainly about very different subjects—first dating experiences, war, and dogs. I used the common thread simply to tie the books together. When you are talking to a large group, it is often a good idea to discuss a variety of books—something for everybody.

BOOKS ON EXHIBIT

BOOKTALK REFERENCES

Adoff, Arnold. *Eats: Poems.* il. by Susan Russo. Lothrop, 1979. "Eats" and "I Am Learning."
A collection of food poems.

Cleary, Beverly. *Fifteen.* il. by Joe and Beth Krush. Morrow, 1956. pp. 121–122.
A light-hearted story about a girl's first romance.

DeJong, Meindert. *The House of Sixty Fathers.* il. by Maurice Sendak. Harper, 1956. pp 128–129.
Tien Pao, separated from his family during World War II, is accompanied by his pet pig through war-torn China.

Hersey, John. *The Wall.* Knopf, 1950. pp 316–319.
A novel about the Warsaw Ghetto.

Holm, Anne. *North to Freedom.* tr. from the Danish by L. W. Kingsland. Harcourt, 1965. pp 35–36.
David, who has spent most of his life in a concentration camp, learns to cope with the outside world.

Holman, Felice. *Slake's Limbo.* Scribner, 1974, pp. 68–70.
Slake hides in a subway station away from the world above ground.

Susann, Jacqueline. *Every Night, Josephine!* Bantam, 1963. pp 117–118.
The author writes with warmth and humor about her pet poodle.

ALTERNATIVE SELECTIONS

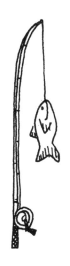

Byars, Betsy. *After the Goat Man.* il. by Ronald Himler. Viking, 1974. pp 60–62, pp 73–74, pp 97–99.
Harold V. Coleman is fat and frustrated until he helps Ada and Figgy search for Figgy's eccentric grandfather.

Heide, Florence Parry. *Banana Twist.* Holiday House, 1978. pp 53–54.
Jonah thinks his neighbor Goober is a real creep, but they both love exotic ice cream concoctions.

Pringle, Laurence. *Wild Foods; A Beginner's Guide To Identifying, Harvesting and Cooking Safe and Tasty Plants from the Outdoors.* il. by Paul Breeden. Four Winds Press, 1978.
Descriptions of easily-found edible plants, with recipes. Show the book's format.

PICTURE BOOKS

Barrett, Judi. *Cloudy With a Chance of Meatballs.* il. by Ron Barrett. Atheneum Pubs., 1978.
In the town of Chewandswallow, the weather comes three times a day as breakfast, lunch, and dinner.

Goffstein, M. B. *Fish for Supper.* il. by author. Dial Press, 1976.
Tiny black and white illustrations are the perfect accompaniment to a day of fishing with grandma.

Heller, Linda. *Lily at the Table.* il. by author. Macmillan, 1979.
The artist shows a miniature girl playing with life-size food in a wordless black and white picture book. Well worth sharing.

Hoban, Russell. *Bread and Jam for Frances.* il. by Lillian Hoban. Harper, 1964.
Definitely a book for young children, it gives a classic cure for finicky eating and would delight any reader.

Hoban, Russell. *Dinner at Alberta's.* il. by James Marshall. Crowell, 1975.
Arthur the crocodile is forced to improve his table manners when he is invited to dinner at Alberta's.

Kunhardt, Dorothy. *Pudding Is Nice.* il. by author. The Bookstore Press, 1975. (First published as *Junket Is Nice.* Harcourt, 1973.)

159

Everyone tries to guess what an old, old man with a red beard and red slippers is thinking while he eats pudding out of a big red bowl.

Lord, John Vernon and Janet Burroway. *The Giant Jam Sandwich.* il. by John Vernon Lord. Houghton, 1973.
The story of how the residents of Itching Down get rid of four million wasps.

Marshall, James. *Yummers!* il. by author. Houghton, 1973.
This picture book explains why some people are fat and others are not; fat people have thin friends who tempt them to eat. Emily Pig takes a walk with Eugene Turtle and stops to eat along the way.

Mayer, Mercer. *Frog Goes to Dinner.* il. by author. Dial Press, 1974.
In this wordless picture book, frog disrupts dinner at a fancy restaurant.

Paterson, Diane. *Eat!* il. by author. Dial Press, 1975.
This is too small to show effectively to a large group, but the graphics are worthwhile. This is a spoof on all the parents who try to force their children to eat.

Stamaty, Mark Alan. *Who Needs Donuts?* il. by author. Dial Press, 1973.
"Who needs donuts? I've got love" is the moral of this picture book, which was awarded a Society of Illustrators Gold Medal. Definitely different graphics.

STORY (optional)

"The Woman Who Flummoxed the Fairies" *in* Nic Leodhas, Sorche. *Heather and Broom; Tales of the Scottish Highlands.* il. by Consuelo Joerns. Holt, 1960.
A delightful (long) Scottish tale about a woman kidnapped by the fairies because of her baking skill. Also in Greene, Ellin. *Clever Cooks: A Concoction of Stories, Charms, Recipes and Riddles.* il. by Trina Schart Hyman. Lothrop, 1973.

MEDIA STORY

Barrett, Judith. *Cloudy With a Chance of Meatballs.* il. by Ron Barnett. Atheneum, 1978.

Tell the story using a cloth-covered oriental straw hat. As each of the foods is mentioned loosen the food (fastened with Velcro) so that it falls down and dangles on the fish wire around the hat. The food is soft sculpture, made of fabric. See photo on page 108.

PICTURE CARDS

Naturally when you give a booktalk you will want to have the actual books to show, exhibit, and offer to the audience to take home to read. You can always simply pick up the book you are discussing and put it down on a table as an exhibit. But what if the book no longer has an attractive book jacket? Or one of the five books you are introducing has been checked out of the library and you want to mention it anyway? Or you would like to prepare a somewhat formal display for your children? All these dilemmas could be solved by exhibiting pictures that represent each book. Use publishers' posters or original pictures, drawn by you or a talented friend, and mounted on poster board.

As you briefly introduce each book, place the picture cards on cardboard stands across the back of your exhibit table. When the books you have presented have been checked out, you will still have a standing exhibit of the books and a permanent ready-to-go booktalk for your collection.

Other Approaches to Booktalking

THE MAILBOX—BOOKTALK AND EXHIBIT

This idea can be used for a booktalk program. The letters can be read aloud to the group if time permits, or they can be left in a mailbag or mailbox for children to read at their leisure.

YOU NEED: A mailbag or box; stationery

HOW TO: Type these letters or others that you have written on stationery. Type the name of the author and title of each book on the envelope flaps. Put the letters into the appropriate envelopes.

PRESENTATION: Extract each letter from its envelope and read it out loud. Give the author and title of the book after you have read each letter. Exhibit the books so the children can read them.

The Law of Gravity, by Johanna Hurwitz. il. by Ingrid Fetz. Morrow, 1978.

Dear Esther,
My letters to you all summer told you all about my project to get my Mom downstairs and out of our apartment for the first time in years, but you ought to read my book to see how I met Bernie and how I was successful with my project, but sorry too.
Love, Margot

The Girls in the Velvet Frame, by Adèle Geras. Atheneum Pubs., 1979.

Dear Aunt Mimi,
You changed everything when you suggested that we five girls get our picture taken! We started a correspondence all the way from Palestine to New York in America to find our lost brother Isaac.
Love, Rifka

162

The Midnight Fox, by Betsy Byars. il. by Ann Grifalconi. Viking, 1968.

Dear Petie,
All through the summer I've written you letters, but now I have to confess that I haven't told you everything. Actually, I left out the most important event of the whole summer: when I saw the black fox and what happened afterwards.
Maybe you better read my book and find out why I didn't write you about it and what really happened.
"Write me a letter" Tom

Julie of the Wolves, by Jean C. George. il. by John Schoenherr. Harper, 1972.

Dear Amy,
Have you any idea what happened when I started off from Alaska to San Francisco to see you? I got lost on the tundra, made friends with a pack of wolves, lost my knapsack, and found out that I am truly an Eskimo even if our old ways are dying.
Your pen pal, Miyax

Dear Wanda,
I wish I had really written this letter. In the book *The 100 Dresses* I teased you because of your funny name and because you always wore the same faded blue dress.
Your letter to Room 13 made me feel better, especially since you gave Peggy and me each one of the drawings of your 100 dresses.
Peggy says that makes it all O.K., but I feel sad and I guess I'll be more understanding next time. Oh well, I loved the book—it made me cry.
Your friend, Maddie

The Hundred Dresses, by Eleanor Estes. il. by Louis Slobodkin. Harcourt, 1944.

The Letter, the Witch and the Ring, by John Bellairs. il. by Richard Egielski. Dial Press, 1976.

Dear Mrs. Zimmermann,
The summer sure did pick up when you received a strange and puzzling deathbed letter from your eccentric uncle.
Good that there were two books before this one because it made the good reading even longer.
Rose Rita Pottinger

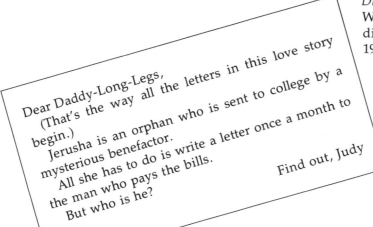

Daddy-Long-Legs, by Jean Webster. il. by Edward Ardizzone. Meredith Press, 1967.

Dear Daddy-Long-Legs,
(That's the way all the letters in this love story begin.)
Jerusha is an orphan who is sent to college by a mysterious benefactor.
All she has to do is write a letter once a month to the man who pays the bills.
But who is he?

Find out, Judy

Letters to Horseface: Being the Story of Wolfgang Amadeus Mozart's Journey to Italy, 1769–1700 When He Was a Boy of Fourteen, by F. N. Monjo. il by Don Bolognese & Elaine Raphael. Viking, 1975.

Horseface,
Here is a whole book of letters from me to you, my sister, the summer I was 14.
I traveled all over Italy meeting famous people *and* I composed my first full-length opera.
Your simpleton brother, Wolferl Mozart

BOOKTALK BOX

Here's an idea that can be used to present one book, several books, or as a book exhibit.

The box contains a collection of found-around-the-house objects that help introduce books to a group. Start by wandering about your home, picking up objects. Ask your children if you can browse through their things as well. As you collect, think how each thing might relate to a book. On a three-by-five-inch index card, write the name of the author, the title, and a short annotation for each book. These will be used to refresh your memory when you use the booktalk box and also to accompany each object as exhibit material.

To use the box, simply extract an object and briefly discuss its relation to the story. Put it down on a table with the book and voilà! your instant booktalk. If you have a bit more time to promote books, do the same thing with several of the objects in the box. No time at all during your jam-packed, curriculum-filled day to take even a minute to present a book? Place the objects, books, and their annotated cards in an exhibit case.

These are a few of the easily found objects in my own booktalk box:

A RUSTY, OLD-FASHIONED KEY [this can be bought at an antique shop, garage sale, or flea market]

The Secret Garden, by Frances Hodgson Burnett. il. by Tasha Tudor. Lippincott, 1962.
Mary finds the key that opens a mysterious walled and locked garden that no one has visited in ten years.

Mary is a willful, unpleasant sort of creature when she first arrives at Misselthwaite Manor. The garden works magic on Mary and on Colin too, who is equally cranky and unpleasant. Maybe it wasn't entirely the magic of the garden; maybe Dickon, the boy who loved animals, helped with the magic. This is the key that Mary Lennox found that leads her to an adventure in a secret garden that no one has been in for ten years. The book is Frances Hodgson Burnett's *The Secret Garden.*

A USED TOOTHPASTE TUBE

The Toothpaste Millionaire, by Jean Merrill. il. by Jan Palmer. Houghton, 1974c1972.
Twelve-year-old Rufus Mayflower and his friend Kate Mackinstrey make a million dollars with their new super good, super cheap toothpaste formula.

This morning when you brushed your teeth did you stop to think about your toothpaste? You didn't? Well, you may never make a million dollars the way Rufus did. *165*

You see, Rufus got upset when he realized that toothpaste cost 79¢ a tube. He thought he might be able to make it for a whole lot less . . . and he did. The cost of the toothpaste was 2¢ a tube. He figured if he sold the toothpaste for 3¢ a tube, with a 1¢ profit, and if just one tenth of the 200 million people in the United States bought a tube of his toothpaste every month, he would make $2.5 million in just one year. Read all about it in Jean Merrill's *The Toothpaste Millionaire.*

AN ENVELOPE ADDRESSED TO MAGGIE MARMELSTEIN

Maggie Marmelstein for President, by Marjorie Weinman Sharmat. il. by Ben Shecter. Harper, 1975.
Maggie is furious that Thad Smith won't let her be his campaign manager, so she decides to run for president of the sixth grade, too. But who sends her such a mean (but funny) note?

[Open the envelope and read the letter—copied from the book—p. 72.]:

The Sixth Grade needs Maggie Marmelstein like

a fatal disease	a rip in their clothes
a room full of fleas	a spike in their bed
an elephant's sneeze	a hole in their head
a wart on their nose	Signed, A Friend

A PEACH PIT

James and the Giant Peach: A Children's Story, by Roald Dahl. il. by Nancy Ekholm Burkert. Knopf, 1961.
Inside a giant peach James meets cheerful Old-Green-Grasshopper, dainty Ladybug, and grumpy Centipede of the multiple boots, and "fabulous, unbelievable" things happen.

I know this looks like an ordinary peach pit, and maybe it is. On the other hand, it may just be from the ordinary peach tree in the garden of nasty old Aunt Sponge and Aunt Spiker, that grows a house-size peach that takes James away on a fabulous, unbelievable adventure. In *James and the Giant Peach,*

We may see a Creature with forty-nine heads
Who lives in the desolate snow,
And whenever he catches a cold (which he dreads)
He has forty-nine noses to blow.

(p. 37)

Here is a list of objects and the books they represent for you to work with:

EYEGLASSES

A Wrinkle in Time, by Madeleine L'Engle. Farrar, Straus, 1962.
When Meg puts on Mrs. Who's glasses, she is able to enter the transparent column where her father is imprisoned (pp. 148–149).
Slake's Limbo, by Felice Holman. Scribner, 1974.
Slake, living underground in a New York subway station, finds a pair of broken eyeglasses and fits some found lenses into the frames. He can now see, not perfectly, but better (pp. 65–66).
Tough Tiffany, by Belinda Hurmence. Doubleday, 1980.
Tiffany is asked to hold Granny's spectacles in church and inadvertently puts them in the collection plate (p. 102).

A BOXFUL OF PENNIES

The Hundred Penny Box, by Sharon Bell Mathis. il. by Leo and Diane Dillon. Viking, 1975.
Each penny represents a story and a year in Great-Great Aunt Dew's life.

A SHINY BLACK ROCK

The Lucky Stone, by Lucille Clifton. il. by Dale Payson. Delacorte Press, 1979.
Three stories represent three generations of luck for those who own the small shiny pebble.

A MINIATURE BATHTUB

The most effective object in my Booktalk Box is a miniature bathtub, bought at a dollhouse shop, to introduce a scene from *Paddington Bear.* I thought it would be amusing to group books with a bath theme.

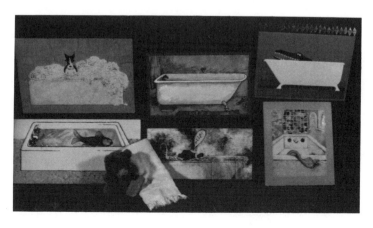

"Mrs. Simkin's Bathtub," by Linda Allen. in *Cricket Magazine,* Volume 7, number 8, April 1980.
A short story about a bathtub that keeps moving around the house until it finds a place to stay.

"The Cleanest Dog in the USA," in *Ribsy,* by Beverly Cleary. il. by Louis Darling. Morrow, 1964.
In this chapter, Henry Huggins' dog Ribsy gets a bubble bath.

The Carp in the Bathtub, by Barbara Cohen. il. by Joan Halpern. Lothrop, 1972.
Two children make a pet of a fish their mother is planning to use for gefilte fish.

Bill and Pete, by Tomie de Paola. il. by author. Putnam, 1978.
The story of William Everett Crocodile. Picture book.

The Champion of Merrimack County, by Roger W. Drury. il. by Fritz Wegner. Little, 1976.
O. Crispin, Mouse, practices his championship bicycling skills on the rim of the Berryfields' bathtub.

The Bear in the Bathtub, by Ellen B. Jackson. il. by Margot Apple. Addison-Wesley, 1981.
Andrew can't take a bath because there is a bear in the bathtub.

"Rikki-Tikki-Tavi," in *The Jungle Book,* by Rudyard Kipling. il. by Fritz Eichenberg. Grosset, 1950.
One of the chapters in *The Jungle Book* relates the story of a not-so-friendly snake.

Harry Cat's Pet Puppy, by George Selden. il. by Garth Williams. Farrar, Straus, 1974.
In the first chapter Huppy is given a bath in a puddle by Tucker Mouse.

Now, start looking for objects, or browse through the library looking for books with memorable objects, and create your own Booktalk Box.

ZIPPER CATS

Introduce each book with cats that rest one inside the other. Acetate pockets on the side of each cat announce the title of each book. The leader unzips each cat as each new book is introduced.

By changing the titles of the books on the cats, you can use this idea for all ages.

The bibliography will give you some suggestions for finding cat books.

BOOKS ABOUT CATS

YOUNGER CHILDREN

Calhoun, Mary. *Cross-Country Cat.* il. by Erick Ingraham. Morrow, 1979.
In an emergency, Henry becomes a cross-country skier.

De Paola, Tomie. *The Kids' Cat Book.* il. by author. Holiday House, 1979.
Information in cartoons.

Feder, Jane. *Beany.* il. by Karen Gundersheimer. Pantheon Bks., 1979.
Small format and detailed drawings of a cat's life with a little boy. Charming.

Gág, Wanda. *Millions of Cats.* il. by author. Coward-McCann, 1928.
The classic cat picture book in which an old man finds "hundreds of cats, thousands of cats, millions and billions and trillions of cats."

Hoban, Tana. *One Little Kitten.* Greenwillow Bks., 1979.
Brief text accompanies black and white photographs of a kitten at play.

Kent, Jack. *The Fat Cat: A Danish Folktale.* il. by author. Parents Mag. Press, 1971.
Tall-tale funny pictures of a cat who eats up everything and everyone he comes across.

Panek, Dennis. *Catastrophe Cat.* il. by author. Bradbury Press, 1978.
Almost wordless picture book. Clear, simple, colorful pictures show a cat getting into mischief.

MIDDLE GRADES

Alexander, Lloyd. *The Town Cats, and Other Tales.* il. by Laszlo Kubinyi. Dutton, 1977.
Delightful short stories in which cats are shown to be more intelligent than humans. Excellent read-alouds. This could be your key book for middle and upper grades.

169

Buchwald, Art. *Irving's Delight.* il. by Reynold Ruffins. McKay, 1975.
A television cat à la Morris is kidnapped and creates a world crisis. Political satire to be enjoyed by younger and older readers.

Cleary, Beverly. *Socks.* il. by Beatrice Darwin. Morrow, 1973.
Socks is the center of the household until the baby arrives.

Clymer, Eleanor. *Horatio Goes to the Country.* il. by Robert Quackenbush. Atheneum Pubs, 1978.
Short, amusing stories about Horatio, the cat hero of several books.

Hurwitz, Johanna. *Much Ado About Aldo.* il. by John Wallner. Morrow, 1978.
Aldo thinks of the family's two cats as his brothers.

Selden, George. *Harry Cat's Pet Puppy.* il. by Garth Williams. Farrar, Straus, 1974.
Harry Cat and Tucker Mouse adopt Huppy the puppy.

Turner, Dona. *My Cat Pearl.* il. by author. Crowell, 1980.
Everyday activities of a little girl and her pet cat.

UPPER GRADES

Goldberger, Judith M. *The Looking Glass Factor.* Dutton, 1979.
In the future, cats will be scientists helped by young Hannah and will be able to walk through walls.

Jones, Diana Wynne. *The Magicians of Caprona.* Greenwillow Bks., 1980.
Benvenuto the senior cat helps Tonino with his magic spells.

Manley, Sean and Gogo Lewis, eds. *Cat Encounters: A Cat-lovers Anthology.* il. with engravings. Lothrop, 1979.
Selections by Jerome K. Jerome, James Thurber, and James Herriot.

Phipson, Joan. *The Cats.* Atheneum Pubs., 1976.
Kidnapped and held for ransom, two captive brothers become the leaders when enormous wild cats attack in the Australian wilderness.

ALL AGES

Bishop, Ann. *Cleo Catra's Riddle Book.* il. by Jerry Warshaw. Elsevier/Nelson, 1981.
A collection of punning cat riddles.

Galdone, Paul. *King of the Cats.* il. by author. Houghton, 1980.
Picture-book version of a popular folktale.

Gantos, Jack. *Rotten Ralph.* il. by Nicole Rubel. Houghton, 1976.
A really wretched cat you will love. Picture book.

Hopkins, Lee Bennett. *I Am the Cat.* il. by Linda Rochester Richards. Harcourt, 1981.
Poems about cats.

Shaw, Richard, ed. *The Cat Book.* Warne, 1973.
Selections of poetry and prose about cats. Illustrations by a variety of artists.

Silverstein, Alvin and Virginia. *Cats: All About Them.* Photographs by Frederick J. Breda. Lothrop, 1978.
Description of the history, breeding, and care of cats.

Taber, Anthony. *Cat's Eyes.* il. by author. Dutton, 1978.
This unique picturebook shows how the world looks to a cat.

PUPPET BOOKTALKS

Puppets can give wonderful booktalks. A puppet skit involves the children in the booktalk presentation. They can write their own skit, you can write one for them, or you can use this one as a start.

FRIENDS: A BOOKTALK

Scene: After school

Charcters: Superwoman }
Wonderman } *puppets or people*

MAN: Hi, Superwoman.

WOMAN: Hello, Wonderman.

TOGETHER: We're friends.

WOMAN: There are friends in books, too.

MAN: I know, like Constance Greene's *I and Sproggy*.

WOMAN: What's a Sproggy?

MAN: Not what, who. You see, Adam is 10 years old and lives in New York City near Gracie Mansion where the mayor of New York lives.

WOMAN: So what's a Sproggy?

MAN: Well, Adam's parents are divorced and his father lives in England with a new wife.

WOMAN: So, what's a Sproggy?

MAN: Adam's Dad comes to visit and takes Adam to this fancy restaurant and asks him to look after his new stepdaughter, who is Adam's stepsister.

WOMAN: I'll bet that's a Sproggy.

MAN: You're right. Sproggy turns out to be two months older than Adam and a whole head taller. She's always saying things like "jolly super" and she asks Adam where the "loo" is.

172

WOMAN:	Does he tell her?
MAN:	That's just it. He says he doesn't have one. And a "loo" turns out to be the bathroom.
WOMAN:	How awful.
MAN:	And then Sproggy rescues Adam from a mugger in the park.
WOMAN:	How humiliating.
MAN:	Actually it's funny.
WOMAN:	I just read about some friends, too.
MAN:	What's the name of the book?
WOMAN:	*A Secret Friend,* by Marilyn Sachs.
MAN:	What's it about?
WOMAN:	Jessica and Wendy have been friends for years and suddenly Wendy starts snubbing Jessica and hanging around with Barbara Wilson.
MAN:	That's terrible.

WOMAN:	Then Jessica starts getting notes that say things like "Wendy Cooper is not your friend. She talks about you behind your back. You have a better friend in this class. A.S.F."
MAN:	Who's A.S.F.?
WOMAN:	Nobody knows. Some of the kids think A.S.F. means "A Secret Friend."
MAN:	We'll *always* be best friends, O.K.?
WOMAN:	Of course, Wonderman. If I send any notes, they'll be to you.
MAN:	Have you read *Beloved Benjamin Is Waiting* by Jean Karl?
WOMAN:	No, is it about friends?
MAN:	Sort of. This girl, Lucinda, runs away from home and hides in an abandoned house in a cemetery.
WOMAN:	Sounds creepy.
MAN:	It is, and lonely too, but then she makes friends with a statue.

WOMAN:	A statue. How can you be friends with a statue?
MAN:	This statue is of a small boy who died in 1889. . . .
WOMAN:	So, and how can Lucinda be friends with it?
MAN:	It turns out that beings from outer space are using the statue to talk to Lucinda.
WOMAN:	What do you mean?
MAN:	Lucinda hears strange noises coming from the statue that turn out to be "things, or people or something from millions or trillions of miles away that are using the statue to talk through."
WOMAN:	I don't understand.

173

MAN:	It's hard to explain; you have to read the book.
WOMAN:	O.K., let's go.
MAN:	Where?
WOMAN:	To the library.
MAN:	Now?
WOMAN:	Yea, sure. I want to read about friends. *I and Sproggy* sounds good, and I want to find out what you mean by the talking statue in *Beloved Benjamin Is Waiting*.
MAN:	All right, and I'll read *A Secret Friend*.
WOMAN:	Come on, friend.
MAN:	Let's go, friend.

They kiss and exit.

THE END

Hint: If you are presenting this to normal sixth-graders, they will probably react loudly to these puppets kissing. Good, it means they're paying attention.

BOOKLIST

Greene, Constance. *I and Sproggy.* il. by Emily McCully. Viking, 1978.

Karl, Jean. *Beloved Benjamin Is Waiting.* Dutton, 1978.

Sachs, Marilyn. *A Secret Friend.* Doubleday, 1978.

FIRST SENTENCES

Look through your library collection for books with intriguing first sentences. Read the sentences from the books, and that's your booktalk, simple and fast. Other uses for your collection of first sentences would be to have the children guess which book they came from, or for a bulletin board exhibit.

If children look for their own first sentences and find a good one, they might just take out that book and read! Here's a starter collection.

MIDDLE-GRADE READERS

"My name is Nate Twitchell, but I can't help that."
From *The Enormous Egg,* by Oliver Butterworth. il. by Louis Darling. Little, 1956.

"There are some people who say that Henry Green wasn't really born, but was hatched, fully grown, from a chocolate bean."
From *Chocolate Fever,* by Robert K. Smith. il. by Gioia Fiammenghi. Coward, McCann & Geoghegan, 1972.

"She had known all along that she was a queen, and now the crown proved it."
From *The Silver Crown,* by Robert C. O'Brien. il. by Dale Payson. Atheneum, 1968.

"My name is Eddie, and I'm not fat."
From *Eddie Spaghetti,* by Edward Frascino. Harper, 1978.

"You are not going to believe me, nobody in their right minds could *possibly* believe me, but it's true, really it is!"
From *Freaky Friday,* by Mary Rodgers. Harper, 1972.

"Where's Papa going with that ax?"
From *Charlotte's Web,* by E. B. White. il. by Garth Williams. Harper, 1952.

175

" 'I shall be a good witch,' said Selina."
From *Mr. McFadden's Hallowe'en*, by Rumer Godden. Viking, 1975.

Here's a long one:

"The Western American Explorer's Club, in the city of San Francisco, was honored as it had never been honored before in the first week of October 1883 by being promised to be first to hear the details of an unexplained, extraordinary adventure; the biggest news story of the year, the story the whole world was waiting impatiently to hear—the tale of Professor William Waterman Sherman's singular voyage."
From *The Twenty-one Balloons*, by William Pène Du Bois. il. by author. Viking, 1947.

OLDER READERS

"They murdered him."
From *The Chocolate War; a novel*, by Robert Cormier, Pantheon, 1974.

"I am afraid."
From *Z for Zachariah*, by Robert C. O'Brien. Atheneum, 1974.

"I hate my father."
From *The Cat Ate My Gymsuit*, by Paula Danziger. Delacorte Press, 1974.

"I always hated summertime."
From *One Fat Summer*, by Robert Lipsyte. Harper, 1977.

"Away in the north of Scotland, in the part they call the Highlands, there is a mountain by the name of Ben MacDui, and this mountain is haunted."
From *The Haunted Mountain: A Story of Suspense*, by Mollie Hunter. il. by Laszlo Kubinyi. Harper, 1972.

"Afterwards, when they asked him, Peter found it very difficult to remember exactly what had happened."
From *Prove Yourself a Hero*, by K. M. Peyton. Collins, 1977.

"Hershy Marko found out a long time ago that if he takes a rubber ball and places it very gently near the top of Market Street Hill, opposite his father's hardware store, he can beat it down the hill, running at top speed, though it's a close race."
From *The Murderer*, by Felice Holman. Scribner, 1978.

BANNER BOOKTALKS

We often use visuals when presenting books to younger children. Using banners as visuals is an effective way of presenting books to older children too. I have several booktalk banners in my collection.

My "Who Lives There?" banner has an appliqued background showing trees, rivers, lakes, and mountains. Small dots of Velcro enable me to add house shapes cut from muslin and decorated with felt-tip pens. As I briefly talk about each book, I affix the houses in which the characters might have lived until the foreground of the banner is filled with houses.

I also have a banner for "Growing Things," but on this banner a garden is permanently sewn so I either point to the objects on the banner while I'm talking about each book or simply use the banner as a background hanging.

My "Pots Around the World" banner is more of a storytelling banner, but I use the stories to introduce each book. I've collected stories about pots from around the world and use the banner as part of a series presentation. Each week I place one of the figures, representing one pot story and the country in which it takes place, on the banner. Then I tell the story and leave the figure on the banner until the next meeting. I keep adding figures as I tell the stories, presenting just one book each session.

My banners are all made of cloth, but the same idea can be used with posterboard.

WHO LIVES THERE?

An old inn: *A Really Weird Summer,* by Eloise Jarvis McGraw. Atheneum Pubs., 1977.

An old Victorian house: *The House in Norham Gardens,* by Penelope Lively. Dutton, 1974.
The House on Mayferry Street, by Eileen Dunlop. il. by Phillida Gili. Holt, 1976.

A fairytale castle: *Beauty; A Retelling of the Story of Beauty and the Beast,* by Robin McKinley. Harper, 1978.

Stone summer cottage: *The TV Kid,* by Betsy Byars. il. by Richard Cuffari. Viking, 1976.

A multistory apartment house: *I Know You, Al,* by Constance C. Greene. il. by Byron Barton. Viking, 1975.

A deluxe N.Y. brownstone: *Harriet the Spy,* by Louise Fitzhugh. il. by author. Harper, 1964.

A small apartment house: *Once I Was a Plum Tree,* by Johanna Hurwitz. il. by Ingrid Fetz. Morrow, 1980.

An elaborate old home with towers: *Noah's Castle,* by John Rowe Townsend. Lippincott, 1976 © 1975.

GROWING THINGS

Burnett, Frances Hodgson. *The Secret Garden.* il. by Tasha Tudor. Lippincott, 1962.

Cleaver, Vera and Bill. *Where the Lilies Bloom.* il. by Jim Spanfeller. Lippincott, 1969.

Holman, Felice. *The Escape of the Giant Hogstalk.* il. by Ben Shecter. Scribner, 1974.

Hunt, Irene. *The Lottery Rose.* Scribner, 1976.

Jobb, Jamie. *My Garden Companion: A Complete Guide for Beginners.* Sierra Club/Scribner, 1977.

Norton, Andre. *Lavender-Green Magic.* il. by Judith Gwyn Brown. Crowell, 1974.

O'Brien, Robert C. *Z for Zachariah.* Atheneum Pubs., 1975.

POTS AROUND THE WORLD

France: *Stone Soup: An Old Tale,* by Marcia Brown. il. by author. Scribner, 1947.

Italy: *Strega Nona: An Old Tale,* by Tomie De Paola. il. by author. Prentice-Hall, 1975.

India: *The Magic Cooking Pot; a Folktale of India,* by Faith M. Towle. il. by author. Houghton, 1975.

Denmark: "The Talking Pot," in *13 Danish Tales,* by Mary C. Hatch. il. by Edgun. Harcourt, 1947.

Japan: "The Dancing Kettle," in *The Dancing Kettle and Other Japanese Folktales,* by Yoshiko Uchida. il. by Richard C. Jones. Harcourt, 1949.

Turkey: "One Candle Power," in *Once the Hodja,* by Alice Geer Kelsey. il. by Frank Dobias. Longmans, 1943.

Germany: *Gone Is Gone; or, The Story of the Man Who Wanted to Do Housework,* by Wanda Gág. il. by author. Coward-McCann, 1935.

Russia: "Who Will Wash the Pot?" in *The Lazies: Tales of the Peoples of Russia,* tr. and ed. by Mirra Ginsburg. il. by Marian Parry. Macmillan Pub. Co., 1973.

China: "Two of Everything," in *The Treasure of Li-Po,* by Alice Ritchie. il. by T. Ritchie. Harcourt, 1949.

USA: *Paul Bunyan Swings His Ax,* by Dell J. McCormick. il. by Lorna Livesley. Caxton Press, 1966 © 1936.
Tall Timber Tales; More Paul Bunyan Stories, by Dell J. McCormick. il. by Lorna Livesley. Caxton Press, 1966 © 1939.

Bengal: *The Old Woman and the Rice Thief,* adapted from a Bengali folktale by Betsy Bang. il. by Molly Garrett Bang. Greenwillow Bks., 1978.

"DEAR ABBY"

Adapt the popular column "Dear Abby" to promote books. Write Dear Abby letters and read them aloud, plant them in the school newspaper, or post them on a bulletin board.

Mama, by Lee Bennett Hopkins. Knopf, 1977.

Dear Abby: My Mama is really lovable, but I suspect that she steals from her employers. What should I do?
—Concerned Son

Winning Kicker, by Thomas J. Duggard. Morrow, 1978.

Dear Abby: This is my last year as football coach at Higgins High. A girl wants to join the team. After 36 years I don't want to make any waves, know what I mean? So, should I let her on the team?
—"No Woman's Libber" Coach

The Amazing Miss Laura, by Hila Colman. Morrow, 1976.

Dear Abby: I really want to earn some money this summer and have a chance to "baby-sit" an old lady. Eccentric widows aren't my thing. Should I take the job?
—Josie (no last name or town please)

179

Dear Abby: My sister, brother, and I have been sneaking into this rich Colonel's yard in the middle of the night to swim in his pool in our underwear. I'm getting scared we'll be caught. How can I tell my sister I don't want to go anymore? —Night Swimmer

The Night Swimmers, by Betsy Byars. il. by Troy Howell. Delacorte, 1980.

A Morgan for Melinda, by Doris Gates. Viking, 1980.

Dear Abby: My father is horse crazy and wants to buy me a Morgan. I'm scared of horses. Should I tell him?

—No Horse Lover

Dear Abby: My parents had a fight last night. I was mad at them for quarreling. Parents are supposed to be perfect. "They should be cheerful, patient, loving, never sick and never tired. And fun too." This morning everything is O.K. Guess I don't have to write to you after all. —Love anyway, An Indignant Daughter

Ramona and Her Mother, by Beverly Cleary. il. by Alan Tiegreen. Morrow, 1979.

SLIDE BOOKTALKS

BOOK JACKET SLIDES

I've had really good success with this booktalk idea. You need to use special equipment or have a good friend help you. The idea is to take slides of the book jackets or covers of the books you are going to talk about. As you discuss each book, a visual image (much larger than the actual book) becomes your background. I used this technique extensively for my classes in children's literature. The image of the bookcover on the screen reinforces the oral citation of the book's author and title. And later, when the students see the real book in the library or on the exhibit table they instantly recognize it.

Pictures taken of related objects also can be used in the slide booktalk. Some of my students accompanied their own slides with taped commentaries, complete with musical backgrounds. Although I find this a very effective method of presentation, I personally prefer to give my own oral presentation because it seems to involve the audience more.

YOU NEED: A 35 mm camera with a close-up lens, or normal lens for large-format books; or a Kodak Ektagraphic Visualmaker kit.

HINTS: You must keep the camera perfectly steady while taking the slides. If you don't have a "copy stand" for this, you can place the camera on a table. You can use daylight for your lighting so long as the front of the book is directly facing the window.

VACATION SLIDES

On your vacation you went to New York or visited the San Diego Zoo. You acquired lots of slides, which you took to your friend's house to show off and your friend's husband fell asleep when the lights were out.

Instead of subjecting a captive audience to an amateur travelogue, put your slides to creative use. Promote books by relating literary settings to the places you've photographed. If you have a copy kit or a 35mm camera, take slides of jackets of the books you're discussing to use along with the vacation slides.

Another use for travel slides is just for setting the scene for a group of books. A trip to a wilderness area could suggest the background for such survival stories as Walt Morey's *Canyon Winter* (Dutton, 1972) or Jean George's *My Side of the Mountain* (Dutton, 1959). Pictures of the beach might be used as an introduction to books such as Natalie Babbitt's *The Eyes of the Amaryllis* (Farrar, Straus, 1977) or Robert Westall's *The Wind Eye* (Greenwillow Bks., 1977). If you are fortunate enough to visit a foreign country, your souvenir slides will make perfect introductions to books set in the same countries. Slides of Japan, for instance, could introduce Katherine Paterson's *The Master Puppeteer* (Crowell, 1976) or Allen Say's *The Inn-keeper's Apprentice* (Harper, 1979). Slides do not have to represent the book exactly to give the flavor of the region or

181

country. You can explain that a slide shows contemporary Japan or the forest before the dam was built.

If you don't travel but your friends do, and they take pictures, borrow theirs. I really wanted to use slides in a talk about Saudi Arabia, so I borrowed a set from someone who had lived there for many years. When my friend Mary wanted to do a booktalk on New York, she felt that her slides wouldn't be satisfactory and borrowed some from a friend.

COMMERCIAL SLIDES

I was jogging in the early morning along the Grand Canal in Venice and thinking of all the wonderful books I've read that take place in Venice. Wouldn't it make a wonderful booktalk to use commercial slides of Venice and excerpt some of the literary descriptions of Venice? I bought slides from a vendor in St. Mark's Square, a cassette of romantic Italian music to use as a background, and was making a list in my head of books when in a bookstall I found that someone had already compiled a collection of stories about Venice: *Venice: A Portable Reader* (edited by Toby Cole. Lawrence Hill, 1979). Everyone who is anybody appears in Cole's anthology: Casanova, Goethe, Dickens, Hemingway, and others.

Voilà! Instant booktalk! And you could do the same for Paris, Rome, Tokyo, and Chicago. Or you could do it for your home town. Here is a list of books for New York and possible location slides to go with them.

NEW YORK FOR YOUNG CHILDREN

SLIDES	BOOKS
Small apartment house on the upper West Side of New York City.	**Hurwitz, Johanna.** *Busybody Nora.* il. by Susan Jeschke. Morrow, 1976.
Neon sign for a nightclub around West 125th–138th St.	**Isadora, Rachel.** *Ben's Trumpet.* il. by author. Greenwillow Bks., 1979.
Financial area with its sky-scrapers.	**Lobel, Arnold.** *On the Day Peter Stuyvesant Sailed into Town.* il. by author. Harper, 1971.
Brownstone apartment house.	**Scher, Paula.** *The Brownstone.* il. by Stan Mack. Pantheon Bks., 1973.
Times Square amusement arcade.	**Steptoe, John.** *Train Ride.* il. by author. Harper, 1971.

NEW YORK FOR MIDDLE-GRADE CHILDREN

SLIDES	BOOKS
Riverside Drive building with pigeons; Greenwich Village with pigeons; West 79th St. entrance to Central Park with pigeons; New York Public Library, 42nd Street and Avenue with pigeons.	**Anderson, Mary.** *Emma's Search for Something.* il. by Peter Parnall. Atheneum Pubs., 1973.
Private brownstone on the upper East Side.	**Fitzhugh, Louise.** *Harriet the Spy.* il. by author. Harper, 1964.

Gracie Mansion, East 88th Street between York Avenue & First Avenue.

Greene, Constance C. *I and Sproggy.* il. by Emily McCully. Viking, 1978.

High-rise apartment building.

Heide, Florence Parry. *Banana Twist.* Holiday House, 1978.

Five-floor apartment house, roof garden, George Washington bridge.

Hurwitz, Johanna. *The Law of Gravity.* il. by Ingrid Fetz. Morrow, 1978.

Metropolitan Museum of Art

Konigsburg, E. L. *From the Mixed-Up Files of Mrs. Basil E. Frankweiler,* Atheneum Pubs., 1967.

Old upper West Side apartment building with a stoop.

Mathis, Sharon Bell. *Sidewalk Story.* il. by Leo Carty. Viking, 1971.

Pushcart peddler; try Delancey St., Central Park, Washington Square, or Herald Square.

Merrill, Jean. *The Pushcart War.* il. by Ronni Solbert. Young Scott Bks., 1964.

Harlem apartment house.

Myers, Walter Dean. *The Young Landlords.* Viking, 1979.

Times Square subway station.

Selden, George. *The Cricket in Times Square.* il. by Garth Williams. Farrar, Straus, 1960.

NEW YORK FOR OLDER CHILDREN

SLIDES

BOOKS

Buildings marked for demolition with Xs on the windows, or pigeons on a building windowsill.

Donovan, John. *Remove Protective Coating a Little at a Time.* Harper, 1973.

The Dakota apartment house (Central Park West and 72nd Street) or Central Park, snow-covered.

Finney, Jack. *Time and Again.* Simon & Schuster, 1970.

Plaza Hotel

Fitzhugh, Louise. *Sport.* Delacorte, 1979.

Riverside Drive, Central Park, Museum of Modern Art garden, Trinity Church cemetery.

Hautzig, Deborah. *Hey, Dollface.* Greenwillow Bks., 1978.

Subway station platform, 42nd Street

Holman, Felice, *Slake's Limbo.* Scribner, 1974.

Grand Central Station, a Woolworth's store	**Hopkins, Lee Bennett.** *Mama.* Knopf, 1977.
Cemetery in Queens.	**Jordan, June.** *His Own Where.* Crowell, 1971.
Empire State Building	**Macaulay, David.** *Unbuilding.* il. by author. Houghton, 1980.
A street in Harlem with stone stoops.	**Myers, Walter Dean.** *It Ain't All For Nothin'.* Viking, 1978.
Fort Lee, New Jersey; George Washington Bridge.	**Zindel, Paul.** *The Undertaker's Gone Bananas.* Harper, 1978.

HINTS: Make a list of the slides you need before you take a trip.

As an alternative to slides, you can use photographs from books.

LIST A BOOK

Lists, Lists, Lists! The grocery list, a Christmas present list, a list of things to do, or a list of lists in books you've enjoyed. Here are a few of my favorites:

HOW TO: Write or type lists on scraps of paper, lined notebook paper strips, or adding machine tape. Pull each list out of a different pocket or out of a bag and simply read the list after a sentence or two (written at the top of the list) that introduces the book.

THE BOOKTALK: In Johanna Hurwitz's *Much Ado About Aldo,* Elaine tries to talk her mother into allowing her to have her ears pierced, and she makes a list of all her friends who already have pierced ears. Karen, her sister, keeps a list of famous names that she finds in the telephone book. Their brother, Aldo, who becomes a vegetarian, makes a list of all the sandwiches his mother can make for his school lunches. The list is on a sheet of paper folded in half. On the left, Aldo has written the YES foods, and on the right, the NO foods. [Pull out the list and read the YES side first.]

185

YES	NO
peanut butter and grape jelly	liverwurst
peanut butter and strawberry jam	salami
peanut butter	baloney
peanut butter and honey	chicken
cream cheese and jelly	roast beef
jelly without peanut butter	ham
jelly without cream cheese	turkey
American cheese	tuna fish
Swiss cheese	

From *Much Ado About Aldo,*
by Johanna Hurwitz. il. by John Wallner.
Morrow, 1978, p. 67.

In *My Father's Dragon,* a boy and his cat pack a knapsack to take with them when they rescue a baby dragon from ferocious beasts. [Read from your list.]

> He took chewing gum, two dozen pink lollipops, a package of rubber bands, black rubber boots, a compass, a toothbrush and a tube of toothpaste, six magnifying glasses, a very sharp jackknife, a comb and a hairbrush, seven hair ribbons of different colors, an empty grain bag with a label saying "Cranberry," some clean clothes, and enough food to last my father while he was on the ship. He couldn't live on mice, so he took twenty-five peanut butter and jelly sandwiches and six apples, because that's all the apples he could find in the pantry.

From *My Father's Dragon*,
by Ruth Stiles Gannett. il. by Ruth Chrisman Gannett.
Random House, 1948, pp. 18–19.

Mr. Popper is really lucky. He receives a penguin as a present. Of course, there are a few problems in keeping a penguin as a pet. First of all, where do you keep a pet that is used to freezing temperatures? Mr. Popper keeps his penguin in the refrigerator. The penguin, Captain Cook, is very curious. Whenever he sees something of interest around the house, he picks it up in his beak and carries it back to his nest in the refrigerator. Mr. and Mrs. Popper eventually discover the penguin's collection. It makes quite a list in *Mr. Popper's Penguins* [Read from your list.]

Two spools of thread, one white chess bishop, and six parts of a jigsaw puzzle . . . A teaspoon and a closed box of safety matches . . . A radish, two pennies, a nickel, and a golf ball . . . Two pencil stubs, one bent playing card, and a small ash tray. . . .

Five hairpins, an olive, two dominoes, and a sock . . . A nail file, four buttons of various sizes, a telephone slug, seven marbles, and a tiny doll's chair. . . .

Five checker pieces, a bit of graham cracker, a Parcheesi cup, and an eraser . . . A door key, a buttonhook, and a crumpled piece of tinfoil . . . Half of a very old lemon, the head of a china doll, Mr. Popper's pipe, and a ginger ale cap . . . An ink-bottle cork, two screws, and a belt buckle. . . .

Six beads from a child's necklace, five building blocks, a darning egg, a bone, a small harmonica, and a partly consumed lollipop . . . Two toothpaste caps and a small red notebook.

From *Mr. Popper's Penguins,*
by Richard and Florence Atwater. il. by Robert Lawson.
Little, 1938. pp. 42–43.

Everybody knows that Harriet keeps a spy notebook in *Harriet The Spy.* She has some interesting lists in it.

NOTES ON WHAT CARRIE ANDREWS
THINKS OF MARION HAWTHORNE

Thinks: is mean
       is rotten in math
       has funny knees
       is a pig

WHAT TO DO ABOUT PINKY WHITEHEAD

1. Turn the hose on him.
2. Pinch his ears until he screams
3. Tear his pants off and laugh at him.

From *Harriet the Spy,*
by Harriet Fitzhugh. il. by author.
Harper, 1964. pp. 183–184. *187*

Gnomes make lots of lists. This is a list of ways to prepare dirt, a gnome diet staple.

GNOMES' 20 FAVORITE WAYS TO EAT DIRT

1. Dirt fried dirt.
2. Dirt topping over fried dirt.
3. Dirt with dirt on the side.
4. Dirt à la dirt.
5. Soup with dirt.
6. Dirt in dirt sauce.
7. Chopped dirt.
8. Dirt spread on dirt.
9. Hot dirt casserole.
10. Dirt lo mein.
11. Scrambled dirt on toast.
12. Scrambled toast on dirt.
13. Bacon-lettuce-dirt (b.l.d.) with mayonnaise.
14. Dirtloaf.
15. Broiled filet of dirt.
16. Dirt à la king.
17. Spaghetti with dirt sauce.
18. Dirt butter and jelly.
19. Dirt with dirt stuffing.
20. Dirt on a seeded bun with lettuce, pickles, onion,
    and special sauce.

From *Gnasty Gnomes,* by Jovial Bob Stine.
il. by Peter Lippman. Random, 1981.

What do witches eat? Here's a list.

WITCHES' MENU

Live lizard, dead lizard
Marinated, fried
Poached lizard, pickled lizard
Salty lizard hide.
Hot lizard, cold lizard
Lizard over ice.
Baked lizard, boiled lizard
Lizard served with spice.
Sweet lizard, sour lizard
Smoked lizard heart.
Leg of lizard, loin of lizard
Lizard a la carte.

by Sonja Kikolay

From *Witch Poems,* edited by Daisy Wallace.
il. by Trina Schart Hyman. Holiday House, 1976. p 23.

This is the list I wrote today:

Walk dog
Pick up Hilary from ice skating
Call lawyer
Make dentist appointment
Do ten sit-ups
Read lists from books and make everyone want to read them.

[Make sure the books you introduce are on exhibit so the group can check them out to read.]

BOOKS THAT CONTAIN LISTS

Atwater, Richard and Florence. *Mr. Popper's Penguins.* il. by Robert Lawson. Little, 1938.

Dahl, Roald. *James and the Giant Peach.* il. by Nancy Ekholm Burkert. Knopf, 1961.

Fitzhugh, Louise. *Harriet the Spy.* il. by author. Harper, 1964.

Gannett, Ruth Stiles. *My Father's Dragon.* il. by Ruth Chrisman Gannett. Random House, 1948.

Holman, Felice. *Slake's Limbo.* Scribner, 1974.

Hurwitz, Johanna. *Much Ado About Aldo.* il. by John Wallner. Morrow, 1978.

Lowry, Lois. *Anastasia Krupnik.* Houghton, 1979.

Sharmat, Marjorie Weinman. *Maggie Marmelstein for President.* il. by Ben Shecter. Harper, 1975.

Thurber, James. *Many Moons.* il. by Louis Slobodkin. Harcourt, 1943.

Wallace, Daisy, ed. *Witch Poems.* il. by Trina Schart Hyman. Holiday, 1976.

OTHER ACTIVITIES

1. Read a list from a book. Ask the children to guess the title of the book.

2. Have the children write original stories around the objects listed in a book.

3. Mix and match exhibit. Post lists (from your booktalk) on a bulletin board. List the titles next to the lists. Have the children match the list with the titles.

COVER STORY: FASHIONS IN CHILDREN'S LITERATURE

A fashion show of book jackets was presented at the Kent County Library System in Grand Rapids, Michigan, and the idea was imported to Oregon by Pat Feehan.

Enlarged book jackets, reproduced with an opaque projector, were worn sandwich-board style and modeled by adults. A "fashion coordinator" then commented on the books as the models walked across the stage.

Categories included headgear (puzzles and riddles), bridle fashions (horse stories), sleepwear (bedtime stories), and playtime fashions (sports books).

190

EXAMPLES OF FASHION COMMENTARY:

Time for a nightcap . . . a good book to share at bedtime or anytime. . . .
Be on the lookout for *Ramona and her Father* by Beverly Cleary (Morrow, 1977).
In an effort to help when money becomes tight at home because her father has lost his job, Ramona lends a hand. She practices rehearsing television commercials hoping that she will be discovered and make a million dollars.
Poor Ramona. All she manages to do is insult her second-grade teacher with memorized lines about "wrinkles in her panty hose."
Beverly Cleary is an author with a reputation for stories that wear well. This book is definitely not a sleeper. Nighty, night!

"Diamonds are forever," and so is the beauty of *The Treasure,* by Uri Shulevitz (Farrar, Straus, 1978). Present this jewel to someone you love in the intimate evening hours before bedtime. The illustrations glowingly illustrate this simple elegant tale so that it will always be in style. You will want to keep this book in a safe place to admire for many years.

BOOKTALK RAW MATERIAL

Start with these ideas to create your own book talks. Add your favorites. Use only those books that you have read or really enjoy.

RUN WITH A BOOK: BOOKS ABOUT RUNNING. Grades 3–7.

> **Adoff, Arnold.** *I Am the Running Girl.* il. by Ronald Himler. Harper, 1979.
>
> **Asch, Frank and Jan.** *Running with Rachel.* Photographs by Jan Asch and Robert Michael Buslow. Dial, 1979.
>
> **Christopher, Matt.** *Run, Billy, Run.* Little, 1980.
>
> **Cragg, Sheila.** *Run Patty Run.* Harper, 1980.
>
> **Fogel, Julianna.** Wesley Paul. *Marathon Runner.* Photographs by Mary S. Watkins. Lippincott, 1979.
>
> **Levy, Elizabeth.** *Running Out of Time.* il. by W. T. Mars. Knopf, 1980.
>
> **Sullivan, George.** *Run, Run Fast.* Crowell, 1980.

MONKEYING AROUND: BOOKS ABOUT MONKEYS, GORILLAS, APES, AND CHIMPANZEES. Grades 4–7.

Armour, Richard. *All Sizes and Shapes of Monkeys and Apes.* il. by Paul Galdone. McGraw, 1970.

Boston, Lucy M. *A Stranger at Green Knowe.* il. by Peter Boston. Harcourt, 1961.

Donovan, John. *Family; A Novel.* Harper, 1976.

Freeman, Dan. *The Great Apes.* Putnam, 1979.

Kevles, Bettyann. *Thinking Gorillas; Testing and Teaching the Greatest Ape.* il. with photographs. Dutton, 1980.

Klein, Norma. *A Honey of a Chimp.* Pantheon, 1980.

Meyers, Susan. *The Truth About Gorillas.* il. by John Hamberger. Dutton, 1980.

Michel, Anna. *The Story of Nim the Chimp Who Learned Language.* Photographs by Susan Kuklin and Herbert S. Terrace. Knopf, 1980.

Teleki, Beza, Karen Steffy, and Lori Baldwin. *Leakey the Elder; A Chimpanzee and His Community.* il. with photographs. Dutton, 1980.

SHOWFOLK: BIOGRAPHIES OF PEOPLE IN SHOW BUSINESS. Grades 7–8.

Arce, Hector. *Groucho.* Putnam, 1979.
Biography of Groucho Marx.

De Veaux, Alexis. *Don't Explain; A Song of Billie Holiday.* Harper, 1980.
A prose poem.

Haskins, James. *I'm Gonna Make You Love Me; the Story of Diana Ross.* Dial, 1980.

Maiorano, Robert. *Worlds Apart; The Autobiography of a Dancer from Brooklyn.* Coward, 1980.

Poitier, Sidney. *This Life.* Knopf, 1980.
Autobiography of Sidney Poitier.

Strasberg, Susan. *Bittersweet.* Putnam, 1980.
Autobiography of Susan Strasberg.

IV PRESENTING POETRY

Poems can be
about anything
but poems FOR CHILDREN
are supposed to be
    cute and sweet and all about
    wee little mice
    and dear little flowers
    and Baby Jesus.

By Siv Widerberg

What goes wrong between childhood and adulthood? We know that small children revel in the sound and rhythm of language, but few grow up to admit a fondness for poetry.

One morning my eight-year-old said she hated poetry. I ignored the statement until that afternoon, when I read her some poems from Jack Prelutsky's *The Snopp on the Sidewalk* (Greenwillow Bks., 1977). She was laughing with great abandon, so I stopped and said that I thought she hated poetry. She replied that that wasn't poetry. "What is?" I asked. She jumped up from her seat and posed with her feet apart, her head thrust forward and her arms flung upward. "Poetry," she said in sonorous tones, "is 'The sky is blue and the clouds are floating through.' "*

What have we done wrong? Actually I'm not sure that I want to find out. Are we still making poetry hated by demanding an analysis of the iambic pentameter? Are we forcing children to write poetry in rigid forms? There have been such fine books written on the enjoyment of children's poetry that it is difficult to believe that we still have children who turn into poetry-haters.

My solution to this problem is not based on any great expertise in po-

---

*Three years later, when Hilary was eleven, she climbed our library ladder to get *Alice in Wonderland*. "Just about every book I read has a quote from *Alice* and I want to memorize some poetry from it!" she said. The next day she came over and asked if I'd like to hear a poem and proceeded to recite "Father William," "How Doth the Little Crocodile," and "Tweedle Dum and Tweedle Dee" from the Lewis Carroll works.

etry. My experience pretty much parallels my daughter's. It wasn't until I found out that poetry didn't have to rhyme that I began expressing my thoughts and feelings privately in poetry.

I think poetry should be fun. If adults could have fun with it, maybe children would enjoy it too. In this section you will find ways to present poetry with informality and abandon. Some of the ideas may not appeal to you, especially if you are used to a more traditional or reverential approach to poetry. In fact, you may find some of these ideas to be on the far side of just plain wacky. I'd like any nonbelievers to try one or two just the same. The ideas have all been tried with adults and children. On the surface they have been roaring successes. If they really instill a permanent fondness for poetry I cannot tell you. We will have to wait and see.

My feeling is that children (and adults) have not been exposed to the delightful aspects of poetry and therefore don't know what they are missing. Years ago I read a Bugs Bunny comic book and the point of the story has stuck with me through the years. Bugs Bunny is in a bunny orphan asylum. At lunch all the orphans are served tasteless gruel. Bugs complains, "But where are the carrots?" "What's a carrot?" ask all the little bunnies. "We like gruel." If you don't know what a carrot or a poem is, how can you possibly know what you're missing?

Usually what happens in today's educational system is that we greet the children in first grade and play a bit with nursery rhymes, and then we ignore poetry until we ask them to analyze Keats or the sonnets of Shakespeare. I don't think it should come as a big surprise that most adults don't cuddle up with a poetry book. Most people don't even read real books, so you can't expect them to read poetry. After all, poetry is for intellectuals . . . or is it?

How can we change almost an entire nation's attitude towards poetry? How can we turn indifference or hatred into appreciation? For starters, I propose taking a "poetry break."

THE POETRY BREAK

You've heard of the coffee break. A poetry break is based on the same principle. Between math and science or between fractions and sets, stop what you are doing and take a minute to present a poem orally and maybe visually. Then go on with your lesson plan. Think how wonderful it would be if the children you are teaching today grow into poetry-loving adults tomorrow because you spent a few minutes a day presenting poetry.

The quickest and easiest way to take a poetry break is to mark poems here and there in an appealing collection of poetry and simply read one of the poems aloud to your students. Start with something simple. If you read aloud consistently throughout the school year, you will be able to read poems of greater sophistication as the year progresses. You don't have to do all the reading yourself, either. Let your students take turns reading or reciting throughout the term.

I'd like you also to encourage children to memorize poems that they like. This activity is definitely out of fashion and there is no justifiable reason for its demise. I call for a revival of poetry memorization. After all, children do not have any of these adult hang-ups about memorizing. I could memorize poetry easily until I was a young adult. Ask me any time and I'll recite, word perfect, those poems that I learned at age ten. The death-blow to memorizing poems comes when we force children to learn poems that are not of their own choosing, imposing our own adult preferences on them. If we present children with some of the superior poetry written especially for them and then let them make their own selections, I think memorizing will not have such unfortunate connotations.

When the school day began with a worship service, the recitation of psalms or prayers often gave children a chance to perform in front of a group. Now, with increased curricular demands, we no longer seem to have any time to give children a chance to perform regularly. But the poetry break can give you an opportunity to let your students perform. Don't insist upon memorization (although you may well recommend it); just give them a chance to present a poem. You don't have to be an English teacher to follow this idea, and you don't have to find poems that have to do with history if you teach social studies. Show your students that you are a real person interested in them as whole human beings.

So, the obvious, most convenient, and probably the most frequently-

195

used way to present poetry is just to read it from a book. (See the bibliography on pages 257–66 for some great collections.)

MEDIA PRESENTATIONS

From time to time you may want to vary your presentations by using some sort of visual or sound effects to get your poem across. You may want to show a picture while presenting a poem, particularly if the poem has been beautifully illustrated. Some traditionalists are shocked when poetry is illustrated. "Poetry should be heard, not seen." One of my friends, for instance, called an illustrated version of Robert Frost's *Stopping by Woods on a Snowy Evening* (Dutton, 1978) a "desecration." She "saw" that poem in her mind's eye in one fashion and she felt that Susan Jeffers (the artist) had ruined it. Of course, the ultimate enjoyment would be to live the poem in your own head, but I think there is room in a brain for several interpretations of a poem. Many children brought up on an overdose of television have trouble visualizing creatively. They are not like the children before the advent of television, whose imaginations could be immediately activated by a few chords of music. The Lone Ranger, Jack Armstrong, Superman, The Inner Sanctum, and The Shadow were all real to us, even though they were only on radio, but it seems to me that many of today's children do not visualize even simple pictures.

Nicola Bayley's small, colorful, detailed drawings for the old country rhyme *One Old Oxford Ox* (Atheneum Pubs., 1977) raise a simple rhyme to greater heights through illustration. You may make your own imaginative pictures when you read Lewis Carroll's *Jabberwocky*, but Jane Breskin Zalben's illustrations give the poem a new dimension (*Lewis Carroll's Jabberwocky*, Warne, 1977).

A most successful anthology, *Reflections on a Gift of Watermelon Pickle* (ed. by Stephen Dunning, Edward Lueders, and Hugh Smith; Lothrop, 1967) is illustrated with photographs that illuminate the meaning of the poems. In their next collection, *Some Haystacks Don't Even Have Any Needle* (Lothrop, 1969), the editors used modern abstract paintings to illustrate the book because they felt that the readers of the first book would have graduated to higher levels of imagination.

Pictures are certainly not always necessary to the presentation of poetry, but they can in many cases play a primary role in attracting readers who are otherwise reluctant to try poetry. In other cases pictures may simply

196

add to the poems in just the way illustrations add to any book, by offering the illustrator's own visual interpretation.

PRESENTATION TECHNIQUES

The ideas for poetry presentation in this chapter were chosen because they are easy to do and the poems work for most audiences. I suggest that you use the media poems sparingly, and intersperse them with simpler recitations. It is better to present a poem without media first and then on a subsequent occasion to present it with the media. Don't be afraid to repeat a media poem. Even though the audience already knows the "surprise," they will still enjoy it. Don't be afraid to repeat a poem many times. A well-chosen poem deserves frequent exposure.

Not all poems lend themselves to media, however. Obviously, in many cases it would be a desecration to munch on a potato chip or wear a silly mask to present a poem. The more serious poems should be introduced with dignity.

As your children grow up with poems, you can recite longer, more sophisticated selections. I'm not suggesting that the beginner in poetry should not hear serious poems, nor am I suggesting that the more advanced student shouldn't play with some of the poems. Just as in anything, I'm promoting a balanced diet.

I think poems containing serious thoughts and complex word play should be presented with as much planning on your part as the lighter poems. Certainly you will want to take time to prepare a serious poem. Read it over several times to make sure that you fully understand it. Practice reading it aloud with expression. If you can possibly memorize the poem, all the better.

Memorizing poetry differs significantly from learning a story. You can't just learn the story line—you must know every word as the poet has written it. I hate to admit this, but although I can memorize pages and pages of a story, I have great difficulty with a two-line poem. I consider this a real infirmity since reciting a poem is obviously a lot more effective than reading one. Recognizing my own failing, I have devised all sorts of ways to present poetry by showing something while I read it. (This does not mean that I think that *you* should not attempt to memorize the poems you present.)

If you are taking the time to prepare a presentation, take time to set the mood. If you don't feel like dimming the lights to create a more formal atmosphere, be sure to pause before you begin the poem, making sure that the audience's attention is directed to you.

Most of the ideas in this section are to be used with single poems presented at the beginning or the end of a book program or story hour, or between school activities as a "poetry break." When you find a poem that fits a season, holiday, subject, or mood, use it. Don't wait until you have time to create a formal program. Once the children get used to the idea of a poetry break, they will look forward to it and be ready to stop running and start listening.

A real necessity is for you to know your poetry collection. The only way to do that is to read poetry in the same way you do mysteries or gothics, with your full attention. Keep a poetry book in the bathroom, kitchen, and in your pocket or purse. When you have a minute or two, start reading. As you search for poems for your poetry projects, you will become more familiar with the literature.

Since I have begun to "think media" when thinking about poems, it is difficult to stop my mind from making the presentation of even the simplest of poems into a celebration. This is not necessary for you. The important thing is simply to share the joys of poetry.

IDEAS FOR PRESENTING POETRY

1. READ POETRY ALOUD often.
2. Poetry Break: Set aside the same time every day to read one poem aloud. Read it at least twice.
3. Act out a poem.
4. Hand out objects, pictures, or miniature animals and ask everyone to find a poem to go with them. Share the poems aloud.
5. Read a poem with a musical background, recorded or live.
6. Use a puppet to recite poems.
7. Draw an illustration for a poem.
8. "Eat a poem." Serve food appropriate to a poem.
9. Have a poetry recitation or reading contest.
10. Show slides as a background to recited poems.
11. Have an on-going poem-of-the-week or poem-of-the-month exhibit in your classroom, library, or child's room.

12. Pick a theme and make an illustrated booklet or exhibit of poems that relate to the theme.
13. Recite a poem in unison or in parts.
14. Memorize a poem a week.
15. Package poetry: Find an object that relates to a poem and copy the poem on a card. Put the object and the poem in a box. Pass the box around for everyone to enjoy.
16. Puzzle poetry: Make a game using original illustrations, picture postcards, or cut-up paperbacks matching the poem to the pictures.
17. Make a puzzle from a poem mounted on posterboard.
18. Have a poetry-writing contest.
19. Ask a guest to share his or her favorite poems aloud with your group.

20. Listen to recordings of poets reading their own works.
21. Show a film or filmstrip featuring poetry.
22. Videotape or record children reading or reciting poetry.
23. Have a poetry election to determine the best-loved poem of the class.
24. Have the children choose a poem to read aloud or recite to a senior citizens' club or to their parents.
25. Plan a poetry program to give at a PTA meeting.
26. Have the children collect poems that their parents or grandparents learned as children. Arrange them in a book.
27. Find someone who can speak a foreign language fluently to recite poems in that language.
28. Pick poems from various sources that you think a friend will like. Copy them into a book and illustrate them, if you wish. Give the book as a gift.

29. Dial-a-poem. Install a telephone-answering device in your library that plays a poem when a number is dialed.

199

30. Have a candlelight poetry reading. Each person who wishes to share a poem lights a candle and then recites a poem. The darker the room, the better the atmosphere.
31. Have a poetry scavenger hunt.
32. Illustrate a poem with transparencies.

Some of these ideas will be discussed more fully in the pages that follow.

Poems and Presentations

In this section, I have collected poems that have been particularly successful in presentations. Although these poems are printed in their entirety so that you do not have to search for the original source, I suggest that you take the time to browse through the poetry section of your library to find other appealing poems.

PRESENTATIONS BY ADULTS

Any poem can be presented by anybody—child or adult—but some poems seem to work best with adult speakers. The next one is a good

example:

SAM AT THE LIBRARY

My librarian
Said to me,
"This is the best book for grade three."
That was the year I was in third,
So I took the book
On her good word.
I hurried home, crawled into bed,
Pulled up the covers over my head,
And turned my flashlight on
And read.

But the book was awful
And icky and bad.
It wasn't funny;
It wasn't sad.
It wasn't scary or terribly tragic,
And it didn't have even an ounce of magic!
No prince,
No dragon,
No talking cat;
Not even a witch in a pointy hat.
Well!
What can you do with a book like that?

My librarian
Tried once more:
"This is the best book for grade four."
That was the year I was in fourth,
So I took her word
For what it was worth;
And I took the book back home to bed,
Draped the covers over my head
Turned my flashlight on,
And read.

But the book was dull as a Brussels sprout.
I couldn't care how the story came out.
It didn't have baseball
Or football or tennis,
It didn't have danger and lurking menace,
Or wicked kings like the ones in history,
And it didn't have even an ounce of mystery!
No midnight moan,
No deserted shack,
No great detective hot on the track,
Nobody tortured on the rack.

201

So naturally
I took it back.

My librarian
Used her head.
When I was in grade five, she said,
"Sam, it's silly to try to pretend
You like the books I recommend,
When it's perfectly,
Patently,
Plain to see—
Your taste and mine will never agree.
You like sports books—
I can't stand them.
I don't like mysteries—
You demand them.
You think fairy tales are for babies.
You hate dog stories worse than rabies.
You're not me,
And I'm not you.
We're as different as pickles and stew.
So from now on, Sam,
You go to the shelf,
And pick out the books you want,
Yourself."

And ever since then
We get along fine.
She reads her books;
I read mine.
And if we choose to converse together,
We smile—
And talk about the weather.

By Carol Combs Hole

PRESENTATION: Just read this one aloud, or better yet
memorize it. The poem is a perfect introduction to a program for adults who work with children and books. It can
also be used with children, as an introduction to your
speech telling them you would be happy to recommend
books, but that you might not always guess their tastes
accurately.

HINT: This is a good poem to use when you don't have
time for a booktalk. Recite the poem and then just let the
children browse through books that you have selected and
placed on an exhibit table or library rack.

MONSTER POETRY

Children will enjoy a playful scare, as long as the "monster" is not genuinely threatening. The first poem here is an old folk rhyme.

> In a dark dark wood
> There was a dark dark house.
> In the dark dark house
> There was a dark dark room.
> In the dark dark room
> There was a dark dark closet.
>
> In the dark dark closet
> There was a dark dark shelf.
> On the dark dark shelf
> There was a dark dark box.
> In the dark dark box
> There was a MONSTER!

PRESENTATION: At the end of the rhyme pick up a black box and extract a MONSTER.

HINT: The monster need not be elaborate since the audience will jump at your loud voice, whatever you pull out of the box. Draw a monster on shelf or adding-machine paper, or use a scary puppet or a feather dust-mop.

THE LURPP IS ON THE LOOSE

Oh the lurpp is on the loose, the loose,
the lurpp is on the loose.
It caused a fretful, frightful fuss
when it swallowed a ship and ate a bus,
and now it's after all of us,
oh the lurpp is on the loose.

Oh the lurpp is on the loose, the loose,
the lurpp is on the loose.
It weighs about a zillion pounds,
it's making loud and lurppy sounds
as it follows us with bumbly bounds,
oh the lurpp is on the loose.

Oh the lurpp is on the loose, the loose,
the lurpp is on the loose.
It's covered with horns and thorns and claws
and razor teeth adorn its jaws,
so everyone's running away, because
the lurpp is on the loose.

By Jack Prelutsky

203

PRESENTATION: On the last line of the poem release a spring snake into the audience. Snakes are available from magic shops or from David Ginn, 5687 Williams Rd., Norcross, GA 30093, or Supreme Magic Company Ltd., 64 High St., Bideford, Devon, England.

TO MAKE YOUR OWN LURPP

YOU NEED: A Slinky
fabric to cover
an empty can with a plastic lid

HOW TO: Stretch the Slinky just enough so that it will still be springy. Cover it with fabric in its extended state. Glue or sew Lurpp features on the fabric. Pack it into a can.

A spring snake is also effective with the following poem.

MOTHER DOESN'T WANT A DOG

Mother doesn't want a dog.
Mother says they smell,
And never sit when you say sit,
Or even when you yell.
And when you come home late at night
And there is ice and snow,
You have to go back out because
The dumb dog has to go.

Mother doesn't want a dog.
Mother says they shed,
And always let the strangers in
And bark at friends instead,
And do disgraceful things on rugs,
And track mud on the floor,
And flop upon your bed at night
And snore their doggy snore.

Mother doesn't want a dog.
She's making a mistake.
Because, more than a dog, I think
She will not want this snake.

By Judith Viorst

PEBBLE POETRY

PEBBLES

Pebbles belong to no one
Until you pick them up—
Then they are yours.

But which, of all the world's
Mountains of little broken stones,
Will you choose to keep?

The smooth black, the white,
The rough gray with sparks
Shining in its cracks?

Somewhere the best pebble must
Lie hidden, meant for you
If you can find it.

By Valerie Worth

PRESENTATION: Recite this poem before you pass around a basket of pebbles. Let the children each choose a pebble. Or recite the poem before you take a walk with your children where they might be able to find their own pebbles.

HINT: If it is not possible to find pebbles, you can purchase them from a garden shop. Ask your friends, neighbors, or patrons if anyone collects and polishes stones as a hobby. They may have leftovers.

205

CANDLE POETRY

The ritual of lighting and blowing out a candle to begin and end a book program or to use as a motif during a program can be very effective. Here are a short collection of poems and a folktale to use with a candle. If possible, use a handcrafted candlestick to maintain the folk spirit of the book program.

THE CONTEST—A FOLKTALE

Once there was a man who lived in a small cottage with his three children. This father wished to will the cottage to the cleverest of his three children. "I will leave my house to whichever of you can fill the cottage with just one thing."

That sounded easy enough. The oldest son brought a flock of chickens into the house. They cackled and scuttled all over the house, nesting in the cupboard and in the man's bed, but they only filled a portion of the house. The second son dumped a load of grain into the house. At first it nearly did fill the house, but soon the chickens began eating the grain—until only the fat chickens and small piles of grain were left.

Now it was the daughter's turn. One evening she lit a single candle and brought it into the cottage. The light of the candle filled every corner of the house.

And so it was that the girl became the new owner of her father's cottage.

PRESENTATION: Light the candle when the girl lights the candle in the story.

Blow out the candle with this poem:

NO ONE

In this room
there's not a
breeze.

No one sneezed
the littlest
sneeze.

No one wheezed
the faintest
wheeze.

The door's shut
tight
with a big brass
handle.

Who?
WHO
BLEW OUT THE CANDLE?

By Lilian Moore

Relight the candle with this poem:

FIRST DAY OF SPRING

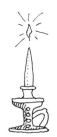

Oh what a beautiful thing
To see on the first day of spring:
   A green thing is sprouting
   And that's why I'm shouting
Happy Birthday dear First Day of Spring!

     By Beatrice Schenk de Regniers

HINT: This poem can also be recited using a bouquet of blooming flowers, a magic trick in which feather flowers seem to bloom from feather leaves. Available from David Ginn, 5687 Williams Road, Norcross, GA 30093.

Blow out the candle with this poem:

Burning
candles
have
no place
to go
but
out.

   By Freya Littledale

To relight or blow out the candle, here's another choice:

THE MONSTER'S BIRTHDAY

Oh, what a party!
They all ate hearty
   of elegant bellyache stew.

Then came the cake
In the shape of a snake
   and trimmed with octopus goo.

The balloons all went BANG!
And everyone sang,
   "Happy birthday, dear Monster
     to you."

   By Lilian Moore

207

HINT: It's very effective to have the people in your audience light and blow out their own birthday candles. Be sure the audience is responsible enough to handle lighted candles. Caution people to hold the candles away from clothing so that wax doesn't spatter when blowing out the candles. Some fire laws may not permit this activity.

Blow out a candle or turn out the electric lights with this poem:

NO DIFFERENCE

Small as a peanut,
Big as a giant,
We're all the same size
When we turn off the light.

Rich as a sultan,
Poor as a mite,
We're all worth the same
When we turn off the light.

Red, black or orange,
Yellow or white,
We all look the same
When we turn off the light.

So maybe the way
To make everything right
Is for God to just reach out
And turn off the light!

By Shel Silverstein

SNACK POETRY

THE LUNCHBOX

I watched my Mommy make my lunch.
Salami sandwich and berry punch
Potato chips and chocolate cake
With icing, that I helped to make.
She added an apple and napkins, too
And closed my lunchbox when she was through.

On the way to school, I smelled the food;
It put me in a hungry mood.
"What could I eat?
What could I take?
I'll only have a bite of cake."

I kept on eating, it was so good
I walked on through the neighborhood.
I got to school;
My lunch was done.
But walking to school
Was super-fun!

By Susan Cohen Field

PRESENTATION: Act this poem out with real food.

YOU NEED: Salami sandwich, berry punch, potato chips, chocolate cake, an apple, napkins packed in a lunchbox.

HINT: Artificial food—a soft sculpture sandwich and cake—could be substituted for real food, but using real food will make it more fun.

SNACK TIME

When the lady next door
Offered me a banana,
I took two—
One for my sister.
She doesn't like
Them.

By Libby Stopple

PRESENTATION: Recite before snack time when you are serving fruit, or afterwards, when at least one child will surely have said, "May I have two?"

BUBBLE GUM

I love bubble gum BUBBLE GUM
Chewy, chewy bubble gum
Bubbles here bubbles there
Pink and blue green purple
Popping and blowing
FUN FUN GUM chewy chewy gum
and it pops in your hair!

Anonymous

PRESENTATION: After you've blown a nice big bubble with your bubble gum, you will have the children's amazed attention.

209

JUNK FOOD

Marshmallow, jelly bean, bubble gum, soup tureen.
Corn dog, pizza pie, onion ring, French fry.
Barbecue, crab-cake, crackerjack, milkshake.
Popcorn, licorice whip, Hershey bar, pickle chip.
Cheeseburger, Jello-jel, Twinkie cake, Taco Bell.
Chocolate malt, Shake n' Bake, Seven-up, STOMACHACHE.
Chorus (*after each line*):
Alka Seltzer, Alka Seltzer, Alka Seltzer, Alka Seltzer!

Anonymous

PRESENTATION: Print the chart on a chalkboard without the Alka Seltzer chorus. The audience recites the chant in unison. The second or third time around, part of the audience can sing the chorus as a surprise.

I discovered this jingle at a Sam Sebesta workshop and loved it so that I have had it upgraded on a cloth banner.

WILLIE ATE A WORM

Willie ate a worm today,
a squiggly, wiggly worm.
He picked it up
from the dust and dirt
and wiped it off
on his brand-new shirt.
Then slurp, slupp
he ate it up,
yes Willie ate a worm today,
a squiggly, wiggly worm.

Willie ate a worm today,
he didn't bother to chew,
and we all stared
and we all squirmed
when Willie swallowed
down that worm.
Then slupp, slurp
Willie burped,
yes Willie ate a worm today,
I think I'll eat one too.

By Jack Prelutsky

PRESENTATION: For strong stomachs only—act this out with cooked spaghetti.

210

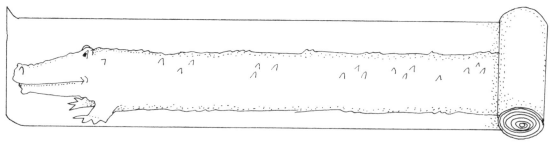

THE CROCODILE

Said a very l–o–n–g crocodile,
"My length is a terrible trial!
I know I should diet
But each time I try it
I'm hungry for more than a mile!"

By Lilian Moore

PRESENTATION: On the last line unroll, with the help of an assistant, a picture of a very long crocodile.

HINT: Use shelf paper. Unroll the paper on the floor and use acrylic paints to draw a crocodile.
An alternative, for those who want their picture to last longer, is to stitch a crococile on a fabric banner.

BUBBLES

BLOWING BUBBLES

Bubbles are big enough
to see your face in
or a real rainbow
and small enough to get lost
almost as fast as they arrive.
How sad . . .
But look! Here comes a new one.

By Kathleen Fraser

211

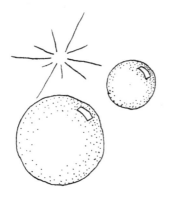
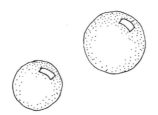
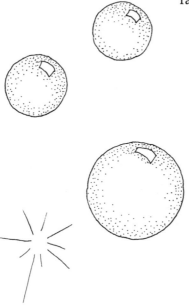

SOAP BUBBLE

The soap bubble's
Great soft sphere
Bends out of shape
On the air,
Leans, rounds again,
Rises, shivering, heavy,
A planet revolving
Hollow and clear,
Mapped with
Rainbows, streaming
Curled, seeming
A world too splendid
To snap, dribble
And disappear.

By Valerie Worth

BUBBLES

Two bubbles found they had rainbows on their curves.
They flickered out saying:
"It was worth being a bubble just to have held that
rainbow thirty seconds."

By Carl Sandburg

BUBBLES

There are big bubbles,
little bubbles,
light bubbles,
cute bubbles,
beautiful bubbles,
colorful bubbles,
sexy bubbles,
smart bubbles, and
friendly bubbles.
Most people don't know
what their bubble is
because they don't look
closely enough.
You should always be careful
with bubbles
because if they don't like you
                                    they
POP!

By Beth

212

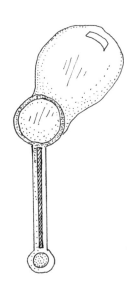

PRESENTATION: At intervals during the program, blow bubbles through a bubble wand—a perfect illustration.

YOU NEED: a bottle of soap-bubble mix and a wand. You can purchase these at a variety store or make your own.

HOW TO MAKE SOAP-BUBBLE SOLUTION:

Combine 1 tablespoon of liquid detergent with 2 table-spoons of water. Mix together gently.

The addition of 4 drops of corn syrup to the solution will create piggyback bubbles, unnecessary for the presentation of the above poems, but fun. If you do include the syrup, use the mixture out-of-doors. It's sticky.

HOW TO MAKE A BUBBLE WAND:

Make a wand with a ring at the end from bent wire or from a coat hanger. The handle is not really necessary; you can also blow bubbles through the metal ring of a home-canning jar lid.

POCKET MONEY

It's a sad commentary on the current state of the world, but money is about the cheapest thing you can purchase these days.

Coins, American and foreign, make marvelous magical souvenirs to give away at book programs.

Ask friends and relatives who travel to a foreign country to buy the smallest coin there. In many cases, a coin will cost less than an American penny. It's fun, too, trying to make a foreign bank teller understand that you want to buy 100 or 500 of the coins that most of his customers are trying to get rid of.

I've been suggesting at various workshops that people give away coins. In Saudi Arabia a group of librarians and teachers started a storytelling league as a result of my visit. At Christmas one of the women planned to tell the Christmas chapter from Laura Ingall Wilder's *Little House on the Prairie*. In the story the children receive shiny new pennies in their stockings, the perfect inexpensive gift for the 200 children that would attend.

But where do you get 200 American pennies when you live in Saudi Arabia? Luckily, Dick, a husband of one of the women, was going to be in Houston, and he went to a bank to buy the pennies. He was told that he would have to go to the main branch for the shiny new pennies. He then walked the few blocks over to the bank headquarters. He was told that the pennies would have to be brought up from the vault and that he should return later in the day to pick them up. That afternoon he returned to the cashier's window for the pennies.

"Excuse me, sir," said the teller. "Have you brought a cart to carry the pennies?"

"What do you mean?" said Dick. "I'll just take the two dollars' worth of pennies in my pocket."

"But sir, we thought you needed two hundred dollars worth of pennies. We've brought them up especially from the vault."

American pennies or foreign coins can take on a special quality too if they are given as a gift to accompany a story or poem such as these.

COINS

Coins are pleasant
To the hand:

Neat circles, smooth,
A little heavy.

They feel as if
They are worth something.

By Valerie Worth

PRESENTATION: Extract a coin or two from a coin purse along with the text of the poem printed on a purse-size card. Read the poem as you weigh the coins in your hand.

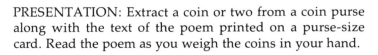

MONEY

Workers earn it,	Heirs receive it,
Spendthrifts burn it,	Thrifty save it,
Bankers lend it,	Misers crave it,
Others spend it,	Robbers seize it,
Forgers fake it,	Rich increase it,
Taxes take it,	Gamblers lose it. . . .
Dying leave it,	I could use it.

By Richard Armour

PRESENTATION: Write each line of the poem on play money. Throw the money into the audience as you read each line. Or wait until the last line and throw the money into the air.

KEEPSAKE

Before Mrs. Williams died
She told Mr. Williams
When he gets home
To get a nickel out of her
Navy blue pocketbook
And give it to her
Sweet gingerbread girl
    That's me
I ain't never going to spend it.

By Eloise Greenfield

PRESENTATION: Open a box of keepsakes and take out a coin. Read the poem, which has been printed on the lid of the box.

LINCOLN PENNY

This bright shiny penny
Shows Abe Lincoln's face
You'll find him in banks
Or most anyplace
Tuck it into your purse
Slip it into your shoe
And always you'll have
Lots of good luck with you.

By Nonie Borba

PRESENTATION: Print the poem on the back of a portrait of Lincoln, which is available at card shops in February.

215

THE LOST PENNY

"Boo-hoo . . ."
"Why are you crying, little boy?"
"Boo-hoo . . . I had a penny and I lost it."
"Here is a penny. Don't cry."
"Thank you-oo . . . Boo-hoo . . ."
"You have a penny. Why are you crying now?"
"If I hadn't lost mine, I'd have two."

By Mirra Ginsburg

PRESENTATION: This little anecdote lends itself to drama. Pretend that you are each person, looking down when you talk as the adult, up when you are the child.

DIGGING FOR TREASURE

I put my hand in
and found—
    a rusty skate key,
    a part of a tool,
    a dead bee I was saving
    to take into school;
my library card
and
a small model rocket,
    I guess it is time
    to clean out
    my pocket.

By Lee Bennett Hopkins

PRESENTATION: Extract items mentioned in the poem from your pocket.

POCKETS

I never knew a kangaroo—
    A sister or a brother—
Who didn't ride, when young, inside
    The pocket of his mother;
And, oh, I'm sure that kangaroos
    Think human folk are funny
To fill their pockets up with things
    As valueless as money.

By Rowena Bennett

PRESENTATION: On the last line take play money out of your pocket and scatter it.

HINT: Play money can be purchased at toy and magic shops, or use real money!

If you'd like to include a story in your coin program, try Sharon Bell Mathis's *The Hundred Penny Box* (il. by Leo and Diane Dillon. Viking, 1975). In this story, great-great aunt June has a penny for every year of her life.

"MODERN TIMES"

Of Quarks, Quasars, and Other Quirks; Quizzical Poems for the Supersonic Age. Collected by Sara and John E. Brewton and John Brewton Blackburn. il. by Quentin Blake. Crowell, 1977.

This is a book I recommend you purchase. There are so many ways you can experiment with the poems in this volume. Obviously, reading them aloud is an excellent way to share poems with a friend or a group, but these are also naturals to use with media. The collection contains poems about all sorts of contemporary subjects, including pollution, supermarkets, computers, and television.

Stack up produce cans and boxes around you while you recite the poems in the section "I'm Lost Among a Maze of Cans," which has amusing poems about supermarkets and shopping.

Retrieve a large carton (refrigerator or filing cabinet box) from the trash, paint it to resemble a computer, and stand inside to perform the poems in the section titled "Where the Neuter Computer Goes Click," which contains funny poems about computers.

Here's a poem to use while you're waiting for the book to arrive.

TEE-VEE ENIGMA

We jeer
And we sneer—
And continue
To peer.
We glare
And we swear—
And continue to stare.
We groan
And bemoan,

We snicker
And scoff—
But we don't
Turn it off.
Maybe what keeps us
Glued to it
Is the joy of being
Rude to it!

By Selma Raskin

PRESENTATION: Decorate a cardboard frame or a picture frame to look like a television set. Hold the frame so that it surrounds your head while you recite the poem. (I stick out my tongue on the last line.)

HINT: If you have trouble memorizing poems, copy the words on the back of the frame.

217

BANNER POEMS

As you recite a poem, place objects that relate to the poem on a background banner. The banner and objects can be cut out of paper, or out of cloth for a more permanent wall hanging.

Recite the poem several times before presenting the poem with the banner. If you use a cloth background, attach the objects to the banner with Velcro. Velcro will also work with paper or poster board.

The banner technique can be adapted for all sorts of poems. The photographs show a banner presentation for the nursery rhyme "Old Mother Hubbard."

Two poems to use in banner presentations follow.

TRUCKS

Big trucks for steel beams,
Big trucks for coal,
Rumbling down the broad streets,
Heavily they roll.

Little trucks for groceries,
Little trucks for bread,
Turning into every street,
Rushing on ahead.

Big trucks, little trucks,
In never ending lines,
Rumble on and rush ahead
While I read their signs.

By James S. Tippett

TRAINS

Over the mountains,
Over the plains,
Over the rivers,
Here come the trains.

Carrying passengers,
Carrying mail,
Bringing their precious loads
In without fail.

Thousands of freight cars
All rushing on
Through day and darkness,
Through dusk and dawn.

Over the mountains,
Over the plains,
Over the rivers,
Here come the trains.

By James S. Tippett

PRESENTATION: On an applique or painted landscape background, attach trucks or trains as the poem is recited.

HINTS: The children can create the trucks and trains, but for a more meaningful presentation, the leader should practice manipulating the objects while reciting the poems.

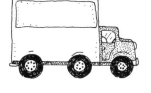

POETRY APRON

Use a felt-decorated apron to make a wearable felt board. As you recite a poem, take felt cutouts from the pocket and attach them to the apron. This apron can also be used to tell simple stories or to introduce a story.

YOU NEED: A bib apron, store-bought or homemade (Simplicity Pattern # 7254, for instance), or bib overalls
An 8″ x 10″ felt square for the "board"
Two 5″ x 5″ fabric squares for pockets
Felt cutouts

HOW TO: Attach the 8″ x 10″ felt square to the bib part of the apron with fabric glue or stitching. (A wide zigzag stitch makes a fun border.)
Glue or stitch the pockets to the skirt part of the apron.
Cut out felt pieces representing objects or thoughts in your favorite poems. Make sure they will fit in the pockets.
Before or during the recitation of a poem, take the appropriate object out of the pocket and place it on the felt board.

HINTS: 1. Pictures can be used on the felt board too. Glue sandpaper on the backs of the pictures to hold them onto the felt. Try using pictures cut from a paperback book of poetry.

2. If you have trouble memorizing a poem, copy it onto an attractive card and keep it in the poetry pocket for reference.

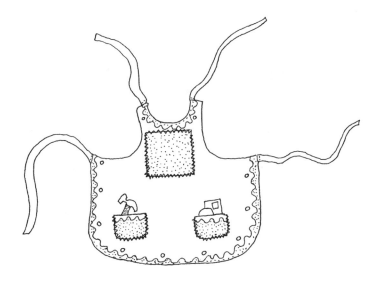

BOOKLIST

HARDCOVER BOOKS:

Adams, Adrienne, comp. *Poetry of Earth.* il. by compiler. Scribner, 1972.
Short poems about nature lend themselves to illustration. White butterflies, bats, and reptiles are among the subjects of these poems.

Brownjohn, Alan. *Brownjohn's Beasts.* il. by Carol Lawson. Scribner, 1970.
Sophisticated, witty poems about animals: mole, mouse, camel, and cow.

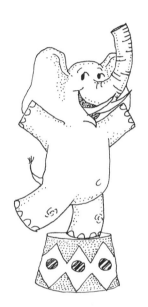

Bruna, Dick. *The Circus: A Toy Box Tale.* tr. by Sandra Greifenstein. il. by author. Follet, 1963.
Simple figures in strong colors offset little rhymes.

Clymer, Theodore, comp. *Four Corners of the Sky: Poems, Chants, and Oratory.* il. by Marc Brown. Little, 1975.
Short American Indian poems illustrated with bright graphics should inspire your imagination.

De Regniers, Beatrice Schenk. *Circus.* Photographs by Al Giese. Viking, 1966.
Lighthearted circus verse.

Larrick, Nancy, comp. *On City Streets: An Anthology of Poetry.* Photographs by David Sagarin. Evans, 1968.
Cut out rectangular shapes to represent tall buildings. Rearrange them as you recite poems about the city.

Shaw, Richard, ed. *The Bird Book.* il. by various artists. Warne, 1974.
Use greeting cards or other pictures of birds to illustrate the bird poems in this book.

PAPERBACK BOOKS:

These are inexpensive, and you can cut out the pictures.

Jones, Hettie, comp. *The Trees Stand Shining: Poetry of the North American Indians.* il. by Robert Andrew Parker. Dial Press, 1974. pa, Dial, 1976.
Short poems. Full-page paintings lend themselves to easy "cut and show".

Preston, Edna Mitchell. *Pop Corn & Ma Goodness.* il. by Robert Andrew Parker. Viking, 1969. pb, Seafarer Viking, 1972.
Use the pictures from the paperback on the felt board while telling this tall tale.

221

Tripp, Wallace, comp. *A Great Big Ugly Man Came Up and Tied His Horse to Me: A Book of Nonsense Verse.* il. by compiler. pa, Little, 1973.
Colorful cartoons illustrate nursery rhymes. The pictures are appropriate for all ages.

GREETING CARDS:

Pictures from Edward Lear's *The Scroobious Pip* (il. by Nancy Ekholm Burkert, Harper, 1968) are available on greeting cards from Sunrise Publications, Inc., Bloomington, Indiana 47401.

Pictures from *The Real Mother Goose* (il. by Blanche Fisher Wright. Rand McNally, 1916) are available on greeting cards from True Inc., Woodstock, Connecticut 06281.

Pictures from Kenneth Grahame's *The Wind in the Willows* (il. by Michael Hague. Ariel Bks. [distributed by Holt], 1980) are available from Sunrise Publications, Inc., Bloomington, Indiana 47401.

OBJECT NURSERY RHYMES

Try something different when you recite a nursery rhyme.

MAGIC FLOWERS

Recite this rhyme several times until the children can chant it with you.

Mary, Mary quite contrary
How does your garden grow?
With silver bells and cockle shells
And pretty maids all in a row.

PRESENTATION: Now repeat the rhyme with a little difference. On the last line, pull a garden from your sleeve. The flowers are feather spring flowers. Feather spring flowers can be hidden in a very small space and grow into a big bouquet when released. They are available at magic shops and from Louis Tannen, Inc., 1540 Broadway, New York, New York 10036; or Abbott's Magic Co., Colin, Michigan 49040.

DOLLS AND A SHOE

There was an old woman who lived in a shoe.
She had so many children
She didn't know what to do.
She gave them some broth
Without any bread,
Whipped them all soundly,
And put them to bed.

PRESENTATION: Find or make miniature dolls (mine were hand-carved and bought at a senior-citizen craft shop). You or your children can sew simple dolls. The shoe can be a rubber boot (mine was bought for fifteen cents at a rummage sale) or a work boot. As you recite the poem, take the dolls out—the more the better—and then replace them in the shoe or boot. You'll probably have to recite the rhyme several times as you take the dolls in or out.

CANDLESTICK

Jack be nimble,
Jack be quick,
Jack jump over the candlestick.

PRESENTATION: The children jump over a candlestick. If there are too many children, choose just one to do the jumping.

223

POETRY MASKS

Wear masks to recite appropriate poems. You can make masks from fabric or decorate large paper bags.

There was a young lady from Niger
Who smiled as she rode on a tiger;
They returned from the ride
With the lady inside,
And the smile on the face of the tiger.

Traditional

What a wonderful bird the frog are.
When he sit he stand almost;
When he jump he fly almost;
When he talk he cry almost;
He ain't got no sense hardly.
He ain't got no tail hardly, either.
He sit on what he ain't got almost.

Traditional

POSTER POETRY

Posters can be used to illustrate poetry. You can acquire them free from publishers, or you can make your own.

UNCLE UMBERT

Here we see old Uncle Umbert,
Wearing such a forlorn frown.
Turn him upside down and you'll see . . .
Uncle Umbert upside down.
What did you expect?

By Shel Silverstein

PRESENTATION: Use an old-timey photograph or drawing of a pompous-looking man, or draw him yourself. Hold the picture facing the audience, then turn it upside down on the fourth line of the poem.

ART CARDS

Choose a poem that you would enjoy illustrating. Draw pictures for the poem and mount them on 8" x 10" cards. Put cardboard stands on the back of your illustrations so that they will stand up on a table.

Present your poem and show the illustrations.

The cards in the photograph illustrate a poem by Ogden Nash.

225

SNAP A POEM

If you are an avid photographer or have a friend who is, here is a way to put your talents to use. Look through a number of poetry collections. Pick poems that lend themselves to visuals. Marchette Chute, Karla Kuskin, A. A. Milne, and Nina Payne are four poets who often write about objects, characters, or scenes that you can find in and around the home. List the scenes you need and then find them in real life and photograph them with 35mm film. Recite poems as you show the slides. This is also an exciting project for children to do themselves.

EXAMPLES:

<table>
<tr><td>AN EVENT</td><td>MY TEDDY BEAR</td></tr>
<tr><td>Something's happened very fine.
   New shoes.
Guess whose?
   Mine!</td><td>A teddy bear is a faithful friend.
You can pick him up at either end.
His fur is the color of breakfast toast.
And he's always there when you need him most.</td></tr>
<tr><td>By Marchette Chute</td><td>By Marchette Chute</td></tr>
</table>

PUPPET POETRY

Nearly all children are enthralled with puppets. In fact, even adults will often listen more closely to what a puppet is saying than to what a real live person is saying. Use finger puppets, hand puppets, picture puppets, or marionettes to recite your favorite poems. The puppet does not have to represent the poem being presented. Any interesting puppet can explore a poem.

If you have a puppet stage that hides the puppeteer, you can read rather than recite a poem, which may make things easier.

You can also turn the program over to the children. Let them make their own puppets, choose their own poems, and put on a poetry puppet show.

PICTURE PUPPETS

These simple puppets will enable you to read, rather than recite, a poem with ease.

YOU NEED: discarded book jackets, greeting cards, or pictures from magazines
tongue depressors, popsicle sticks, or dowels
craft glue
poster board
poetry collections

HOW TO: Cut out a picture and a matching piece of poster board.

Glue the poster board to the back of the picture, with tongue depressor between. The tongue depressor should protrude from the bottom of the reinforced picture to form a handle. Print a poem on the back of the board.

USE: Read the poem aloud while holding the picture up. Move the picture around, if that is appropriate.

HINT: If you use pictures from book jackets, you will be introducing a book and a poem at the same time.

227

POEMS FOR BEDTIME

A model bed makes a poetry exhibit.

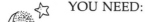

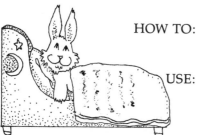

YOU NEED: a doll's bed, a dollhouse bed, or a small bed you've made yourself
white muslin sheets cut to fit the bed
a typewriter
a collection of poems about the night, bedtime, sleep

HOW TO: Type bedtime poems on the muslin sheets. You may need to use a sheet of paper to feed the fabric into the typewriter.

USE: Use the bed as an exhibit, or as the basis for a nighttime poetry reading or story hour. Take the sheets off the bed and read the poems to the group. Share picture books between poetry readings.

GOODNIGHT DAVID—A PUPPET ROUTINE

I use a puppet to introduce and end the bedtime story/poetry program. My puppet is a rabbit hand puppet that works perfectly for a nighttime story program, since I almost always use Margaret Wise Brown's *Goodnight Moon* (il. by Clement Hurd, Harper, 1947). The main character in this book is a bunny who is saying goodnight to the objects in his room. I use a Steiff hand puppet* imported from Germany. These puppets are expensive (perhaps you can get one as a birthday present) and are available from fine toy shops such as FAO Schwarz (745 Fifth Avenue, New York, NY 10022; or 180 Post Street, San Francisco, CA 94108). A less expensive rabbit puppet can be made by splitting the back and removing some of the stuffing from a stuffed bunny toy (usually available in stores around Easter).

Begin the program with the rabbit puppet asleep in the bed covered with the poetry sheets. Display the rabbit in his bed and ask the children if they would like to meet the bunny. "This is his bed. He's very shy, so when I bring him out whisper very quietly, 'Hello, David.' " Take the puppet out of the bed. You can turn your back on the audience while you are putting the puppet on your arm.

The puppet acts shy. He hides his head in his paws and peeks out now and then; then he waves. My rabbit doesn't do any talking. He speaks only to me and I tell the audience what he says.

---

228 *Useful also as the main character in Charlotte Zolotow's *Mr. Rabbit and the Lovely Present.* il. by Maurice Sendak. Harper, 1962.

"David wants to know your name. On the count of three, everyone shout out your name. Don't be scared, David. Ready? One, two, three . . . thank you! David likes to be petted. Would you like to pet him?" The children in the front row get to pet David, but he acts shy, hiding behind your arm and his paws.

"Now would you like to hear some stories? How about you, David? Sit right here." Place the puppet over a stand or an empty pop bottle so he can see and hear the stories too. He is not used again until the end of the program.

Now proceed to read the poems typed on the muslin sheets and share the picture books. Each time you use a sheet from the puppet's bed, mention him, saying "I'm sure David won't mind if we use one of his sheets." Or, "This is one of David's favorite nightime poems." Involve the children, too—"This poem was originally written in Swedish. Do you ever feel this way?"

NOT BEING ABLE TO SLEEP

The worst thing about
not being able to sleep
I think
is
when suddenly you realize
that you're not going to be able
to sleep.

By Siv Widerberg

"This poem was first published in 1885. Has this ever happened to you?"

BED IN SUMMER

In winter I get up at night
And dress by yellow candle-light.
In summer, quite the other way,
I have to go to bed by day.

I have to go to bed and see
The birds still hopping on the tree,
Or hear the grown-up people's feet
Still going past me in the street.

And does it not seem hard to you,
When all the sky is clear and blue,
And I should like so much to play,
To have to go to bed by day?

By Robert Louis Stevenson

229

At the conclusion of the program, use David again. "The stories and poems are over for tonight. Let's put David back to bed." Turn your back on the audience as you put the rabbit back into position on your hand.

"Time to go to sleep." Bunny shakes head No. "Aren't you tired?" Bunny shakes head No. "Yes you are, you must be. Come on, get ready for bed." Bunny picks up pillow. "Is that your pillow? It's a pretty color." Bunny hits you with pillow. "Hey, what are you doing? We're not going to have a pillow fight." He hits you again. "All right, that's enough. Promise not to do that again." You turn and get hit again. "That's enough. Now get into bed." Bunny lies down. Sits up. "What? You want a drink of water?" Give him a glass. "Now goodnight." "What? Now you need your stuffed animal?" Hand him his animal (I have a small rabbit). Sits up again. "Now what? Oh, you want a goodnight story. You've just had one. Oh well, here's a book to sleep with. It will give you happy dreams. It's called *A Taste of Carrot*." Hand him the book. "Now are you ready to go to sleep? What? Oh, of course, you want a goodnight kiss." Bunny kisses you and blows kisses to the children. "Goodnight."

BOOKLIST

These books are short collections of poems about night and bedtime. Picture books are listed on page 315.

Fisher, Aileen. *In the Middle of the Night.* il. by Adrienne Adams. Crowell, 1965.

Fox, Siv Cedering. *The Blue Horse, and Other Night Poems.* il. by Donald Carrick. Seabury [distributed by Houghton], 1979.

Hill, Helen, Agnes Perkins and Alethea Helbig. *Dusk to Dawn: Poems of Night.* il. by Anne Burgess. Crowell, 1981. A short collection of poems with night themes by Randall Jarrell, Archibald MacLeish, Langston Hughes, and others. For the older child.

Hopkins, Lee Bennett, comp. *Go To Bed!* il. by Rosekrans Hoffman. Knopf, 1979.

Payson, Dale and Karen Maxwell Wyant, comps. *Sleepy Time Treasury.* il. by Dale Payson. Prentice-Hall, 1975.

Plath, Sylvia. *The Bed Book.* il. by Emily Arnold McCully. Harper, 1976.

Russo, Susan, comp. *The Moon's the North Wind's Cooky.* il. by compiler. Lothrop, 1979.

TRANSPARENCY POETRY

Make transparency overlays to use with an overhead projector when reciting poetry.

YOU NEED: acetate sheets cut to fit an overhead projector
permanent-ink felt-tip pens
overhead projector

HOW TO: Draw pictures that go with a poem on separate sheets of acetate. Place each picture in a different area of the acetate "page." If you have access to a Thermo-Fax machine, you may want to type the lines of the poems onto the sheets with the pictures. Tape the sheets together on one side to make a "book."

When you project the pictures, flip each sheet over separately until all sheets are overlaid and projecting at the same time.

PRESENTATION: Recite the poem, adding a new picture when appropriate.

HINTS: Recite the poem without the transparencies as an introduction and to allow the audience to "see" the pictures in their mind's eye before they see the transparency version.

231

EXAMPLES:

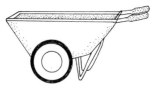

SPRING AND ALL

So much depends   glazed with rain
upon   water
a red wheel   beside the white
barrow   chickens.

By William Carlos Williams

You need separate transparencies of a red wheelbarrow, rain, and white chickens.

POEM

As the cat   carefully
climbed over   then the hind
the top of   stepped down
the jamcloset   into the pit of
first the right   the empty
forefeet   flowerpot.

By William Carlos Williams

You need separate transparencies of a cat, a jamcloset, and a flowerpot.

TABLE

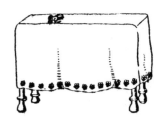

Table, I've got my eye on you,
Hoping there may be pie on you.
And if there isn't, fie on you!
Right now there's a fly on you.

By David McCord

You need separate transparencies of a table, a pie, and a fly.
Take away the pie and replace it with the fly.

HINT: You can also make slides to illustrate poems by copying pictures onto transparency film with a Thermo-Fax machine, coloring them with felt-tip pens, and mounting the film in cardboard slide mounts (available at photography shops).

232

Exhibits

This section gives a few ideas on using poems for bulletin boards and other exhibits. Perhaps you can think of other ways to bring poetry to the attention of your library or classroom. Try posting short poems in the telephone booths, on circulars, or on the lunch tables.

BULLETIN BOARD—POEMS AND PHOTOS

Select poems to establish a theme and pin them on the bulletin board; then ask the children to bring in appropriate photographs. You might use baby pictures with poems about babies, cat pictures with poems about cats. Since I'm a dog lover, I've used dog poems as the central theme for the first exhibit. The children could bring in pictures of their dogs or draw pictures of the "ideal" dog. Cats or other pets can be given equal time on your next bulletin board.

DOGS

BIRTHDAY PRESENT

White?
Oh yes, a woolly white one.

Black?
Oh yes, a black-as-night one.

Tan?
I think a tan or brown one
perfect for a farm or town one.

Sleek?
Oh yes, a sleek and trim one.

Shaggy?
Any her or him one.

Tousled, frowzled,
big or small.

I'd like any kind at all—
just so it's a dog.

By Aileen Fisher

233

DOGS

The dogs I know
Have many shapes.
For some are big and tall,
And some are long,
And
some
are thin,
And some are fat and small.
And some are little bits of fluff
And have no shape at all.

By Marchette Chute

HINT: Be sure to read the poem aloud each time someone brings in a dog picture . . . or at least once.

CLOTHES

Once
I kept my Sunday clothes on
All day long,
And no one came to
See us.

By Libby Stopple

PRESENTATION: Exhibit with class photographs, or have the children bring in snapshots of themselves in party clothes.

BULLETIN BOARD—POCKET POEMS

Use Beatrice Schenk de Regniers's poem below as the focal point of your bulletin board. Let the children design and make their own pockets to go on the board. (They can glue material scraps together.) The children may write original poems or copy their favorites from a book to place in the pockets.

KEEP A POEM IN YOUR POCKET

Keep a poem in your pocket
and a picture in your head
and you'll never feel lonely
at night when you're in bed.

The little poem will sing to you
and the little picture bring to you
a dozen dreams to dance to you
at night when you're in bed.

By Beatrice Schenk de Regniers

234

POEM-OF-THE-MONTH

Every library and classroom should have one of these posters or banners hanging on the wall. Make your own design. Mine is a house with a clear acetate window in which to place the poems. It is made on poster board, but I also have a cloth banner that serves the same purpose. Again, it is up to you to decide if you want to trade up or down, depending on the relative importance of the project in your situation. But remember, once you've made the basic exhibit, you can use it forever.

While you are making the basic exhibit, be sure that you take the time to collect the poems. Place the poems that are not being used in a manila envelope glued to the verso side of your poster so that you can easily change the poem.

Children also can find poems for you and be made responsible for changing the poems each month.

Poem of the Month

Activities and Games

In this section, you will find ways of playing with poems.

EAT A POEM

Serve a meal and recite a poem before each course. (The recipes are all fantastic favorites from my secret file. Do not use these recipes unless you also use the poem in some way or I'll be very sad I gave the recipes away.) Copy the poems and let each dinner guest read one aloud or recite a poem yourself as you bring in each course. For a large group, divide the cooking up as you would for a potluck dinner, providing each cook with a copy of one recipe. If you don't want to cook from scratch (shame on you!) good canned and packaged foods can be substituted for some of the recipes.

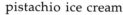

EAT A POEM MENU

SOUP

choice of mandarin mushroom soup with singing rice,
or
beautiful green soup

SPAGHETTI

choice of clam sauce or chestnut meatballs

SALAD

tomato and sunflower salad

DESSERT

choice of chocolate cake, vanilla cookies, or

pistachio ice cream

MILK

Begin with Marchette Chute's "Dinnertime"—a short poem about table manners.

DINNERTIME

I am told
    To sit up nicely.
I am told
    I should not stuff
All my dinner
    In a minute
And three helpings
    Are enough.

No one says,
    "Do have another.
You can hardly
    Stop at three."
No one wants
    Me to be happy
In the way
    I want to be.

By Marchette Chute

Now start your meal with a hot bowl of soup. Choose between Sandburg's "Soup" and Lewis Carroll's "Beautiful Soup."

SOUP

I saw a famous man eating soup.
I say he was lifting a fat broth
Into his mouth with a spoon.
His name was in the newspapers that day
Spelled out in tall black headlines
And thousands of people were talking about him.

When I saw him,
He sat bending his head over a plate
Putting soup in his mouth with a spoon.

By Carl Sandburg

RECIPE FOR MANDARIN MUSHROOM SOUP
WITH SINGING RICE

SINGING RICE

Begin this recipe well in advance of your dinner.

YOU NEED: 1 cup rice   salad oil
               4 cups water   greased cookie sheet
               2 teaspoons salt

HOW TO: Mix rice, water, and salt in a saucepan. Let stand for ½ hour. Bring to a boil, cover, and simmer for ½ hour. Drain. Spread evenly on a heavily greased cookie sheet. Bake at 250° for 8 hours, turning occasionally with a spatula. Remove from oven. Break into bite-size pieces. Pour

2 inches of salad oil into a 6-quart saucepan. Heat to 425°. Fry rice for about 4 minutes, or until golden brown. Drain and keep hot until ready to serve.

MANDARIN MUSHROOM SOUP

YOU NEED: 3½ cups chicken broth
⅓ lb. lean pork, diced fine
1 clove garlic, crushed
1 tablespoon soy sauce
¼ cup sliced fresh mushrooms
¼ cup sliced water chestnuts (these are available canned)
¼ cup frozen grean peas

HOW TO: Combine broth, pork, garlic, and soy sauce in a saucepan. Simmer for 10 minutes. Remove garlic, add remaining ingredients, and simmer 2 minutes more.

Place the rice in a casserole. At the table, pour the soup over the rice and listen to it "sing." Serves six.

BEAUTIFUL SOUP

Beautiful Soup, so rich and green,
    Waiting in a hot tureen!
Who for such dainties would not stoop?
Soup of the evening, beautiful Soup!
Soup of the evening, beautiful Soup!
    Beau–ootiful Soo–oop!
    Beau–ootiful Soo–oop!
Soo–oop of the e–e–evening,
    Beautiful, beautiful Soup!

Beautiful Soup! Who cares for fish,
    Game, or any other dish?
Who would not give all else for two p—
ennyworth only of beautiful Soup?
Pennyworth only of beautiful Soup?
    Beau–ootiful Soo–oop!
    Beau–ootiful Soo–oop!
Soo–oop of the e–e–evening,
    Beautiful, beauti–FUL SOUP!

By Lewis Carroll

RECIPE FOR GREEN SOUP

YOU NEED:

1½ cups of dry split peas   2 to 3 qts. of water
1 ham bone   ½ cup tomato purée
1 stalk celery   ½ cup heavy cream
1 onion, stuck with cloves   salt
1 bay leaf   croutons

Soak peas in water to cover overnight in a large kettle. Drain; then combine with ham, onion, celery, water, and spices. Bring to boil, then lower heat and simmer until peas are soft. Remove the ham bone and purée the soup in blender (or put through a sieve). Add the tomato purée and cream. Salt to taste. Return to stove, bring to boil. Serve with croutons—enjoy! Serves six.

For a main course, serve spaghetti, as inspired by Shel Silverstein's poem.

SPAGHETTI

Spaghetti, spaghetti, all over the place,
Up to my elbows—up to my face,
Over the carpet and under the chairs,

Into the hammock and wound round the stairs,
Filling the bathtub and covering the desk,
Making the sofa a mad mushy mess.

The party is ruined, I'm terribly worried,
The guests have all left (unless they're all buried).
I told them, "Bring presents." I said, "Throw confetti."
I guess they heard wrong
'Cause they all threw spaghetti!

By Shel Silverstein

RECIPE FOR SPAGHETTI WITH CLAM SAUCE

YOU NEED: 2 (7 or 8 oz.) cans minced clams
2 tablespoons olive or vegetable oil
3 tablespoons butter or margarine
2 cloves garlic, minced
1 (8 oz.) package spaghetti
¼ teaspoon salt
pinch of pepper
3 tablespoons chopped parsley

HOW TO: Bring a large pot of water to a boil. Drain clams, reserving juice. In a saucepan heat oil and 2 tablespoons of butter, and sauté garlic until tender. Add clam juice and cook at a slow boil until reduced to about one cup (3 or 4 minutes). Cook spaghetti according to directions and drain. Return spaghetti to pot and toss with remaining butter and keep warm. Reduce heat under clam juice and stir in clams, seasonings, and parsley. Serve over spaghetti. Serves four.

239

RECIPE FOR CHESTNUT MEATBALLS AND SPAGHETTI

MEATBALLS

YOU NEED: 2 cups soft bread crumbs
½ cup milk
1 tablespoon soy sauce
½ teaspoon garlic salt
¼ teaspoon onion powder
1 pound ground beef
½ pound bulk pork sausage
6 oz. canned water chestnuts, drained and chopped

HOW TO: Mix all ingredients together. Form into small meatballs and bake at 350° for 18–20 minutes.

SPAGHETTI WITH GARLIC AND OIL

YOU NEED: 1 (8 oz.) package spaghetti
½ cup olive oil
2 cloves garlic
salt and pepper

HOW TO: Boil spaghetti according to package directions. Shell and crush garlic. Heat the oil and garlic, pressing the garlic slightly to extract the juice. Season with salt and pepper. Serve with the meatballs. Serves six.

HINT: The meatballs can be served with buttered spaghetti for those who like things "plain".

Accompany the spaghetti with tomato sunflower salad, but first recite Myra Cohn Livingston's "Tomato Time" and Kaye Starbird's "Sunflowers".

TOMATO TIME

On a summer vine, and low,
The fat tomatoes burst and grow;

A green, a pink, a yellow head
Will soon be warm and shiny red;

And on a morning, hot with sun,
I'll find and pick a ripened one.

Warm juice and seeds beneath the skin—
I'll shut my eyes when I bite in.

By Myra Cohn Livingston

240

SUNFLOWERS

The sunflowers in our garden
Have stems that are tall as stilts
And sunshiny blossom-faces
And dresses of leaves, like kilts.

It's funny about the sunflowers.
You don't even know they're there,
Until some morning you notice
They're five feet up in the air.
And maybe a short time later,
You look as you wander by
And suddenly you see them standing
Eleven or twelve feet high.

The sunflower plants remind me
Of Amy and Joanie Brown,
Who probably do more growing
Than anyone else in town.
Their mother is just exhausted
From letting down hems each fall,
And can't understand the reason
Her daughters are both so tall.

Although I would hate to tattle
On neighbors like Joan and Amy
(Because—if we had a battle—
Undoubtedly, they'd outweigh me)
I happen to know the reason
The two of them grow like weeds:
Whenever they're here each autumn,
They eat a few sunflower seeds.

By Kaye Starbird

RECIPE FOR TOMATO AND SUNFLOWER SEED SALAD

YOU NEED: 1 (8 oz.) container cottage cheese
4 ripe tomatoes, cut in wedges
4 tablespoons sunflower seeds
1 tablespoon minced parsley
salt and pepper

HOW TO: Mix sunflower seeds and parsley. Blend into cottage cheese; salt and pepper to taste. Scoop cottage cheese mixture onto tomato wedges. Healthy as well as good. Serves six.

241

Recite this old Mother Goose rhyme and serve ice-cold milk to drink—the real thing, not skim or low-fat milk.

Cushy cow bonny, let down thy milk,
And I will give thee a gown of silk:
A gown of silk and a silver tee,
If thou wilt let down thy milk to me.

To end the meal, choose between David McCord's "Pistachio Ice Cream," Eve Merriam's "A Vote for Vanilla," and Nina Payne's "Chocolate Cake."

PISTACHIO ICE CREAM

Pistachio ice cream, all green;
And I am pausing now between
Two spoonfuls just to say I wish
You had the money for a dish.

By David McCord

RECIPE FOR PISTACHIO MARSHMALLOW ICE CREAM

YOU NEED: 2 cups light cream
30 miniature marshmallows
¼ teaspoon green food coloring
⅛ teaspoon salt
½ teaspoon almond extract
½ teaspoon vanilla extract
2 cups heavy cream whipped
1 cup ground pistachio nuts (Shell nuts, place in strainer. Pour boiling water over nuts, then cold water. Remove skins and then grind nuts.)

HOW TO: In the top of a double boiler combine light cream and marshmallows. Heat and stir until marshmallows are melted. Cool 20 minutes. Add remaining ingredients and mix well. Freeze in mold or ice tray in freezing compartment of refrigerator. Makes a half gallon.

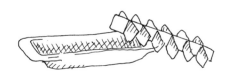

242

A VOTE FOR VANILLA

Vanilla, vanilla, vanilla for me,
That's the flavor I savor particularly
In cake or ice cream
Or straight from the bean
In pudding, potatoes, in fish or in stew,
In a sundae, a Monday, the whole
        week-long through!

I care not a sou, a hoot, or scintilla,
A fig or a farthing—except for vanilla!
Boo, foo, eschew, sarsaparilla;
More, adore, encore vanilla!
From the Antarctic to the Antilles,
Vive Vanilles!
On the first of Vanilla I'll write to you
At half-past vanilla we'll rendezvous;

By the light of vanilla we'll dance and we'll
        fly
Until vanilla dawns in the sky.
Then to a vanilla villa we'll flee
By the vanilla side of the sea,
With vanilla tables, vanilla chairs,
Vanilla carpeting on the stairs,
Vanilla dogs, vanilla cats,
Vanilla shoes, vanilla hats,
Vanilla mice in vanilla holes,
Vanilla soup in vanilla bowls:

Vanilla, vaniller, vanillest for me,
The flavor I favor most moderately!

By Eve Merriam

RECIPE FOR VANILLEKIPFEL (VANILLA CRESCENTS)

YOU NEED: 1 pound butter (do not substitute)
½ cup powdered sugar
1 cup chopped walnuts
4 cups flour
1 teaspoon vanilla

HOW TO: Cream butter and sugar. Add flour slowly, then nuts and
vanilla. If dough gets too soft, it can be put in refrigerator
to harden. Roll dough between hands to form a snake.
Break off two-inch pieces and shape into crescents. Bake
on ungreased cookie sheet at 350° for approximately 15
minutes. Roll in powdered sugar while still warm. Makes
about 6 dozen cookies, but they disappear very fast!

CHOCOLATE CAKE

Chocolate cake
Chocolate cake
that's the one
I'll help you make
Flour soda
salt are sifted
butter sugar
cocoa lifted
by the eggs

then mix the whole
grease the pans
I'll lick the bowl
Chocolate caked
Chocolate caked
that's what I'll be
When it's baked.

By Nina Payne

243

RECIPE FOR CHOCOLATE CHERRY CAKE

YOU NEED: ¼ pound butter
¾ cup chocolate chips
¾ cup sugar
4 egg yolks
½ cup flour
4 beaten egg whites
1 can sour cherries, drained

HOW TO: Melt butter and chocolate chips in a double boiler. Mix sugar, egg yolks, and flour together and add to butter-chocolate mixture. Fold in the egg whites. Butter a square baking dish and spoon in the batter. Add drained cherries. They will sink to the bottom. Bake at 325° for 45 minutes. This is a Viennese chocolate cake. Serves eight.

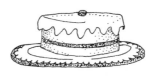

After dinner recite Walter de la Mare's "Miss T" and Kaye Starbird's "Eat-it-all Elaine."

MISS T.

It's a very odd thing—
    As odd as can be—
That whatever Miss T. eats
    Turns into Miss T.;
Porridge and apples,
    Mince, muffins, and mutton,
Jam, junket, jumbles—
    Not a rap, not a button
It matters; the moment
    They're out of her plate,
Though shared by Miss Butcher
    And sour Mr. Bate;
Tiny and cheerful,
    And neat as can be,
Whatever Miss T. eats
    Turns into Miss T.

By Walter de la Mare

EAT-IT-ALL ELAINE

I went away last August
To summer camp in Maine,
And there I met a camper
Called Eat-it-all Elaine.
Although Elaine was quiet,
She liked to cause a stir
By acting out the nickname
Her camp-mates gave to her.

The day of our arrival
At Cabin Number Three
When girls kept coming over
To greet Elaine and me,
She took a piece of Kleenex
And calmly chewed it up,
Then strolled outside the cabin
And ate a buttercup.

Elaine, from that day forward,
Was always in command.
On hikes, she'd eat some birch-bark.
On swims, she'd eat some sand.

At meals, she'd swallow prune-pits
And never have a pain,
While everyone around her
Would giggle, "Oh, Elaine!"

One morning, berry-picking,
A bug was in her pail,
And though we thought for certain
Her appetite would fail,
Elaine said, "Hmm, a stinkbug."
And while we murmured, "Ooh,"
She ate her pail of berries
And ate the stinkbug, too.

The night of Final Banquet
When counselors were handing
Awards to different children
Whom they believed outstanding,
To every *thinking* person
At summer camp in Maine
The Most Outstanding Camper
Was Eat-it-all Elaine.

By Kaye Starbird

Books about food and eating are listed on pages 159 and 317.

A PLATE OF POETRY

You can copy your favorite poem, draw your own illustration for it with felt-tip pens, and have it all printed on a plastic dinner plate.

Kits are available from Make-a-plate, 9 Kane Industrial Drive, Hudson, MA 01749; and from Small Fry Originals, Plastic Manufacturing Co., 2700 S. Westmoreland Ave., Dallas, TX 75224.

SLEEP ON A POEM

Decorate a pillowcase with your favorite poem. These pillowcases make fine presents for parents, grandparents, or yourself.

YOU NEED: text of a favorite poem or quote from a poem
a white pillowcase
permanent ink felt-tip pens

HOW TO: Copy the poem on the pillowcase with the felt-tip pen. Draw a picture on the pillowcase to illustrate the poem.

HINT: Choose a short poem or you'll have to stay up too late reading it!

Pillowcases can also be decorated using fabric crayons available from art supply shops. With the crayons, art is drawn on paper and then transferred with a hot iron on the fabric. The advantage of the crayons over the felt-tip pens is that if you make a mistake you can discard your picture and begin again without ruining the fabric.

JUMP A POEM

A PLAYTIME SKIP

When I get sick
Of arithmetic
And reading and writing
Don't seem exciting,
I jog my brain
To keep me sane,
And skip and skip
And skip and skip,
And never stop
Until I drop
And when I do,
It's strange but true,
My lazy brain
Starts work again.

By Cynthia Mitchell

PRESENTATION: Jump rope while reciting this poem or others from *Halloweena Hecatee*, by Cynthia Mitchell (il. by Eileen Browne. Crowell, 1979). Or ask the children to contribute their own favorite jump-rope rhymes.

HINT: Let some children jump while others recite, especially if you are out of shape.

BOUNCE A POEM

BOUNCING SONG

Hambone, jawbone, mulligatawney stew,
Pork chop, lamb chop, cold homebrew,
Licorice sticks and popsicles, ice cream pie:
Strawberry, chocolate, *vanilla!!!*

By Dennis Lee

PRESENTATION: Bounce a ball while reciting this poem.
Ask the children if they know other bouncing rhymes.

BIRTHDAY BOX

Copy poems onto birthday
cards. Place them in a pretty box
or a cardboard box covered with
wrapping paper and tied up with
a bow.

Whenever a child in your group has a birthday, celebrate the occasion
with a special poem that you choose from the birthday box.

The poems do not necessarily have to be about birthdays; it might be
better if they were about the interests of the child. The birthday box could
be filled with poems about sports, holidays, animals, and outer space.

Change the collection or add poems as you come across suitable ones.

POEMS AS PRESENTS

Memorize a poem and recite it as a gift.

Or, collect poems on a single theme, such as baseball, autumn, or love.
Copy and illustrate the poems and place them in a booklet to present as a
gift.

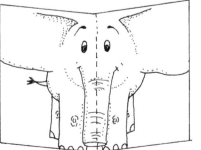

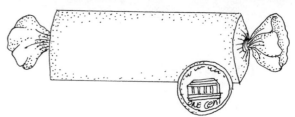

POETRY PARTY FAVOR

Directions for a poetry activity are hidden inside the party favors.

YOU NEED: For each favor:
an empty piece of cardboard tubing about 5" long—from a toilet roll, towel roll, etc.
a square of colored tissue paper
small sheets of paper
balloons or other small favors (optional)
Poetry books

HOW TO: Print directions for the game on small sheets of paper and put a separate sheet inside each piece of tubing, along with a party surprise (balloon, penny, candy) if you like. Wrap the tubes with colored tissue paper, twisting the ends to make them look like party-poppers. Pass out the party favors. Each child opens one favor and performs the task. Use your own collection of poetry books to make up tasks. Sample directions: "Find a rain poem and read it aloud to the class"; "Find page 31 in X collection; read the poem and tell the class what the poet was trying to say." Or you might hide a different poem in each favor and let the children read the poems through a few times and then read them aloud to the class.

The poems and favors can be re-used. Each time a child will get a different poem.

HINT: Don't try to collect all the tubing by yourself. Simply ask your class or library club to bring cardboard tubes to the school or the library. Collecting by many people is much more efficient than collecting by one person or one family.

PACKAGED POETRY

Selecting the poems and exchanging the boxes stimulates interest in poetry.

YOU NEED: an assortment of small empty boxes (discarded gift boxes are excellent)
poetry books
small objects, such as pebbles, feathers, charms, and miniature animals; or small pictures from magazines or greeting cards
glue
felt-tip pens or acrylic paints

HOW TO: Divide the children into groups of two or three, or let them participate individually.

Provide each child or each group with an empty box and let them choose an object or picture.

Have the children find a poem to complement the object. Then let them copy the poem on a small piece of paper, decorate the box, and place the poem and the object inside. Then everyone should exchange boxes and enjoy the poems.

HINT: You can package poetry yourself and use the boxes as an exhibit. Almost everyone will want to look inside the boxes, and then may read and think about the poems.

COLOR BOX POETRY

Read a poem and then arrange pictures to illustrate it on a felt-covered box top. Or let the child read the poem and then find the appropriate pictures to mount on the felt board.

YOU NEED: a cigar box (available from a tobacconist)

black or white felt

envelopes

small pictures (drawn or collected from magazines, greeting cards, or photographs)

Rubber cement, or pattern spray (available from a fabric shop)

HOW TO: Cover the inside cover of the box with black or white felt to make a small individual felt board.

Find poems about colors.

Now draw or collect small pictures representing objects of these colors.

To affix small picture to the individual felt board, coat the back of the picture with rubber cement. When it dries, it will be tacky enough to adhere to the felt board. Pattern spray works the same way.

Store the pictures in separate envelopes, and place envelopes and poems in the cigar box.

HINT: Object shapes cut from colored felt will adhere to the felt board too, without any glue.

249

MATCH-UP PUZZLES

Cut up a paperback book of poetry or collect poems from various sources. Find or draw a picture to illustrate each poem. Mount the poem and the illustration for it on separate pieces of poster board. Let the children match each poem to its illustration.

PAPERBACKS

Fisher, Aileen. *Cricket in a Thicket.* il. by Feodor Rojankovsky. Scribner, 1963.

Krauss, Ruth. *Somebody Else's Nut Tree and Other Tales for Children.* il. by Maurice Sendak. The Bookstore Press (Lenox, MA), 1971.

Tripp, Wallace, comp. *A Great Big Ugly Man Came Up and Tied His Horse to Me: A Book of Nonsense Verse.* il. by compiler. Little, 1973.

Widerberg, Siv. *I'm Like Me: Poems for People Who Want to Grow Up Equal.* tr. by Verne Moberg. il. by Claes Bäckström. The Feminist Press, 1973.

You can also attach magnets or sandpaper to the back of the pictures and use them for poetry presentations on a magnetic or felt board.

POSTAGE STAMP POETRY

Find a poem to illustrate a stamp.

YOU NEED: A picture stamp for each child
Poetry books

HOW TO: 1. Let each child choose a stamp and use the library resources to find a poem to go with it, or
2. Make this into a simpler individual game. Using an inexpensive snapshot album, mount a different stamp on each page. Find poems yourself for each stamp. Type title of the poem and the book in which it appears next to the stamp. The object of the game is to find the book on the shelves and then locate the poem.

250

HINT: An excellent source of stamps is the local variety store. Stamps are often packaged by subject (animals, airplanes, sports, dolls) or by country. They are still inexpensive to buy—you can purchase 150 flag stamps for just 59¢. Dealers sometimes advertise cheap packets of stamps on the covers of matchbooks, or in the classified section of the newspaper. You can also acquire some free stamps by sending out a call to parents.

EGG THOUGHTS

This activity uses one title to stimulate interest.

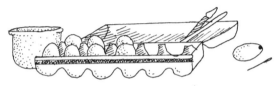

YOU NEED: blown-out eggs (To blow out an egg, allow it to reach room temperature. Pierce it at each end with a long pin, making one hole slightly larger than the other. Be sure that you pierce the yolk, so that it will blow out easily. Place a bowl underneath the egg and gently blow into the smaller hole until the shell is entirely empty. If you wish to use the egg as a hanging decoration, insert a ribbon into the larger hole and affix it with a dab of Epoxy.)
felt-tip pens
the poetry anthology *Egg Thoughts and Other Frances Songs,* by Russell Hoban (il. by Lillian Hoban. Harper, 1972).

HOW TO: Use the felt-tip pen to write titles or quotes from *Egg Thoughts* on the eggs.
Store the finished eggs in an empty egg carton.
Let each child choose an egg from the box and carefully bring it to you.
Read the poem referred to aloud to the group.

HINT: Impress on the children the need to be gentle with the blown-out eggs.

RELATED ACTIVITY: Read Dr. Seuss's *Horton Hatches the Egg* (il. by the author. Random House, 1940) aloud to the children. The rhymed text tells how an elephant hatches an egg. The children can decorate their own elephant-bird eggs afterwards (hardboiled eggs may be best for this activity).

251

PARODIES

We don't think of parody when we think of poetry, but poking fun in rhyme and rhythm can be a delight. Try this experiment in the collection of folklore. Begin by reciting or singing your favorite examples of parody. Can the group come up with other parodies? Ask friends, students, or colleagues if they know any for your collection. Here are a few to begin with.

THE TWELVE DAYS OF HALLOWEEN
(to the tune of "The Twelve days of Christmas")

On the twelfth day of Halloween my true love gave to me:

12 witches cackling

11 masks a-leering

10 ghouls a-groaning

9 ghosts a-booing

8 monsters shrieking

7 pumpkins glowing

6 goblins gobbling

5 scarey spooks

4 skeletons

3 black cats

2 trick or treaters

and a screech-owl in a dead tree

More parodies of "The Twelve Days of Christmas" can be found in:

Knight, Hilary. *A Firefly in a Fir Tree.* il. by author. Harper, 1963.
This is a mouse's version. Since the book is very small (2" x 3"), you may want to pass it around for individual viewing.

252

Mendoza, George. *A Wart Snake in a Fig Tree.* il. by Étienne Delessert. Dial Press, 1968.
Highly imaginative text and pictures. The paperback edition (Dial/Pied Piper, 1976) can be cut up and placed on an exhibit board.

RUDOLPH THE RED-NOSED COWPOKE
(to the tune of "Rudolph the Red-Nosed Reindeer")

Rudolph the red-nosed cowpoke
Had a very shiny gun
And if you ever saw it
You would turn around and run.

All of the other cowpokes
Used to laugh and call him names
They never let poor Rudolph
Join in any poker games.

Then one foggy Christmas Eve
Sheriff came to say
"Cowpoke, with your gun so bright
Won't you kill my wife tonight?"

Then how the cowpokes loved him
As they shouted out with glee,
"Rudolph the red-nosed cowpoke
You'll go down in history!"

An even more gruesome ditty goes to the tune of "Santa Claus is Coming to Town."

You better not cry
You better not shout
Santa Claus is
DEAD [speak this line]

MOTHER GOOSE PARODIES

Mary had a little lamb
Her father shot it dead,
And now it goes to school with her
Between two chunks of bread.

Hickory dickory dock
Three mice ran up the clock
The clock struck one
And the other two escaped with minor injuries.

Mary had a little lamb,
A little pork, a little jam,
An ice-cream soda topped with fizz,
And Boy! how sick our Mary is!

Mary had a little lamb—
the doctor was surprised.
But Old McDonald had a farm—
the doctor nearly died.

253

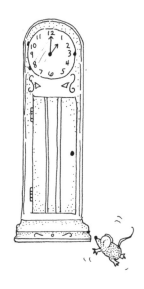

Little Miss Muffet sat on a tuffet,
Eating her curds and whey.
Along came a spider and sat down beside her—
And she picked up a spoon and
    beat the daylights out of it.

More Mother Goose parodies can be found in:

Arneson, D. J. *Mother Goose is Dead.* il. by Tony Tallarco. Dell, 1967.

Jacobs, Frank. "If Famous Poets Had Written Mother Goose," *Mad* (Sept., 1967)

Kelly, Walt. *The Pogo Stepmother Goose.* il. by author. Simon & Schuster, 1954.

Merriam, Eve. *The Inner City Mother Goose.* il. by Lawrence Ratzkin. Simon & Schuster, 1969.

HALLOWEEN POETRY READ-IN

There are so many excellent books of Halloween poetry it seems a pity to choose just one. Why not have a poetry read-in? Have as many books as you can available. Let the children and the leader take turns reading poems. Intersperse the poetry readings with the shorter riddles. The poems should be copied onto individual sheets and put into a pumpkin. Each child chooses a poem from the pumpkin. I use a cloth pumpkin, but a ceramic or plastic jack-o-lantern could be used for the same purpose.

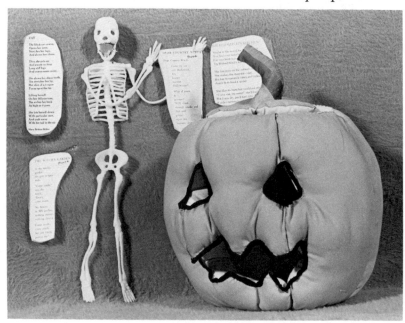

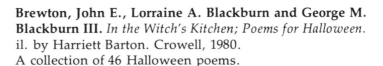

BOOKLIST

Brewton, John E., Lorraine A. Blackburn and George M. Blackburn III. *In the Witch's Kitchen; Poems for Halloween.* il. by Harriett Barton. Crowell, 1980.
A collection of 46 Halloween poems.

Hopkins, Lee Bennett. *Hey-how for Halloween.* il. by Janet McCaffery. Harcourt, 1974.
Short collection.

Moore, Lilian. *See My Lovely Poison Ivy and Other Verses About Witches, Ghosts and Things.* il. by Diane Dawson. Atheneum Pubs., 1975.
Amusing poems excellent for reading aloud.

Moore, Lilian. *Spooky Rhymes and Riddles.* il. by Ib Ohlsson. Scholastic, 1972.
Some of these poems are repeated in *See My Lovely Poison Ivy,* but it's a good collection with spooky riddles too.

Pretlutsky, Jack. *Nightmares: Poems to Trouble Your Sleep.* il. by Arnold Lobel. Greenwillow Bks., 1976.
Longer, more sophisticated poems than those in the Moore and Wallace collections. Rhythmical and scarey. Trolls, ghouls, skeletons, and a haunted house.
Also, *The Headless Horseman Rides Tonight: More Poems to Trouble Your Sleep.* il. by Arnold Lobel. Greenwillow Bks., 1980.

Riley, James Whitcomb. *The Gobble-uns'll Git You Ef You Don't Watch Out!* il. by Joel Schick. Lippincott, 1975.
The black and white line drawings are suitable to share with a small group. This is the old "Little Orphan Annie" poem, written in the 1800s.

Sarnoff, Jane and Reynold Ruffins. *The Monster Riddle Book.* Rev. ed. Scribner, 1978.
Riddles about vampires, ghouls and goblins.

Serraillier, Ian. *Suppose You Met A Witch.* il. by Ed Emberley. Little, 1973.
An illustrated version of a poem about how two children outwit a witch. Rehearse this before you read it aloud, so you can read while sharing the pictures.

Wallace, Daisy, ed. *Ghost Poems.* il. by Tomie de Paola. Holiday House, 1979.
See also *Witch Poems* (il. by Trina Schart Hyman. Holiday House, 1976) and *Monster Poems* (il. by Kay Chorao. Holiday House, 1976). Short theme collections.

TREAT   GHOST POPS

YOU NEED (for each child):
a ball lollipop
a white cocktail-size paper napkin
a black felt-tip pen
a 6" piece of orange yarn
a 6" piece of black yarn

HOW TO: For each ghost, wrap the napkin around the lollipop. Twist the yarn together and tie the napkin in place. Draw two ghost eyes on the napkin.

PUMPKIN DROP COOKIES

YOU NEED: ½ cup butter or margarine
1½ cups sugar
1 egg
1 cup cooked or canned pumpkin
1 teaspoon vanilla
2½ cups all-purpose flour
1 teaspoon baking powder
1 teaspoon baking soda
½ teapoon salt
1 teaspoon nutmeg
1 teaspoon cinnamon
½ cup diced roasted almonds
1 cup chocolate pieces

HOW TO: Cream butter and sugar until light and fluffy. Beat in egg, pumpkin and vanilla. Mix and sift flour, baking powder, baking soda, salt, nutmeg, and cinnamon. Add to creamed mixture; mix well. Add almonds and chocolate pieces; mix thoroughly. Drop dough by teaspoons onto well-greased cookie sheets. Bake at 350° for 15 minutes or until lightly browned. Remove from cookie sheets while still warm; cool on racks. Makes about 6 dozen cookies.

GRANDPARENT POETRY

In the olden days, memorizing poetry was a part of the regular classroom routine. Ask the children to visit older people, perhaps in a senior center, and collect poems that the people remember from their own childhoods.

POETRY RECITATION CONTEST

A natural outgrowth of memorizing poems is presenting them to an audience. Why not have a good old-fashioned poetry recitation contest? If participation is voluntary, you won't feel quite so dated. At our school when I was a child, the recitation contest was an annual event. There were two categories: English and French. Since I really enjoyed this contest as a student (I *never* won), I reinstated the idea as a school librarian. I think I was surprised myself that it was so successful. The school was small, one classroom per grade. The classroom teachers ran an in-class contest, and the winners competed before the entire school. We gave upper, middle, and lower school prizes—books, of course.

If you decide to do this, have plenty of poetry books on hand, so that the children will have a wide range of choice. Help those who are looking for poems to recite.

Poetry for Programs—A Bibliography

In creating this bibliography, I've tried to include books that you will actually use (more than once!) in your poetry programs. These books are my first choices for selecting poems that turn kids on to poetry. They are particularly appropriate for children who have had little previous experience with poetry because they include poems that are easy to relate to, funny, or have a certain charm. Some of the books are serious, but most published in the last fifteen years have tended to be humorous.

This list is especially for poetry presentations; however, you might want to refer to a more balanced list if you are looking for a core collection. The Library of Congress sells such a bibliography:

Haviland, Virginia and William Jay Smith, comps. *Children and Poetry: A Selective, Annotated Bibliography.* Library of Congress, 1979. (for sale by Superintendent of Documents, U.S. Government Printing Office, Washington, DC 20402).

In the following list, I have starred (*) the items that I find most valuable, but I use all the books extensively. The books are for children and adults to share aloud.

ANTHOLOGIES

The Charge of the Light Brigade and Other Story Poems. Scholastic, 1969.
"Paul Revere's Ride," "Casey at the Bat," and other traditional story poems.

257

*Dunning, Stephen, Edward Lueders, & Hugh Smith, comps. *Reflections on a Gift of Watermelon Pickle and Other Modern Verse.* Lothrop, 1967.
Still the best collection for young adults.

Janeczko, Paul B., comp. *Don't Forget to Fly: A Cycle of Modern Poems.* Bradbury, 1981.
Seventy modern poets are represented.

Koch, Kenneth and Kate Farrell, comps. *Sleeping on the Wing: An Anthology of Modern Poetry With Essays on Reading and Writing.* Random, 1981.
Excellent essays elucidate the poetry.

Larrick, Nancy, comp. *Crazy to be Alive in Such a Strange World: Poems About People.* photographs by Alexander L. Crosby. Evans, 1977.
Funny, poignant poems about all kinds of people.

Plotz, Helen, comp. *As I Walked Out One Evening: A Book of Ballads.* Greenwillow Bks., 1976.
The words of the most famous ballads. Also see other collections by Plotz.

Wilner, Isabel, comp. *The Poetry Troupe: An Anthology of Poems To Read Aloud.* il. by compiler. Scribner, 1977.
Lots of good stuff for the poetry program.

POETRY AND MUSIC

Blyton, Carey. *Bananas in Pyjamas: A Book of Nonsense With Words and Music.* il. by Tom Barling. Faber [distributed by Merrimack Bk. Serv.] 1976.
Silly rhymes set to music.

Crofut, William. *The Moon on the One Hand; Poetry in Song.* arr. by Kenneth Cooper & Glenn Shattuck. il. by Susan Crofut. Atheneum Pubs., 1975.
Serious poetry set to music.

Keller, Charles, comp. *Glory, Glory, How Peculiar.* il. by Lady McCrady. Prentice-Hall, 1976.
"On Top of Spaghetti," and "Found a Peanut" are among the children's folksongs in this book.

POETRY WITH PICTURES

Carroll, Lewis. *Lewis Carroll's Jabberwocky.* il. by Jane Breskin Zalben. Warne, 1977.
Illustrated version of Carroll's poem.

Charlip, Remy and Burton Supree. *Mother, Mother I Feel Sick, Send for the Doctor Quick Quick Quick: A Picture Book and Shadow Play.* il. by Remy Charlip. Parents Mag. Press, 1966.
Many household objects appear to have been swallowed by a boy. The book includes suggestions for presenting the story as a shadow play.

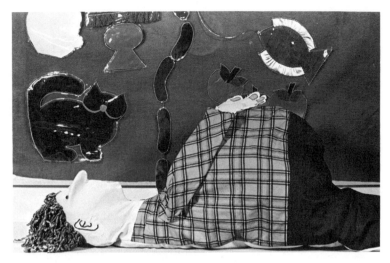

Craft, Ruth. *Pieter Breughel's "The Fair."* Lippincott, 1976.
Poems inspired by a Breughel painting.

Frost, Robert. *Stopping by Woods on a Snowy Evening.* il.
by Susan Jeffers. Dutton, 1978.
The famous poem illustrated in picture-book format.

Griego, Margo C., et al. *Tortillitas para Mamá.* il. by Barbara Cooney. Holt, 1981.
Nursery rhymes in English and Spanish.

Highwater, Jamake. *Moonsong Lullaby.* Photographs by
Marcia Keegan. Lothrop, 1981.
A Native American lullaby.

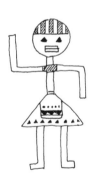

Jones, Hettie, comp. *The Trees Stand Shining: Poetry of the
North American Indians.* il. by Robert Andrew Parker. Dial
Press, 1971.
Full-color paintings illustrate these short traditional
poems.

Lear, Edward. *The Owl and the Pussy Cat and Other Nonsense.* il. by Owen Wood. Viking, 1979.
A famous nonsense poem lavishly illustrated.

*****Lewis, Richard (ed.).** *In a Spring Garden.* il. by Ezra Jack
Keats. Dial Press, 1965.
Haiku selections for many varied moods of a single day.

Litchfield, Ada B. *It's Going to Rain.* il. by Ruth M. Hart-
shorn. Atheneum Pubs., 1980.
Cape Cod fishermen discuss the weather in a rhythmic
picture book with a surprise ending.

Lobel, Arnold, comp. *Gregory Griggs and Other Nursery
Rhyme People.* il. by author. Greenwillow Bks., 1978.
Lesser-known Mother Goose illustrated with fun.

Thayer, Ernest Lawrence. *Casey at the Bat: A Ballad of the Republic, Sung in the Year 1888.* il. by Wallace Tripp. Coward, McCann & Geoghegan, 1978.
The classic baseball saga is illustrated with cartoon animals.

Tripp, Wallace, comp. *Granfa' Grig Had a Pig and Other Rhymes Without Reason From Mother Goose.* il. by compiler. Little, 1976.
Mother Goose for all ages with funny pictures.

*__Willard, Nancy.__ *A Visit to William Blake's Inn: Poems for Innocent and Experienced Travelers.* il. by Alice and Martin Provensen. Harcourt, 1981.
A lovely picture book inspired by William Blake's poetry.

*__Zemach, Harve.__ *The Judge; An Untrue Tale.* il. by Margot Zemach. Farrar, Straus, 1969.
Picture poetry tale about an official who refuses to believe that a monster is coming.

POETRY WITH A THEME

*__Adoff, Arnold.__ *Eats: Poems.* il. by Susan Russo. Lothrop, 1979.
Love affair with food.

Adoff, Arnold. *Friend Dog.* il. by Troy Howell. Lippincott, 1980.
A girl and a dog share adventures.

*__Adoff, Arnold.__ *All the Colors of the Race.* il. by John Steptoe. Lothrop, 1982.
Poems about Adoff's interracial family.

Adoff, Arnold. *Tornado! Poems.* il. by Ronald Himler. Delacorte Press, 1977.
A family's experience with a tornado in the Midwest.

Baylor, Byrd. *Desert Voices.* il. by Peter Parnall. Scribner, 1981.
Poems about desert animals.

Belting, Natalia. *Whirlwind Is a Ghost Dancing.* il. by Leo and Diane Dillon. Dutton, 1974.
North American Indian poems vividly illustrated.

*__Brewton, Sara, John E. Brewton, and John Brewton Blackburn.__ *Of Quarks, Quasars, and Other Quirks; Quizzical Poems for the Supersonic Age.* il. by Quentin Blake. Crowell, 1977.
Supermarkets, television, and computers are featured here.

Cole, William, comp. *Good Dog Poems.* il. by Ruth Sanderson. Scribner, 1981.
Poems about dogs by various authors, from A. A. Milne to Robert Frost.

Cole, William. *Poem Stew.* il. by Karen Ann Weinhaus. Lippincott, 1981.
Poems about food.

Cole, William, comp. *The Poetry of Horses.* il. by Ruth Sanderson. Scribner, 1979.
Extensive collection of horse poems.

Fox, Siv Cedering. *The Blue Horse, and Other Night Poems.* il. by Donald Carrick. Seabury [distributed by Houghton], 1979.
Sleeping and dreaming.

Hoberman, Mary Ann. *Bugs: Poems.* il. by Victoria Chess. Viking, 1976.
Poems about . . . (yes) bugs.

Hoberman, Mary Ann. *A House Is a House for Me.* il. by Betty Fraser. Viking, 1978.
Rhymes about different houses—". . . pockets are houses for pennies/And pens can be houses for ink."

Hopkins, Lee Bennett, comp. *Good Morning to You, Valentine.* il. by Tomie de Paola. Harcourt, 1976.
Short collection of Valentine verse. Easy to recite. Other holiday collections by Hopkins are *Sing Hey for Christmas Day!* (il. by Laura Jean Allen. Harcourt, 1975.); *Beat the Drum: Independence Day Has Come.* (il. by Tomie de Paola. Harcourt, 1977.); *Hey-How for Halloween!* (il. by Janet McCaffery. Harcourt, 1974.); *Merrily Comes Our Harvest In: Poems for Thanksgiving.* (il. by Ben Shecter. Harcourt, 1978.); and *Easter Buds Are Springing: Poems for Easter.* (il. by Tomie de Paola. Harcourt, 1979.).

Hughes, Ted. *Under the North Star.* il. by Leonard Baskin. Viking, 1981.
Each of these serious poems is a song to an animal or bird of the far north. Large powerful drawings accompany each poem.

Livingston, Myra Cohn. *No Way of Knowing: Dallas Poems.* Atheneum Pubs., 1980.
The poet remembers with warmth and clarity her experiences in the black community during a twelve-year period.

Livingston, Myra Cohn, ed. *Poems of Christmas.* Atheneum Pubs., 1980.
A varied collection of Christmas poems capture the holiday's many moods.

*Mitchell, Cynthia. *Halloweena Hecatee and Other Rhymes to Skip To.* il. by Eileen Browne. Crowell, 1979.
Rhymes to chant as you skip rope.

*Moore, Lilian. *See My Lovely Poison Ivy, and Other Verses About Witches, Ghosts and Things.* il. by Diane Dawson. Atheneum Pubs., 1975.
Every poem a gem to use with children . . . or anybody.

Moore, Lilian. *Think of Shadows.* il. by Deborah Robison. Atheneum Pubs., 1980.
Original poems explore shadows cast by mice and astronauts, children at play, and giraffes.

Moore, Vardine, comp. *Mice Are Rather Nice: Poems About Mice.* il. by Doug Jamison. Atheneum Pubs., 1981.
A collection of poems about mice.

Morrison, Lillian. *Overheard in a Bubble Chamber and Other Sciencepoems.* il. by Eyre De Lanux. Lothrop, 1981.
Science is the theme of this collection.

Mother Goose. *If Wishes Were Horses: And Other Rhymes.* il. by Susan Jeffers. Dutton, 1979.
Mother Goose rhymes with horse themes. For horse lovers.

Ness, Evaline, comp. *Amelia Mixed the Mustard and Other Poems.* il. by compiler. Scribner, 1975.
Girls in poetry; funny, poignant, and proud. For contrast, see Prelutsky's *Rolling Harvey Down the Hill.*

*O'Neill, Mary. *Hailstones and Halibut Bones: Adventures in Color.* il. by Leonard Weisgard. Doubleday, 1961.
The classic collection of poems about color.

Plotz, Helen, comp. *Gladly Learn and Gladly Teach: Poems of the School Experience.* Greenwillow Bks., 1981.
An anthology emphasizing teaching and school.

Prelutsky, Jack. *Circus.* il. by Arnold Lobel. Macmillan Pub. Co., 1974.
Long poems about the circus accompanied by lively pictures.

Prelutsky, Jack. *Rolling Harvey Down the Hill.* il. by Victoria Chess. Greenwillow Bks., 1980.
Poems about a gang of boys—the nice guys and the bully. See Ness's *Amelia.*

*Worth, Valerie. *Still More Small Poems.* il. by Natalie Babbitt. Farrar, Straus, 1979.

Poems about everyday objects. Companion to *Small Poems* (1972) and *More Small Poems* (1976).

SILLY STUFF

Asch, Frank. *Country Pie.* il. by author. Greenwillow Bks., 1979.
Companion to *City Sandwich* (1978). Short, surprising poems.

*****Brewton, Sara, John Brewton, and G. Meredith Blackburn III.** *My Tang's Tungled and Other Ridiculous Situations.* il. by Graham Booth. Crowell, 1973.
Excellent collection of funny poems.

Cole, William, comp. *I'm Mad At You!* il. by George MacClain. Collins [distributed by Philomel Bks.], 1978.
One of Cole's many humorous collections.

Gage, Wilson. *Down in the Boondocks.* il. by Glen Rounds. Greenwillow Bks., 1977.
Rhythmic story to read aloud and read together.

Nash, Ogden. *Custard and Company.* il. by Quentin Blake. Little, 1980.
Lighthearted poems illustrated appropriately with cartoon drawings.

*****Prelutsky, Jack.** *The Sheriff of Rottenshot.* il. by Victoria Chess. Greenwillow Bks., 1982.
"The Spaghetti Nut," "Sadie Snatt," "Philbert Phlurk," and other ridiculous characters.

Smith, William Jay. *Laughing Time: Nonsense Poems.* il. by Fernando Krahn. Delacorte Press, 1980.
A collection of one poet's favorite nonsense poems. Short poems about animals (yak, goony bird), people (Mr. Smith), and things (hats, dictionary, toaster).

Tripp, Wallace, comp. *A Great Big Ugly Man Came Up and Tied His Horse to Me: A Book of Nonsense Verse.* il. by compiler. Little, 1973.
Nonsense poems with colorful illustrations.

COLLECTIONS BY A SINGLE POET

Chute, Marchette. *Rhymes About Us.* il. by author. Dutton, 1974.
"Teddy Bear," "At the Library," "My Little Brother."

Clifton, Lucille. *Some of the Days of Everett Anderson.* il. by Evaline Ness. Holt, 1970.
A six-year-old boy romps through these pages.

263

Fisher, Aileen. *Out in the Dark and Daylight.* il. by Gail Owens. Harper, 1980.
Poems of nature and now.

Giovanni, Nikki. *Vacation Time; Poems for Children.* il. by Marisabina Russo. Morrow, 1980.
A short collection that includes "Jonathan Sitting In Mud" and "Kisses."

Greenfield, Eloise. *Honey, I Love, and Other Love Poems.* il. by Diane and Leo Dillon. Crowell, 1978.
A child's likes—riding on a train, listening to music.

Grimes, Nikki. *Something on my Mind.* il. by Tom Feelings. Dial Press, 1978.
The poet was inspired by the illustrations to write her poems.

Holman, Felice. *I Hear You Smiling and Other Poems.* il. by Laszlo Kubinyi. Scribner, 1973.
"The Flower Trap" (about a carpet) and "Coca-Cola Sunset" are examples of these spritely contemporary poems.

Kuskin, Karla. *Any Me I Want To Be.* il. by author. Harper, 1972.
Thoughts by dogs, clocks, and birds expressed in short poems.

Lee, Dennis. *Alligator Pie.* il. by Frank Newfeld. Houghton, 1975.
"On Tuesdays I Polish My Uncle," and others by a Canadian poet. Also, *Garbage Delight* (Houghton, 1978).

Littledale, Freya. *I Was Thinking: Poems.* il. by Leonard Kessler. Greenwillow Bks., 1979.
Short, easy-to-read poems.

Livingston, Myra Cohn. *O Sliver of Liver; Together With Other Triolets, Cinquains, Haiku, Verses and a Dash of Poems.* il. by Iris Van Rynbach. Atheneum Pubs., 1979.
Diverse forms and subjects in a short collection.

*McCord, David. *One at a Time: His Collected Poems for the Young.* il. by Henry B. Kane. Little, 1977.
Poems by one of America's best-known children's poets.

Merriam, Eve. *A Word or Two With You: New Rhymes for Young Readers.* by John Nez. Atheneum, 1981.
Just one of Merriam's excellent collections. "A" for use of language.

*Milne, A. A. *Now We are Six.* il. by Ernest H. Shepard. Dutton, 1961. See also *When We Were Very Young.* il. by Ernest H. Shepard. Dutton, 1961.
Outstanding poems about children.

Payne, Nina. *All the Day Long.* il. by Laurel Schindelman. Atheneum Pubs., 1973.
Everyday thoughts—going to school, pancakes, tag-along.

Pomerantz, Charlotte. *The Tamarindo Puppy and Other Poems.* il. by Byron Barton. Greenwillow Bks., 1980.
Poems written in English with a sprinkling of Spanish.

Prelutsky, Jack. *Rainy Rainy Saturday.* il. by Marylin Hafner. Greenwillow, 1980.
"Read alone" collection

*Prelutsky, Jack. *The Snopp On the Sidewalk, and Other Poems.* il. by Byron Barton. Greenwillow Bks., 1977. Excellent collection of funny, scarey poems.

*Silverstein, Shel. *Where the Sidewalk Ends.* il. by author. Harper, 1974.
Every poem in this collection is guaranteed to make you laugh, or at least smile.
See also *A Light in the Attic* (il. by author. Harper, 1981).

Starbird, Kaye. *Don't Ever Cross a Crocodile, and Other Poems.* il. by Kit Dalton. Lippincott, 1963.
Camp and people.

Thurman, Judith. *Flashlight, and Other Poems.* il. by Regina Rubel. Atheneum Pubs., 1976.
Skinned knees, spills, oil slicks.

Tippett, James S. *Crickety Cricket!* il. by Mary Chalmers. Harper, 1973.
For pre-primary.

Viorst, Judith. *If I Were in Charge of the World and Other Worries.* Atheneum, 1981.
Laugh-aloud poems about everyday life.

*Widerberg, Siv. *I'm Like Me: Poems For People Who Want to Grow Up Equal.* tr. by Verne Moberg. il. by Claes Bäckström. Feminist Press, 1973.
Translated from the Swedish, these are realistic sentiments.

265

ADULT REFERENCES—

INDEXES

Index to Poetry for Children and Young People, 1976–1981. Edited by John E. Brewton, G. Meredith Blackburn III, and Lorraine A. Blackburn. H. W. Wilson, 1982.

Indexes poetry by title, subject, author, and first line.

Subject Index to Poetry for Children and Young People, 1957–1975. Compiled by Dorothy B. Frizzell Smith and Eva L. Andrews. American Library Assoc., 1977.

Lists poems found in 263 anthologies by subject.

Using an index to find a poem can be efficient. However, just browsing through the books in the poetry section can also be extremely useful. You will get to be thoroughly familiar with the books and find poems the indexers forgot, overlooked, or didn't choose to include.

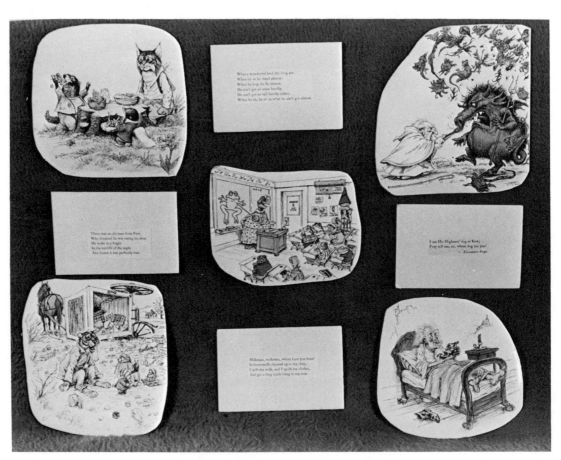

V GAMES

This section is for those children who respond well to a slightly competitive atmosphere. The object of the games is to make reading fun and at the same time inspire the child toward a reading goal. Most of these games are really book report ideas in attractive packaging. It is no secret that millions of dollars are spent each year to design new and stunning packaging to encourage consumers to buy, buy, buy. Let's borrow from Madison Avenue and package our "goods" in attractive ways to encourage our children to read, read, read.

Use greeting cards, board games, and small objects that relate to books. Try one of these games and see how your children respond to it. If you like the idea, you or your students can spend some time developing your own games so that you can eventually have an entire reading-game corner in your library or classroom. Ideally these games should be "played" for fun or extra credit, not as a regular assignment. Although these games offer practice in writing, speaking, research, and artistic skills related to books, the emphasis should always be on *fun*.

Party Games

Use these games as sources of book report or presentation ideas, or use them as I do—as party games. Invite your teenagers for hot spiced cider and doughnuts (homemade?) and direct the conversation to books. The first game, which calls for matching annotations to books, features science fiction titles. Display the books and the annotations separately, in your classroom or library. Encourage the students to figure out which annotation goes with which book. Several weeks later, after they have read most of the books, give your party and play the game.

SCI-FI MATCH-UP

Match the annotations with the book titles.

1. ___ Ann Burden believes she is the last person alive when one day a stranger in a safe-suit appears in her peaceful valley.

2. ___ A voice from Outer Space helps Lucinda survive in an abandoned caretaker's house located in a neighborhood cemetery.

3. ___ Escape from the plastic world of supermarkets and TV to the eternal twilight of Tembreabrezi.

4. ___ Francine and Paul each were experiencing the same frightening dream.

5. ___ Outside the protective walls of the city Harmony and Vector (who are Persons) discover how the natives of earth survive.

6. ___ The plague kills nearly everyone; how will the survivors adjust to the new world?

7. ___ Life at Harper Hall with nine fire lizards could never be dull.

8. ___ Varina and two children are held hostage while revolution brews on Earth.

9. ___ Kathleen befriends a homeless pup who turns out to be Sirius, the Dog Star sent to earth to find the Zoi.

10. ___ Fernfeather wonders if it is true that there is nothing outside her world of caverns and semi-darkness.

11. ___ A twelfth century legend haunts a twentieth century inventor of a time machine.

12. ___ Creep wanders into the England of the Industrial Revolution where children work twelve hours a day in factories and coal mines.

13. ___ Elana was a stowaway on a dangerous mission to the medieval planet of Andrecia. Could she help control the dragon?

14. ___ The visitors are so different. Do they come from another country, or another planet?

a. *The Beginning Place,* by Ursula K. LeGuin. Harper, 1980.

b. *Beloved Benjamin Is Waiting,* by Jean E. Karl. Dutton, 1978.

c. *A Chance Child,* by Jill Paton Walsh. Farrar, Straus, 1978.

d. *The Creatures,* by John Rowe Townsend. Lippincott, 1980.

e. *The Delikon,* by H. M. Hoover. Viking, 1977.

f. *Dogsbody,* by Diana Wynne Jones. Greenwillow Bks., 1977.

g. *Dragonsinger,* by Anne McCaffrey. Atheneum Pubs., 1978.

h. *Empty World,* by John Christopher. Dutton, 1978.

i. *Enchantress from the Stars,* by Sylvia Louise Engdahl. il. by Rodney Shackell. Atheneum Pubs., 1970.

j. *Into the Dream,* by William Sleator. il. by Ruth Sanderson. Dutton, 1979.

k. *The Shadow of the Gloom-World,* by Roger Eldridge. Dutton, 1978.

l. *Time Piper,* by Delia Huddy. Greenwillow Bks., 1979.

m. *The Visitors,* by John Rowe Townsend. Lippincott, 1977.

n. *Z for Zachariah,* by Robert C. O'Brien, Atheneum Pubs., 1975.

Answers: 1-n, 2-b, 3-a, 4-j, 5-d, 6-h, 7-g, 8-e, 9-f, 10-k, 11-l, 12-c, 13-i, 14-m

STORY-PLACE MATCH-UP

Match the place with the book.

1. ___ *Exit From Home,* by Anita Heyman. Crown, 1977.

2. ___ *The Haunting of Kildoran Abbey,* by Eve Bunting, Warne, 1978.

3. ___ *Let a River Be,* by Betty Sue Cummings, Atheneum Pubs., 1978.

4. ___ *The Master Puppeteer,* by Katherine Paterson. il. by Haru Wells. Crowell, 1976.

5. ___ *The Moonclock,* by Claudia Von Canon. Houghton, 1979.

6. ___ *The Road From Home: The Story of an Armenian Girl,* by David Kherdian. Greenwillow Bks., 1979.

7. ___ *A String in the Harp,* by Nancy Bond. Atheneum Pubs., 1976.

8. ___ *Tornado! Poems,* by Arnold Adoff. il. by Ronald Himler, Delacorte Press, 1977.

9. ___ *Sweet and Sour,* by Carol Kendall and Yao-wen Li. il. by Shirley Felts. Seabury, 1979.

a. Austria
b. Ohio
c. Florida
d. China
e. Ireland
f. Turkey
g. Japan
h. Wales
i. Russia

Answers: 1-i, 2-e, 3-c, 4-g, 5-a, 6-f, 7-h, 8-b, 9-d

Playing With Language

GIVE A BOOK A NEW NAME

How do you choose a book to read? Often you just look at the cover or jacket and the title. Try to show the importance of a good title by having children retitle books they have read. Or read a picture book without mentioning the title. Let the group of children invent a title for the book. (If there are children in the room who are familiar with the real title, caution them not to reveal it.) Now compare the group's title with the author's. Whose is better?

This activity also works with poetry, which is often untitled. Read poems aloud and let your group come up with ideas for titles.

BOOK TITLE SENTENCES

Compose sentences using book titles (it's just as much fun to write the sentences as to play the game!). Exhibit the unmarked sentences on a bulletin board near a display of the books. Pass out copies of the sentences and let the children find the titles and underline them.

It was dawn. Below the root the town cats, George and Martha and Mama, were watching Daniel's duck escape to freedom from under the wagon wheels of the freight train.

Ramona and her father asked, "Will I like it?" when they heard that there was fish for supper just before the best Christmas pageant ever.

In Bert Breen's barn on Humbug Mountain a very hungry caterpillar beat the turtle drum.

Beloved Benjamin is waiting near the pyramid to see the amazing dandelion.

It was <u>dawn</u>. <u>Below the root</u> the <u>town cats</u>, <u>George and Martha</u> and <u>Mama</u>, were watching <u>Daniel's duck</u> <u>escape to freedom</u> from under the <u>wagon wheels</u> of the <u>freight train</u>.

<u>Ramona and her father</u> asked <u>Will I like it?</u> when they heard that there was <u>fish for supper</u> just before <u>the best Christmas pageant ever</u>.

270

In Bert Breen's barn on Humbug Mountain a very hungry caterpillar beat the turtle drum.

Beloved Benjamin is waiting near the pyramid to see the amazing dandelion.

For a variation on this game, write the titles on separate slips of paper. Let the children draw slips and make up sentences; or work with the class to create a silly story using all the titles.

BETTY BOTTER TONGUE TWISTER SKIT
by Annelise Wamsley

This skit uses a familiar tongue twister as its central theme. Easy to stage and perform, it will give children a chance to act before a group.

Stage setting:	*A chair on the left and a chair on the right with a small table next to each one and a phone on each table.*
Enter MATILDA.	*She plops down in one chair and dials awkwardly.*
Enter HARRIETTA.	*She sits down daintily in the other chair and answers the phone.*

MATILDA: 'Ullo Harrietta. Yeh, this is Matilda.

HARRIETTA: Oh hello, Matilda. And how are you today?

MATILDA: Pretty good. How ya doin'?

HARRIETTA: Just fine, Matilda.

MATILDA: (*laughs in a screechy voice*) I've got the best gossip for ya. (*laughs*) It's so funny, listen to this, Harrietta. Betty Botter bought some butter. (*She's laughing so hard that she can hardly keep from falling off her seat.*)

HARRIETTA: (*in an unsure, scared voice*) Betty Botter bought some butter?

MATILDA: Yeh, ain't that funny (*laughs again*). But she said (*laughs*), she said (*laughs*), she said this butter's bitter! (*in hysterics*)

271

HARRIETTA: But she said this butter's bitter? (*She's very unsure if this is funny. She's almost crying.*)

MATILDA: If I put it in my batter (*laughs*)

HARRIETTA: If I put it in my batter?

MATILDA: It will make my batter bitter. (*She can't stand it and her chair almost falls over backwards*)

HARRIETTA: (*starts crying*) It will make my batter bitter!

MATILDA: Ain't it a riot? (*laughs*) Listen to the rest.
But a bit of better butter.

HARRIETTA: (*brightens up*) But a bit of better butter?

MATILDA: (*laughs*) Will make my batter better. (*in hysterics again*)

HARRIETTA: (*Smiles faintly, content*) Will make my batter much, much better.

MATILDA: That's right (*laughs*). Yeh. Here's the rest.
So Betty bought some better butter and made her batter much better.

HARRIETTA: (*more confident, smiles*) And made her batter so-o-o much better!

MATILDA: (*laughing so hard she's about to cry*) Well . . . see ya later Harrietta, bye now.
They hang up and Matilda walks off.

HARRIETTA: (*walks up to the center of the stage and puts her hands over her heart*) Oh, how I love a happy ending!

For more tongue twisters see:

Schwartz, Alvin. *A Twister of Twists, A Tangler of Tongues: Tongue Twisters.* il. by Glen Rounds. Lippincott, 1972.

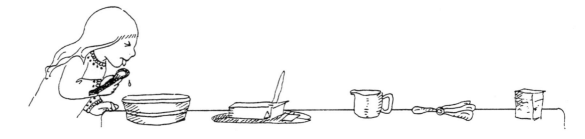

PADDINGTON BEAR WORD FIND

by Donata Chaffin

This puzzle is based on *Paddington Helps Out,* by Michael Bond (il. by Peggy Fortnum. Houghton, 1961).

Read the book and then find the answers to the questions in the puzzle below horizontally, vertically or diagonally.

1. Paddington lived with Mr. & Mrs. _____. (Brown)

2. Bear's name _____. (Paddington)

3. Paddington comes from _____ territory. (Peruvian)

4. What did Paddington lose when he went fishing? (hat)

5. Paddington's friend's name is Mr. _____. (Gruber)

6. At the auction Paddington bids on a _____ stand. (preserves)

7. Paddington makes a _____ rack for Mr. Brown. (magazine)

8. In the process of making Mr. Brown's rack, he accidently saws Mr. Curry's kitchen _____. (table)

9. At the cinema, Paddington saves the day and gets to ride on the _____. (organ)

10. Mr. & Mrs. Brown catch a "nasty wee bug . . ." and Paddington sets out to cook _____. (dumplings)

11. Paddington celebrates his _____ by going to Porchester, an exclusive restaurant. (birthday)

12. What does Paddington order for dinner? (marmalade sandwich)

13. During the course of the dinner Paddington loses one of his _____. (onions)

14. Where was Paddington's missing hors d'oeuvre? (saxophone).

P	R	E	S	E	R	V	E	S	B	A	C	A
A	B	G	O	T	R	O	S	P	E	D	S	T
D	X	Y	Z	E	W	R	P	S	T	V	A	R
D	O	M	B	Z	F	E	I	O	S	U	X	E
I	T	U	W	B	R	O	W	N	G	Z	O	N
N	R	S	T	U	E	R	I	O	N	N	P	D
G	U	X	V	L	Y	G	Z	O	I	F	H	S
T	H	I	B	G	H	A	T	O	L	J	O	E
O	A	A	K	L	J	N	N	M	P	V	N	L
N	T	E	N	I	Z	S	G	A	M	N	E	I
O	V	S	R	T	S	E	E	R	U	Z	Y	D
B	I	R	T	H	D	A	Y	M	D	X	J	S
A	V	E	A	T	O	S	G	A	J	B	U	W
Z	W	I	M	W	K	Y	X	L	I	O	B	J
T	A	I	R	A	Z	V	R	A	D	E	N	A
X	H	L	L	U	S	A	N	D	W	I	C	H
Z	X	U	B	C	Q	R	U	E	V	W	X	Y

273

CROSSWORD PUZZLE

This puzzle is based on well-known children's books.

ACROSS

1. This elephant lived in Paris
6. He lost a shoe in Mr. McGregor's garden
11. Hamelin's rat expert
16. Birthplace of Hans Christian Andersen
17. Famous stalk
18. Leo Politi describes Mexico in the story ____ ____
19. What a "Wind in the Willows" character was
20. River in the Grimm Brothers' homeland
21. Grown-up version of Bambi
22. Famous author of collie stories
26. The (Fr.)
27. Dorothy's Woodman without a heart
29. Little Toot
30. "Amahl and the Night Visitors"
32. Ferdinand el ____ (Sp.)
34. Creator of 1 Across, ____ Brunhoff
35. Author ____ ____ Alcott (inits.)
36. What Lassie was never doing (2 words)
39. Kjelgaard's Irish Setter
41. Part of Dumas's Count's title
42. Regarding
43. Charlotte A. Cavatica was familiar with things of a ____ sort
45. He went a-courtin'
46. What Laura and Mary lived in, in the Big Woods of Wisconsin

48. Long John Silver's destination
49. With 52 Across, part of the sequel to "The House on East 88th Street"
52. See 49 Across
53. Other half of 15 Down
55. Mr. Popper's pets like this
57. Familiar sight for Heidi
59. A beautiful swan started out like this
61. Son of 7 Down
62. Negative

64. Captain Nemo's creator
66. Signature of one of the creators of a curious monkey
68. Pinocchio's nose started to ____
70. A Nigerian people
71. Going from frying pan to fire
72. Compass direction
73. What "The Tomahawk Family" was
74. Apparel of Dr. Seuss's fox

DOWN

1. The Owl and the Pussy-cat had a pea-green one.
2. What Alice's adventure really was.
3. Gentle Ben
4. A collection of stories
5. Author of " __ __'s Best Word Book Ever." (inits.)
7. The d'Aulaires wrote a picture book about this President who was often called ____
8. The great one at Bow says, "I'm sure I don't know"
9. Huge companion of a legendary lumberman
10. Suffix meaning belonging to
11. Author of *The Proof of the Pudding* (inits.)
12. Government agency (abbr.)
13. Author for 6 Across as it would appear in an index
14. Twin of Jacob, whom you can find in *The Rainbow Book of Bible Stories*
15. Half of a tattered pair
23. One of the opening words of many children's stories
24. Home for Little Robin Redbreast
25. Canal traveled by a mule named Sal
27. Connected with "I think I can . . . I think I can. . . ."
28. Suffix meaning one who does (var.)
31. Folk tale trickster, __ ansi
33. Old English (abbr.)

35. Creator of Dab-Dab and Gub-Gub
37. Color of Brighty of the Grand Canyon
38. What Tweedledum was to Tweedledee
40. Author of *Stuart Little*, __ __ White (inits.)
41. Friend of 19 Across
44. Old word for old times
46. *Ride on the Wind* is the story of this famous aviator (inits.)
47. Composer of *Peer Gynt*, Edvard Gr ____
50. __ Fontaine
51. Shoemaker's helpers
53. Captain Ahab might say "yes" this way
54. Letters from Joan Aiken's name
56. "This is the farmer sowing his __" (nursery rhyme)
58. Prefix meaning feet
60. Udry–Sendak title, ____ *Be Enemies*
63. What Mary's little pet might have become
65. Friend of Christopher Robin
66. Authors of *How Big Is Big* and other science books (inits.)
67. Much ____ about nothing
69. Initials of popular poet who wrote: "Children aren't happy with nothing to ignore / And that's what parents were created for."

Solution to puzzle on page 274.

1 B	2 A	3 B	4 A	5 R		6 R	7 A	8 B	9 B	10 I	T		11 P	12 I	13 P	14 E	15 R
16 O	D	E	N	S	E		17 B	E	A	N		18 O	F	R	O	S	A
19 A	R	A	T			20 E	L	B	E				21 S	T	A	G	
22 T	E	R	23 H	24 U	25 N	E		26 L	E		27 T	28 I	N		29 T	U	G
	A		30 O	P	E	R	A		31 A		32 T	33 O	R	O		34 D	E		E
35 L	M		36 L	O	S	I	N	G	37 H	E	A	R	T		38 T		39 R	40 E	D
O		41 M	O	N	T	E		42 R	E		I		43 W	44 E	B	B	Y
45 F	R	O	G			46 C	A	B	I	47 N		48 I	L	E		A
T		49 L	50 Y	51 L	E		52 L	Y	L	E		53 A	N	D	54 A	N	N
55 I	56 C	E		57 A	L	58 P		59 U	G	60 L	Y		61 T	A	D
62 N	O		63 E		64 V	65 E	R	N	E	E		66 H	67 A	R	E	Y
68 G	69 R	O	W		70 E	D	O		71 O	U	T	A	N	D	I	N
	72 N	N	E		73 S	I	O	U	X		S		74 S	O	X

BOOKLIST
USING LANGUAGE CREATIVELY

These books feature inventive and uncommon ways of using language. The books can serve as an exhibit, as booktalk material, or as examples of a creative approach to words and communication.

Adams, Richard. *Watership Down.* Macmillan Pub. Co., 1974.
The author creates an entire rabbit civilization complete with lapine language, and some linguistic rules to go with it.

Babbitt, Natalie. *The Search for Delicious.* il. by author. Farrar, Straus, 1969.

Gaylon, the king's messenger, sets off on a quest for the definition of the word "delicious."

Bielewicz, Julian A. *Secret Languages; Communicating in Codes and Ciphers.* il. with drawings and photographs. Elsevier/Nelson, 1980.
An overview of the use of codes.

Carroll, Lewis. *Lewis Carroll's Jabberwocky.* il. by Jane Breskin Zalben with annotations by Humpty Dumpty. Warne, 1977.
A picture-book version of the famous nonsense poem.

Charlip, Remy. *Arm in Arm; A Collection of Connections, Endless Tales, Reiterations and Other Echolalia.* il. by author. Parents Mag. Press, 1969.
Word play drawn as pictures. A picture book for browsing.

Charlip, Remy, Mary Beth, and George Ancona. *Handtalk: An ABC of Finger Spelling & Sign Language.* il. with photographs. Four Winds, 1980.
Full-page color photographs teach the language of the deaf.

Fisher, Cyrus. *The Avion My Uncle Flew.* il. by Richard Floethe. Appleton, 1946.
Read this mystery carefully and you will be able to read two pages of a story entirely in French.

George, Jean Craighead. *Julie of the Wolves.* il. by John Schoenherr. Harper, 1972.
An Eskimo girl learns to communicate with a pack of wolves through careful observations of their habits.

Godden, Rumer. *Mr. McFadden's Hallowe'en.* Viking, 1975.
Scottish dialect adds to the charm of this book about an inheritance, a pony, a spunky girl, and a cranky elderly man.

Holm, Anne. *North to Freedom.* tr. by L. W. Kingsland. Harcourt, 1965.
David's knowledge of many foreign languages is a tremendous help in his quest for freedom.

Juster, Norton. *The Phantom Tollbooth.* il. by Jules Feiffer. Random House, 1961.
Play on words is an important part of Milo's visit to the Lands of Beyond, which include the Foothills of Confusion, the Mountains of Ignorance, the Lands of Null, the Doldrums, and the Sea of Knowledge.

Karl, Jean. "Over the Hill," in *The Turning Place; Stories of a Future Past.* Dutton, 1976.

In this short story, Carpa meets a boy who does not speak her language and she longs to communicate with him.

277

Keller, Charles. *Daffynitions*. il. by F. A. Fitzgerald. Prentice-Hall, 1976.
Silly word definitions: caterpillar—an upholstered worm; undercover agent—a spy in bed.

Krauss, Ruth. *A Hole Is To Dig; A First Book of First Definitions*. il. by Maurice Sendak. Harper, 1952.
Nursery-school children inspired this beginning dictionary of "logical" definitions.

Lear, Edward. *The Pelican Chorus & The Quangle Wangle's Hat*. il. by Kevin W. Maddison. Viking, 1981.
Two of Edward Lear's classic nonsense poems illustrated with charm.

MacLachlan, Patricia. *Arthur, For The Very First Time*. il. by Lloyd Bloom. Harper, 1980.
Arthur's family speaks French to the family chicken.

Neufeld, John. *Freddy's Book*. Random House, 1973.
A young boy asks his friends and relatives the meaning of a four-letter word scrawled on a wall. (Adults: read this before recommending.)

Orgel, Doris. *A Certain Magic*. Dial Press, 1976.
Aunt Trudi's copybook written during World War II reveals her first efforts at writing English and a lot more.

Raskin, Ellen. *Figgs & Phantoms*. Dutton, 1974.
A wacky mystery, maybe, but definitely an experiment in language.

Schwartz, Alvin, comp. *Flapdoodle: Pure Nonsense From American Folklore*. il. by John O'Brien. Lippincott, 1980.
Word play collected by a folklorist.

Steptoe, John. *Marcia*. Viking, 1976.
"The beginning of me gettin' into growin' up" written in Black English. (Adults: read this before recommending.)

Sullivan, Mary Beth and Linda Bourke. *A Show of Hands; Say It In Sign Language*. il. by Linda Bourke. Addison-Wesley, 1980.
Cartoon drawings illustrate hand signals for words and letters.

Thurber, James. *The Wonderful O*. il. by Marc Simont. Simon & Schuster, 1957.
What happens when the letter "O" is forbidden on the island of Coroo?

Watson, Clyde. *Quips & Quirks*. il. by Wendy Watson. Crowell, 1975.
Rarely heard but wonderful words to explore for fun.

Weston, John. *The Boy Who Sang The Birds.* il. by Donna Diamond. Scribner, 1976.
"Words aren't the only language," says Mrs. Boniharder about Dorkle's strange birdlike speech.

Williams, Barbara. *Albert's Toothache.* il. by Kay Chorao. Dutton, 1974.
A toothless turtle insists that he has a toothache; a lesson in language.

Yep, Laurence. *Dragonwings.* Harper, 1975.
Moon Shadow must learn the language of the American Demons.

Playing With Pictures

These games foster visual literacy.

PICTURE SEQUENCING GAME

Buy three identical paperback picture books (wordless picture books are good for this game). Cut out the pictures in two of the copies and mount them on poster board or construction paper. (You will need two copies to get both sides of each page.) If you have access to a laminating machine, laminate the pictures. Make sure to cover or cut off the page numbers.

Then have the children try to place the pictures in logical order. Keep the third copy of the book intact so that you can show the children the proper sequence of the pictures at the end of the game (and so you will know the sequence yourself!).

You will find many other uses for these mounted pictures. They can serve as a bulletin board display or as storytelling props. You can also give a set of pictures to a child and ask the child to tell the story.

PICTURE MEMORY GAME

This game focuses on the illustrator's role and demands close attention from the players.

YOU NEED: Pictures drawn by children, representing books they have read.

279

HOW TO: Each child entering the game draws a picture of a scene or character from a book.

All pictures are laid out on the floor.

Give the players one minute to familiarize themselves with the pictures.

Now gather up the pictures.

Shuffle them and place them face down.

Remove three of the pictures and turn the remaining pictures over.

Players call out the missing pictures and receive one point for each picture correctly named.

Repeat the shuffle until one or more players has earned ten points.

Now players must each describe their own picture and its relationship to the book they have read.

HINT: Fifteen or more players make the memory part of this game more challenging. However, it may be tiring to have too many players describing pictures. Therefore, if you have a large group, describe only those pictures that have been removed during the game. This game can also be played with book jackets.

BOOKLIST

USING PICTURES CREATIVELY

This is a short selection of books that give experience in seeing what you look at.

Ahlberg, Janet and Allan. *Each Peach Pear Plum; An "I Spy" Story.* Viking, 1979.
An "I Spy" picture book using nursery rhyme characters.

Anno, Mitsumasa. *Anno's Animals.* Collins, 1979.
Sophisticated drawings make the reader really work to find the hidden animals.

Areugo, Jose, and Ariane Dewey. *We Hide, You Seek.* il. by authors. Greenwillow Bks., 1979.
Similar to Anno's book, but much easier to find the animals.

Bester, Roger. *Guess What?* Photographs by author. Crown, 1980.
Photographic riddles.

Grillone, Lisa and Joseph Gennaro. *Small Worlds Close Up.* il. with photographs. Crown, 1978.
Spectacular close-up photographs help the reader realize the delights of microscopic viewing.

Hoban, Tana. *Take Another Look.* Photographs by author. Greenwillow Bks., 1981.
Small cut-outs enable the viewer to see only a portion of the entire picture on the next page. See also *Look Again!*

Oakley, Graham. *Graham Oakley's Magical Changes.* il. by author. Atheneum Pubs., 1980.
Split pages display a series of imaginative full-color drawings that enable the reader to make numerous combinations.

Pienkowski, Jan. *The Haunted House.* il. by author. Dutton, 1979.
Fabulous three-dimensional cutouts in a witty romp through a haunted house.

Rauch, Hans-Georg. *The Lines Are Coming: A Book About Drawing.* Scribner, 1978.
This is a book about drawing, but it is also a superb examination of the versatility of line.

Schaaf, Peter. *The Violin Close Up.* Photographs by author. Four Winds, 1980.
Careful photographs examine the parts of a violin.

Map Games

American children and adults often have an appalling lack of geographic sense. Most people simply cannot point out Austria or Poland on a map and certainly have no idea about the geography of Africa. Even more surprising, they have no clear idea of the location of, say, Oregon or Iowa, in their own country. It might be argued that a person can get through life without ever knowing the capital of Spain, but there is a practical application. How many times have you been misdirected after you've asked for help? How many times have you become tongue-tied when giving directions? Most of us need a bit of practice in giving and following directions.

Many popular books for children contain maps to aid in following a character's journey or to set the action of the story.

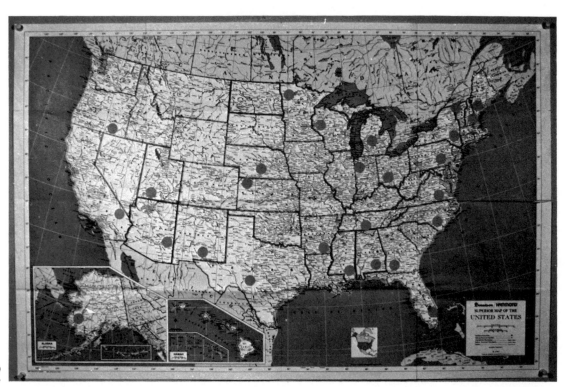

PLAN A TREASURE HUNT

Give directional clues on index cards placed in envelopes. Send children individually or in groups from clue to clue until they find the treasure (why not try cookies shaped like Treasure Island?). Each child can be working through the same set of clues in a different order, i.e., Group A can be working through clues 1–10 while Group B follows clues 10–1. You can send the children out of the room into the street, around the neighborhood, or play the game in a small area ("Go three steps, turn right, go straight to the second window"). The clue might be anywhere along the path. You can also have the children write the clues for their teammates, giving them a chance to practice giving directions.

MARK A MAP

At home or in school, hang a map on the wall. Whenever you read a story with a distinctive setting, find the country, state, or city on the map and mark it.

DRAW A MAP

Make a map for a book that doesn't already include one. Draw routes for the characters and use miniature paper dolls or colored discs to represent them. Use the map for a bulletin board display.

BOOKLIST

Make your own maps for these books.

Burnford, Sheila. *The Incredible Journey.* Little, Brown, 1961.
Two dogs and a cat find their way home, 250 miles away, in a journey that takes them through the Canadian wilderness.

Fitzhugh, Louise. *Harriet the Spy.* Dell, 1964.
Harriet's spy route would provide a challenge for a mapmaker.

McCloskey, Robert. *Lentil.* Viking, 1940.
A boy saves the day with his harmonica. Map the small town where the story takes place.

McGowen, Tom. *Odyssey From River Bend.* Little, 1975.
A group of civilized animals search for a city of the past.

Morey, Walt. *Kavik the Wolf Dog.* Dutton, 1968.
Kavik's travels back to Alaska can be charted.

Steig, William. *Dominic.* Farrar, 1972.
Funny adventures with Dominic, a dog.

283

DESIGN A BOARD GAME

Make a board game based on the travels of characters in a book. The object of such a game might be for the characters to get to a common destination or to separate places as fast as possible. For younger children, use colored cards to match the squares ("move to the red square"); for older children, use place names ("move to Eeyore's house"). Set up cards that send players back or ahead. Following is a game based on *Ribsy*, by Beverly Cleary (il. by Louis Darling, Morrow, 1964).

RIBSY GAME

YOU NEED:

1. Index cards. Mark three each with the following numbers: 1,2,3,4. Write instructions like those listed below on other cards (one move per card).

   Stop to scratch a flea. Lose next turn.

   Go back to the shopping center to search for the Huggins family.

   Take a ride in the Dingley's station wagon. Move forward four spaces.

   Mrs. Frawley buys you a new coat. Move to her house.

   Mrs. Frawley serves you a big meal. Go to her house.

   Stay where you are and recite the Pledge of Allegiance as you would in Mrs. Sonchek's class.

   Danny brings his squirrel to school for Show and Tell. Chase him ahead four spaces.

   Stop to beg a sandwich from a workman. Lose a turn.

   Go to the football field to eat a hot dog.

   Run for a touchdown. Move five spaces ahead.

   Ribsy's picture is in the newspaper. Wait at the Saylor's for one turn.

   Ribsy hears Henry's voice on the phone. Run to Henry. Move ahead three spaces.

   Take a ride in the elevator of Larry's apartment house. Stay there for the next turn.

2. A board for the game. Draw a series of squares. Include nine stops, in this order:

The shopping center (first square)
The Dingley's bathtub
Mrs. Frawley's house
Construction site—workmen at lunch
Mrs. Sonchek's second grade
The high school football field
Joe Saylor's house
Larry's apartment house
Henry Huggins' home (last square)

3. Markers. Make miniature Ribsy dog cut-outs, each in a different color, for the players to use as markers.

OBJECT OF THE GAME: Your Ribsy must get from the shopping center to Henry Huggins' home first.

HOW TO PLAY: Shuffle the cards. Each player takes one card in turn. If the card has a number, the player moves the number of spaces indicated. If it has directions, these must be carried out. If a player has only two spaces to go before he gets to the end and draws a "three" card, he waits where he is until the next turn.

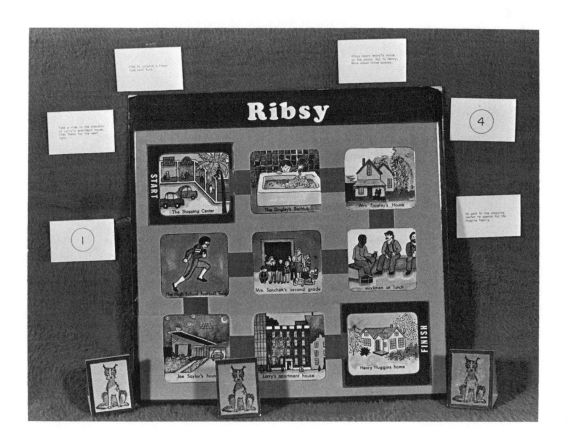

285

BOOKLIST

Maps appear in these books. Choose one to make your own map game.

> Time is going,
> Never staying,
> Always flowing,
> Ever saying:
> Gone!

Adams, Richard. *Watership Down.* MacMillan, 1972.
A maverick band of rabbits set off to find a new home.

Brown, Palmer. *Hickory.* il. by author. Harper, 1978.
A field mouse leaves his home (a grandfather clock) for the outdoors.

Chute, Marchette. *The Innocent Wayfaring.* Dutton, 1943.
Travel through fourteenth-century England with Anne.

Dickinson, Peter. *The Dancing Bear.* Little, Brown, 1972.
Travel through the past with a slave and his performing bear.

Fife, Dale. *North of Danger.* Maps and decorations by Haakon Soether. Dutton, 1978.
Two hundred miles of frozen wasteland lie between Arne and his father.

Finlayson, Ann. *Rebecca's War.* Warne, 1972.
America at the time of the Revolution.

Gray, Elizabeth. *Adam of the Road.* Viking, 1970.
Medieval England.

Juster, Norton. *The Phantom Tollbooth.* Collins, 1972.
Dictionopolis is one of the lands you'll visit.

Kendall, Carol. *The Gammage Cup.* Harcourt, 1959.
Find your way to the land of the Minnipins.

Kherdian, David. *The Road From Home; the story of an Armenian Girl.* Greenwillow, 1979.
Biography of a young Armenian girl deported from Turkey in 1916.

Lagerlof, Selma. *The Wonderful Adventures of Nils.* Pantheon, 1963.
Through Sweden on the back of a goose.

LeGuin, Ursula K. *A Wizard of Earthsea.* Parnassus, 1968.
Islands in a fantasy land.

Milne, A. A. *Winnie the Pooh.* Dutton, 1926.
The hundred-acre wood and all that.

Stevenson, Robert Louis. *Treasure Island.* Hamlyn, 1967.
The classic treasure-map story.

Reading Games

HORSE READING GAME

Capitalize on the interest in horse stories with this reading game for grades 1–4.

YOU NEED: Poster board
Felt-tip pens
Horse pictures or original art
Glue
Game tokens or checkers
Laminating press or clear contact paper to cover board (optional)

HOW TO: Make a game board with room for twenty-five moves.
Rules and booklist should be printed on the game board.
Cover game board with clear contact paper for protection (optional).

HINT: Substitute books available in your library for those listed below.

OBJECT OF THE GAME: To get your horse home to the pasture by getting twenty-five points.

RULES: Children move their tokens one space for each point they make.

FIVE POINTS are received for reading three of these books:

Anderson, C. W. *Billy and Blaze.* il. by author. Macmillan Pub. Co., 1962.

Anderson, C. W. *A Pony for Linda.* il. by author. Macmillan Pub. Co., 1951.

Brown, Paul. *Pony Farm.* il. by author. Scribner, 1948.

Dennis, Wesley. *Flip.* il. by author. Viking, 1941.

Doty, Jean Slaughter. *Can I Get There By Candlelight?* il. by Ted Lewin. Macmillan Pub. Co., 1980.

Hopkins, Lee Bennett, comp. *My Mane Catches the Wind: Poems About Horses.* il. by Sam Savitt. Harcourt, 1979.

Krementz, Jill. *A Very Young Rider.* Photographs by author. Knopf, 1977.

287

MacClintock, Dorcas. *Horses As I See Them.* il. by Ugo Mochi. Scribner, 1980.

Pender, Lydia. *Barnaby and the Horses.* il. by Inga Moore. Oxford, 1980.

Rabinowitz, Sandy. *The Red Horse and the Bluebird.* il. by author. Harper, 1975.

FIVE POINTS are received for reading one of these books:

Aldridge, James. *A Sporting Proposition.* Little, 1973.

Anderson, Lonzo. *Ponies of Mykillengi.* il. by Adrienne Adams. Scribner, 1966.

Bødker, Cecil. *Silas and the Black Mare.* tr. by Sheila La Farge. Delacorte Press/Seymour Lawrence, 1978.

Campbell, Barbara. *A Girl Called Bob and a Horse Called Yoki.* Dial, 1982.

Farley, Walter. *The Black Stallion.* il. by Keith Ward. Random House, 1944.

Gates, Doris. *A Morgan for Melinda.* Viking, 1980.

Henry, Marguerite. *King of the Wind.* il. by Wesley Dennis. Rand McNally, 1948.

Morey, Walt. *Run Far, Run Fast.* Dutton, 1974.

FIFTEEN POINTS for writing one book report including answers to the following:

What were the title and the author of the book?

What was the story about?

Who were the characters?

Where did the story take place?

Did you like the book? Why or why not?

FIVE POINTS for reading aloud to a friend part of one of the books you have chosen.

TWO POINTS for doing one of these activities:

Draw a picture of part of the story.

Make a game for others to play about a horse book you have read.

Write a story about a horse.

Write a report called "How to Take Care of a Horse." Look in these books if you need help:

Chase, Edward L. *Big Book of Horses.* il. by author. Grosset, 1971.

Copper, Marcia S. *Take Care of Your Horse.* Scribner, 1974.

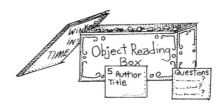

OBJECT READING GAME

This game for older children is fun to put together. You can also use the game materials in a display.

YOU NEED:

Any object or miniature that relates to a book. If you enjoy little things, or have a young child at home and are something of a pack rat, this game will be easy for you to assemble. Walk around the house looking for broken jewelry, discarded objects, small treasures. Now try to relate each of the objects to a book. Collect:

A pretty box or other container
Stickers or tags
Index cards

HOW TO:

Attach a sticker or tag to each of the objects.
Use the stickers to number the objects.
Make an index card for each book. On one side, list the author and title and the number you have assigned to the object that goes with that book; on the reverse side write questions for the reader to answer. The nature of the questions will depend on how much you wish the readers to do or tell. You may want to ask a factual question about the plot to ensure that the book has actually been read. In addition, you might ask the children a research question or have them do some creative writing, perhaps only indirectly related to the book.
Finding objects is more fun than making up questions, so write down questions as soon as you find each object. Change the objects and questions frequently. Make sure the books are available. Sample questions appear below.

RULES:

The reader picks an object and then looks for the corresponding card. After reading the book, he or she answers the questions on the back of the cards.

289

SAMPLE OBJECTS AND BOOKS

MODEL SHEEP
Krumgold, Joseph. . . . *And Now Miguel.* il. by Jean Charlot. Crowell, 1953.
Miguel begs to be allowed to tend his father's sheep.

STONE CAT
Stolz, Mary. *Cat in the Mirror.* Harper, 1975.
A pet cat is the link between modern-day New York and Ancient Egypt.

PIG
Peck, Robert Newton. *A Day No Pigs Would Die.* Knopf, 1973.
A poignant account of growing up in a Shaker family.

White, E. B. *Charlotte's Web.* il. by Garth Williams. Harper, 1952.
Wilbur, a friendly pig, is saved from becoming ham by a spider.

THREE MINIATURE DOLLS
Sachs, Marilyn. *Dorrie's Book.* il. by Anne Sachs. Doubleday, 1975.
Dorrie, accustomed to being an only child, is suddenly confronted with triplets in the family.

EYEGLASSES
L'Engle, Madeleine. *A Wrinkle in Time.* Farrar, Straus, 1962.
Meg uses magic glasses to see her father inside a column.

Holman, Felice. *Slake's Limbo.* Scribner, 1974.
Slake fashions glasses from discards found in a subway station in New York City.

A RING
Green, Alexander. *Scarlet Sails.* tr. by Thomas P. Whitney. il. by Esta Nesbitt. Scribner, 1967.
Asole wakes up with a ring on her finger. Is the prophecy coming true?

A VALENTINE CANDY BRACELET
Degens, T. *Transport 7–41–R.* Viking, 1974.
A candy bracelet is a thirteen-year-old girl's only link with home as she travels on a train crowded with World War II evacuees.

SAMPLE QUESTIONS

The Cat in the Mirror, by Mary Stolz.
Plot question: What is the significance of the cat in the title?
Research question: Look up the history of cats. Did they have a special role in Ancient Egypt? Or, look up Ancient Egypt and report on its art.

Creative writing project: If you could be transported back in time, which period would you pick? Write a story about an adventure you might have in that era.

Slake's Limbo, by Felice Holman.
Plot question: What is the relationship between the motorman named Willis Joe Whinny and Slake?
Research question: Many large cities have underground railways like New York City's. Find out about the construction and use of these subterranean trains in Paris, London, San Francisco, or New York.

Creative writing project: If you were to run away in your home town, where would you go? How would you live? Or, write a continuation to *Slake's Limbo.* Where do you think Slake would have spent his first night in his new life?

BIRD READING GAME

Every year we receive numerous greeting cards for occasions of every sort. There are cards for birthdays, cards for holidays such as Valentine's Day and Christmas, and cards that just say hello. If you take my advice and become a saver, you will soon have a box or drawer filled with cards. What do you do with them? One Christmas seemed to be "the year of the bird." Since I received at least twenty cards that featured birds in some way, here is a "game" or book-report idea made from these cards.

YOU NEED: A notebook or presentation book
Bird cards or bird pictures
8″ × 10″ ring binder acetate sheets
Typewriter
Glue
Poems about birds

HOW TO: On each righthand page of the notebook, glue a bird card or bird picture.
Write the title of a book and the author's name beneath it.

291

On the reverse side of the page, write a question that the reader can answer orally (to discover if the child has read the book). Then ask a question that will become a writing project.

Intersperse the book pages with poems about birds. Use the poetry indexes to find poems, or let the children search for them.

HINT: Use books that are accessible to your group (*i.e.*, be sure they are in your own library). Book titles need not match up with the pictures exactly.

USE: The notebook can serve as a bibliography or as the basis for a game. Ask each child to choose one picture, read that book, and answer the questions.

BOOKLIST AND SAMPLE QUESTIONS

Notice that the list includes books that have to do with birds only incidentally. The object is to encourage wider reading. The oral questions are "recall," have-you-read-the-book sort of questions. The creative writing questions are inspired by the books, but are not directly related to them.

Andersen, Hans Christian. *The Nightingale.* tr. by Eva Le Gallienne. il. by Nancy Burkert. Harper, 1965.

The classic tale of the Emperor of China and a nightingale.

Tell: Why is the nightingale unhappy at the Emperor's court?

Why does he return after his escape?

Write: An essay comparing something natural with something artificial.

Byars, Betsy. *The House of Wings.* il. by Daniel Schwartz. Viking, 1972.

A rebellious boy and his bird-loving grandfather spend a summer together.

Tell: How does the crane change the relationship between Sammy and his grandfather?

What happened in the past to make grandfather treat birds with particular kindness?

Write: A story in which a third person, an animal, or an object is instrumental in bringing two people closer together.

Burnett, Frances Hodgson. *The Secret Garden.* il. by Tasha Tudor. Lippincott, 1962.

Mary hears a noise in the night and discovers a boy as unpleasant as herself.

    Tell: Why is the robin important to the story?

           Mary is a cranky little girl when she arrives in Yorkshire. What happens to change her into a loveable and memorable heroine?

Write: An essay about your first impressions of a new place.

Donovan, John. *Remove Protective Coating a Little at a Time.* Harper, 1973.

Harry, a loner, meets Amelia, an elderly New York vagrant.

    Tell: What is the significance of the birds in the story?

           Describe Harry's changing relationship with Bud and Toots.

Write: A story about how two lonely people meet.

DuMaurier, Daphne. "The Birds," in *Kiss Me Again, Stranger: A Collection of Eight Stories Long and Short.* il. by Margot Tomes. Doubleday, 1952.

Birds attack a town.

    Tell: How did the author build up suspense in the story?

           How did the children react when the birds attacked?

Write: A story in which something you take for granted acts strangely.

Farmer, Penelope. *The Summer Birds.* il. by James J. Spanfeller. Harcourt, 1962.

Children are taught to fly during one glorious summer.

    Tell: Why are the children afraid grown-ups will find out about their flying?

           What did the children learn from the "war"?

Write: An essay telling how you would feel if you could fly.

George, Jean. *My Side of the Mountain.* il. by author. Dutton, 1959.

Sam leaves the city to live alone in the wilderness.

    Tell: Describe the training of Frightful.

           Mention some of the things Sam eats during his stay in the Catskills.

Write: A story about being on your own in the city or the country.

293

George, Jean. *Who Really Killed Cock Robin? An Ecological Mystery.* Dutton, 1971.
Two children investigate the death of a robin on Mayor Joe's property.

    Tell: What are some of the possible causes of Cock Robin's death?
           Describe the town's attitude toward a clean environment.
    Write: An essay supporting an organization fighting for anti-pollution laws, protection of wildlife, or some other environmental cause.

Stanger, Margaret A. *That Quail, Robert.* il. by Cathy Baldwin. Lippincott, 1966.
A quail is born on a kitchen sink and lives a happy life with a Cape Cod family.

    Tell: What happens during Christmas with Robert?
           What does the family do with Robert when they leave for a vacation?
    Write: Describe an incident with a pet you own or imagine an incident with a pet you would like to own.

Weston, John. *The Boy Who Sang the Birds.* il. by Donna Diamond. Scribner, 1976.
Dorkle seems to have a strange affinity to birds.

    Tell: How does Dorkle communicate?
           Tell about Dorkle's relationship with animals.
    Write: Make up your own language and write a paragraph in it. Be sure to translate it for your friends.

White, E. B. *The Trumpet of the Swan.* il. by Edward Frascino. Harper, 1970.
Louis is a trumpeter swan who uses a trumpet to communicate with his friends.

    Tell: How did Louis earn money?
           Tell about Louis's night at the Ritz.
    Write: Plan a scheme for earning money and tell what you would do with the money once it was earned.

Yashima, Taro. *Crow Boy.* il. by author. Viking, 1955.
Classmates gain respect for a boy who can imitate bird calls.

    Tell: Can you distinguish between liking someone and respecting them?
           What did the class learn about their behavior towards "Crow Boy"?

Write: Look back on your own school days. Have you ever been teased by anyone? Have you seen somebody else being treated unfairly? Write about a true incident of this type in your own class or school.

MORE BIRD BOOKS

Buchwald, Emilie. *Floramel and Esteban.* il. by Charles Robinson. Harcourt, 1982.
An adventurous cow finds a friend and learns to become a musician . . . honest!

Bunting, Eve. *Blackbird Singing.* il. by Stephen Gammell. Macmillan Pub. Co., 1980.
A blackbird infestation disrupts a family's relationships.

George, Jean Craighead. *The Cry of the Crow.* Harper, 1980.
Mandy makes a pet of a baby crow.

Langton, Jane. *The Fledgling.* il. by Erik Blegvad. Harper, 1980.
Georgie Hall is taught to fly by a goose.

Levine, Betty K. *Hawk High.* il. by Louise E. Jefferson. Atheneum Pubs., 1980.
Toni tries to prove her capability by climbing a cliff to see into a bird's nest.

Pringle, Laurence. *Listen to the Crows.* il. by Ted Lewin. Crowell, 1976.
An examination of the crow's "language."

OLD AND YOUNG READING GAME

In the olden days, in a less mobile era, children lived with or near their grandparents. Today children are likely to grow up with little or no influence from older people. Books featuring children in meaningful relationships with older people can help fill this void.

YOU NEED: Glue
Scissors
Drawing paper
Felt square

HOW TO: Make a folder out of felt, by folding a big rectangle in half.
Type or print the rules of the game on a piece of drawing paper.

Glue the paper on the left side of the opened folder and cover it with a felt flap.

Make small felt folders.

Type or print the author and title of a book on paper to fit the inside of each "miniature book."

Glue the paper inside the small felt books, and glue them to the right side of the opened felt folder.

HINT: This can also be used to encourage reading from any subject bibliography.

RULES (to be listed under the felt flap):

Each of these books tells of an older person's relationship with a younger person.

To complete this game you will need fifteen points.

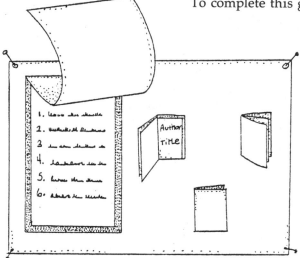

FIVE POINTS: Read one of these books.

TWO POINTS: Tell how the relationship in the story changed one of the people.

FIVE POINTS: Choose one project.

1. Write a poem about old age.

2. Rewrite part of the book as a skit.

3. Write an essay about an incident involving you and an older person, perhaps a grandparent.

4. Pretend that you are the younger person in the book you read. Write a letter to the older character telling what happened after the book ended.

THREE POINTS: Choose one project.

1. Make a poster advertising the book.

2. Draw a map of the book's setting.

3. Draw a portrait of a character in the book.

BOOKLIST

Books about older people.

Blue, Rose. *Grandma Didn't Wave Back.* il. by Ted Lewin. Watts, 1972.
Grandma begins to act strangely, forgetting important things, and it worries Debbie and her family.

Burch, Robert. *Two That Were Tough.* il. by Richard Cuffari. Viking, 1976.
Mr. Hilton and his rooster, Wild Wings, wish to retain their independence.

Byars, Betsy. *After the Goat Man.* il. by Ronald Himler. Viking, 1974.
Harold and Ada search for Figgy's eccentric grandfather.

Cawley, Winifred. *Gran at Coalgate.* il. by Fermin Rocker. Holt, 1974.
Dad disapproves of Gran's "modern" household, which features bobbed hair, short skirts, the moving pictures, and the Charleston.

Colman, Hila. *The Amazing Miss Laura.* Morrow, 1976.
Josie, as a companion to the eccentric widow of a famous painter, learns to relate to her own crusty grandfather.

Cleaver, Vera and Bill Cleaver. *Queen of Hearts.* Lippincott, 1978.
Granny Lincoln is 79 when she has a mild stroke. Wilma is 12 when she comes to stay with her. They have a battle of wills.

Cornish, Sam. *Grandmother's Pictures.* il. by Jeanne Johns. Bookstore Press, 1974.
Grandma's scrapbook gives a young boy a picture of the past.

Cummings, Betty Sue. *Let a River* Be. Atheneum Pubs., 1978.
Ella is a spunky 76-year-old conservationist. Reetard is her ally in a fight to save Indian River.

De Paola, Tomie. *Nana Upstairs & Nana Downstairs.* il. by author. Putnam, 1973.
A young boy and his relationship with his two grandmas.

297

Donnelly, Elfie. *Offbeat Friends.* tr. by Anthea Bell. Crown, 1982.
Mari, an Austrian schoolgirl, befriends Mrs. Panacek, a 78-year-old "crazy."

Farber, Norma. *How Does it Feel to be Old?* il. by Trina Schart Hyman. Dutton, 1979.
A little girl and her grandmother discuss old age.

Godden, Rumer. *Mr. McFadden's Hallowe'en.* Viking, 1975.
Selina, "a solid child," and Haggis, her pony, reform a recluse.

Gonzalez, Gloria. *The Glad Man.* Knopf, 1975.
Melissa and her brother, Troy, bring trouble to an old man living in a dilapidated bus.

Hurmence, Belinda. *Tough Tiffany.* Doubleday, 1980.
Tiffany's Granny is a cantankerous, sprightly, fascinating character.

Jones, Weyman. *Edge of Two Worlds.* il. by J. C. Kocsis. Dial Press, 1968.
The only survivor of a Comanche massacre meets a Cherokee Indian in search of the origins of his people.

Konigsburg, E. L. "At the Home" in *Throwing Shadows.* Atheneum Pubs., 1979.
Phillip brings his tape recorder to an old folk's home and gets involved with the residents.

Krumgold, Joseph. *Onion John.* il. by Symeon Shimin. Crowell, 1959.
Andy's father and his friends try to reform Onion John's way of life.

Mathis, Sharon Bell. *The Hundred Penny Box.* il. by Leo and Diane Dillon. Viking, 1975.
Great-great-aunt Dew is 100 years old and a special person to Michael, who tries to protect her from adults who "know best."

Schellie, Don. *Kidnapping Mr. Tubbs.* Four Winds, 1978.
Two teenagers kidnap a man who is nearly 100 years old from a nursing home and learn that "you can't go home again."

Shannon, Monica. *Dobry.* il. by Atanas Katchamakoff. Viking, 1934.
Grandfather emerges as the leading character in a warm family story that takes place in Bulgaria.

Taylor, Theodore. *The Cay.* Doubleday, 1969.
Philip, a young white boy blinded in a shipwreck, is aided on a tropical island by Timothy, an elderly black man.

Tolan, Stephanie S. *Grandpa—and Me.* Scribner, 1978.
Kerry's grandpa begins to change, and now he says and does strange things.

Turner, Ann. *A Hunter Comes Home.* Crown, 1980.
Fifteen-year-old Jonas returns from school to his Eskimo village and struggles to make peace with his grandfather.

Wersba, Barbara. *The Dream Watcher.* Atheneum Pubs., 1972.
Albert meets Mrs. Woodfin, who doesn't think he is strange at all.

Zolotow, Charlotte. *My Grandson Lew.* il. by William Pène Du Bois. Harper, 1974.
Lewis and his mother share memories of Grandpa.

FILM CAN GAME

The element of chance turns a book report assignment into a game.

YOU NEED: empty film cans (available from your local film processor)

slips of paper bearing questions or instructions

HOW TO: Tell the children to prepare for the game by reading a book.
Put a slip of paper in each can.
Let each child choose a can, open it, and follow the instructions or answer the question inside.

SAMPLE INSTRUCTIONS:

Write a skit to introduce the book to a group.

Make up a poster or a singing commercial for the book.

Design a book jacket. Don't forget to describe the book on the flap.

How did the story end? Would you change the ending?

Pick one word to describe each character in the book.

Find an interesting conversation in the book. Read it aloud with expression.

What was your favorite part of the story? Why?

Which picture did you like best? Why?

Write a description of an animal, a child, or an adult in the book.

Do an imitation of a character in the book.

Where did the story take place? Describe the setting.

How did the story make you feel?

Which character did you like most? Why?

Which character did you like least? Why?

Have any of the characters changed their ways or learned something by the end of the story? Discuss.

Choose three main events in the story. Draw a picture and write a sentence for each event.

Find your favorite description in the book. Read it aloud.

Find another book by the same author in the library.

Below: Readopoly, adapted from a board game developed by the Library Services division of the Wisconsin Department of Public Instruction.

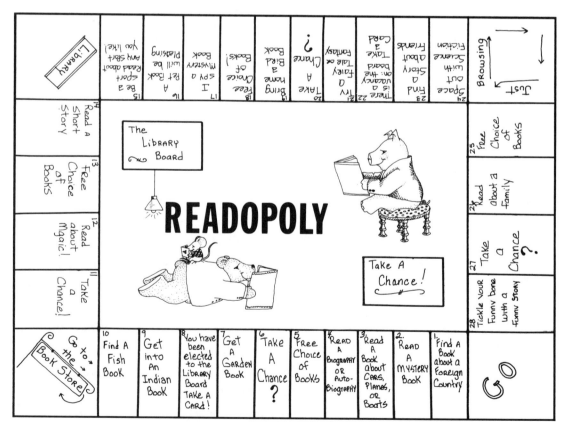

"Give a Quote" Presentation*

This presentation introduces a quest that a child can pursue alone or with friends, through some favorite books. It is a good game for children who are put off by competitive situations.

Are you looking for an unusual present for your mom, your dad, or your best friend? Give a favorite quote from a book you read this year. Maybe you can remember a sentence that impressed you; if not, look through some of your favorite books again for a special phrase or paragraph. Copy the quote in your best handwriting and decorate it with pictures or a border so that it can be framed and hung on the wall.

Here are some quotations I remember. This one is for my uncle who travels a lot.

> No matter where There is,
> when you arrive it becomes Here.

It's from *The Gammage Cup:* Carol Kendall, illustrated by Erik Blegvad; Harcourt Brace Jovanovich. The Minnipins are a race of little people who live in an isolated mountain valley. They never question the authority of the Periods (the leading family), only Muggles is different. She really believes in this quote. It will make a good present for Uncle Peter.

My friend Ione will like this sentence, because she loves giraffes.

> The giraffe is God's special comic miracle.

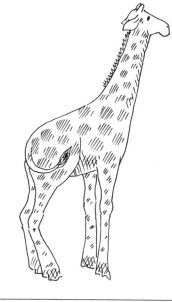

Uncle C.C. says it in a book called *Good-bye, Chicken Little:* Betsy Byars; Harper and Row. He is a wacky character who comes to stay with Jimmie's family after Uncle Pete dies. Uncle C.C. often says things that seem incredibly truthful, and in this case he said the perfect quotable sentence for my friend Ione.

I may give the next quote to myself.

> I'm glad I'm not perfect, I'd be bored to death.

It's from *Harriet the Spy:* Louise Fitzhugh; Harper and Row. Harriet's book is full of sentences that might make

*Reprinted from *Cricket, The Magazine for Children*, vol. 7, no. 4, Dec. 1979. © 1979 by Open Court Publishing Company.

good gifts; here's one that could be just right for your mother.

> You're never too old to spy . . . except maybe if you're over fifty you might fall off fire escapes. But you could spy around on the ground a lot.

My brother annoys me sometimes, but he's smart, so I'm going to give him this quote to put over his desk.

> Don't pretend to be stupider than you really are.

Mr. Badger said that in *Wind in the Willows:* Kenneth Graham, illustrated by Ernest Shepard; Scribner's. If you can't find an appropriate quote in any other book, read this one. All the animals are always making comments you wish you had made.

Anyone would like the next quote, I think. But you have to remember to hang it upside down.

> The world looks so different upside down. The sky is on the ground, and the grass is in the sky.

That's the kind of thing you'd be likely to say after hanging upside down too long. But Randolph doesn't have that problem; he finds it impossible to hang by his tail the way other possums do. You can read about him in a picture book called *Impossible Possum:* Ellen Conford, illustrated by Rosemary Wells; Little, Brown.

Here's a quote about nothing.

> Nothing is absolutely the limit of nothingness—it's the lowest you can go. If there were something that was left or less than nothing—then nothing would be something (even though it's just a very little bit of something).
>
> —Wilbur Pig

I'm not sure what all this means, and it would take a long time to copy and decorate, but it's a great quote. It's from *Charlotte's Web:* E. B. White, illustrated by Garth Williams; Harper and Row. Do you recognize it?

Stuck for a terrific quote? Go to the library and ask the reference librarian for *Familiar Quotations* by John Bartlett. It's a huge book filled with quotes.

Happy gift giving!

VI CRAFTS

Handicrafts have always been a popular leisure activity in America, for both children and adults. When a craft can be related to books and reading, the resulting art objects will become effective advertisements for books. If you are going to do a craft—decorate a table, appliqué a shirt, or create something out of old egg cartons—why not use a book theme?

My own house has many decorative objects that relate to books. It is much more meaningful to me to have a framed Winnie the Pooh poster or a Leo the Late Bloomer wall hanging that reminds me of a good book than to have an *objet d'art* that relates to nothing in particular.

When I do crafts, I usually make something that relates to books: a tote bag to carry story props, a tissue box to use with "sob stories." I wear vests and jackets decorated with book illustrations and jewelry that reminds me of my favorite books.

If you follow me into a hotel, be prepared for some odd confrontations.

In an elevator at the MGM Grand Hotel, a man says, "Excuse me, but does that dog on your jacket have any significance?" "I'm really glad you asked," I say. "This is Harry the Dirty Dog, the hero of a really wonderful children's picture book. Have you read it?" "Excuse me, Miss, I get off on this floor," says my elevator companion suddenly. But I don't worry; I've done my daily job for The Cause of Books and Reading.

This section will give you some ideas for making things that relate to books—things to keep and enjoy. (If you want to sell these items, you must have the permission of the copyright holder.) The craft and exhibit projects are accompanied by lists of books that you can use for instant displays or for booktalks.

Some of the book themes suggested here relate in only a tangential way to the craft. But I think we should grasp every opportunity to promote books. When you are cutting and pasting, drawing or painting, or stitching and patching, have a theme book table set up with books either to discuss while you're working or to take home to read when you've finished creating. It might seem a bit farfetched to tie in books that give you an old-fashioned cry with the making of a tissue box, but the books are all worth reading *And* it just so happens that *The Lottery Rose* is at least a two-hundred-tissue read.

Please try not to use these craft ideas without relating them to reading, but feel free to use the booklists for booktalks, exhibits, or handouts.

GREETING CARD PROJECTS

Absolutely splendid greeting cards are available in gift and stationery shops these days. There are many cards with pictures by nineteenth-century children's book illustrators and contemporary artists such as Wallace Tripp. Purchase your own cards or start a correspondence with a friend who will send you cards. When I'm in a store I always seem to find the perfect card for Johanna, or Lloyd, or Wendi, but when I get home I'm reluctant to send such great artwork away to even the best of friends, so I use the cards to promote books.

EXHIBITS

Find cards that remind you of a particular book. A drawing of two hippopotamuses could represent *George and Martha,* by James Marshall. The photograph of a ballet dancer might remind you of *A Very Young Ballet Dancer,* by Jill Krementz. Or the picture of a dragon might represent *The Truth About Dragons,* by Rhoda Blumberg.

Simply type the author's name, the title, and an annotation on a piece of paper and glue it over the greeting inside the card. Tack the cards on a bulletin board and you have a professional-looking exhibit that invites people to come closer and look. (After all, they must open the card to read what's inside it.)

CREATIVE WRITING

Pictures have long been used to spark creative writing. Magazine clippings are not very good candidates for imaginative pictures to use in this project, but greeting cards are. Also, they are easily available and they can be reused. Gather a number of provocative cards. Duplicate the directions below on a piece of paper and place them in the envelopes with the cards. Each child chooses an envelope from a basket and uses the picture and the directions to write a story.

This picture is an illustration for the story you are about to write. Look at the picture. What will the story be about? Where will it take place? Who are the characters? What happened before the picture? What will happen after it? Is there conversation in your story? Don't forget to put a title on your composition. Put your name on the story. You are the author. Think *before* you write. Copy your story on a fresh piece of paper. Check it for good grammar and spelling.

PUZZLES

Greeting cards are the perfect size and weight to use in making individual picture puzzles. Simply cut a picture into pieces and house them in their own envelope. To make this a book-oriented project, write clues to a related book on the envelope. When the puzzle is put together, the picture serves as an introduction to the book. You might also want to write the book's title on the picture before you cut it up.

305

To give an example of a puzzle, a picture of a lion could represent *The Lion, the Witch and the Wardrobe,* by C. S. Lewis, and all those snow scenes you receive around Christmas time could be used with such books as *Day of the Blizzard,* by Marietta Moskin, and *North of Danger,* by Dale Fife.

PROMOTIONAL MATERIALS OR SOUVENIRS

Cards, particularly holiday cards, can be used for publicity. Cut off the greeting and use the picture as a give-away to advertise the next story-hour or book program. Rubber stamps are quite inexpensive and can be used to stamp "Library Program, Wednesday" on the back of the picture. Or use the pictures as souvenirs at a program. Stamp "Thanks for coming to the library" or "Use me as a bookmark" on the card. An almost limitless supply of cards can be acquired around holiday time by letting it be known that you have a use for them.

BOOKTALKS

Collect cards on a single subject, for instance, cats or the circus, and use the cards to hold the text of your booktalks. Quotes from the books you wish to promote can be pasted inside the cards so that the audience will be looking at something interesting while you talk about the books. Display the cards with the books at the end of your talk.

PROJECTS

Collect cards with a theme: rabbits, mice, autumn. Glue the picture from the card on a larger piece of poster board. Type a card to go underneath the picture with the name of the author, the title, and an annotation of a thematically related book. Add projects, such as the film can game (see page 299), that children can do in unstructured time.

CHILDREN'S ART ON GREETING CARDS

Janice Jensen, a first-grade teacher, uses library books to teach reading. Her children draw pictures illustrating the books they have read, and Janice duplicates them on colored paper, buys envelopes, and sells them at cost to the children's parents. Who wouldn't want to send cards with their own children's art?

TISSUE BOX DÉCOUPAGE

A handy tissue box to keep at home, at school, or in the library can be decorated to remind you of a favorite book.

YOU NEED: a precut wooden boutique tissue box (available at a hobby shop, or write Heirloom Wood Products, Boxwood Lane, R.D. #9, York, PA)
acrylic paint
pictures cut from books or original art
scissors
craft glue
Varathane varnish, acrylic finish, or other protective coating

HOW TO: Paint the box in any color and let dry.
Cut pictures to fit box.
Glue pictures to box
Cover pictures with Varathane varnish or other finish.

HINTS: To glue small pieces without tearing them, cover the picture with wax paper and use a roller or pencil to smooth out corners. Acrylic paints and finishes are water-soluble and they dry very quickly, for a one-day project.

BOOKLIST

Books for those who would like a "good old-fashioned cry." Keep your tissue box within reach. (These books are for the middle grades.)

Alcott, Louisa May. *Little Women.* il. by Barbara Cooney. Crowell, 1955.
A warmhearted account of a family of girls. Beth's death is a memorable chapter for all who read this book.

Hunt, Irene. *The Lottery Rose.* Scribner, 1976.
Georgie is an abused child who finds a new life. Be sure to have a full box of tissues at your side.

Lowry, Lois. *A Summer to Die.* il. by Jenni Oliver. Houghton, 1977.
Meg is envious of her pretty and popular sister, Molly, until Molly becomes ill.

Magorian, Michelle. *Good Night, Mr. Tom.* Harper, 1982.
An English World War II evacuée finds a home with an old man.

Paterson, Katherine. *Bridge to Terabithia.* il. by Donna Diamond. Crowell, 1977.
Leslie shows Jess a fantasy world, but then an accident changes Jess's outlook.

Rawls, Wilson. *Where the Red Fern Grows; the Story of Two Dogs and a Boy.* Doubleday, 1961.
Billy trains Old Dan and Little Ann to be fine hunting dogs.

Ross, G. Max. *When Lucy Went Away.* il. by Ingrid Fetz. Dutton, 1976.
No one knows where Lucy, the family cat, has gone.

Sewell, Anna. *Black Beauty.* il. by John Groth. Macmillan Pub. Co., 1962.
First published in 1877, this classic horse story has been bringing tears and joy to generations of readers.

ANIMAL CRACKER PINS

Here is an animal pin that is quick to make.

YOU NEED: animal crackers
clear varnish or acrylic finish
pin backs
craft glue
paintbrush

HOW TO: Paint both sides of the animal crackers with the finish and let dry.
Affix pin with craft glue.

HINT: Several coats of varnish will give a smoother finish to the pin.

ACTIVITIES

1. After the pins have been made, each child must find a book in the book display or library shelves featuring the animal on his or her pin.

2. Each child finds and reads aloud an animal poem.

3. Each child imitates his or her animal.

4. Have a zoo storyhour, and then make the pins.

BOOKLIST

Animal books to use on exhibit, to share, or to search for animal poetry.

309

ANIMAL PICTURE BOOKS:

Adizzone, Edward. *Diana and Her Rhinoceros.* il. by author. Walck, 1964.
A little girl befriends a rhinoceros with a terrible cold.

Barrett, Judi. *Animals Should Definitely Not Wear Clothing.* il. by Ron Barrett. Atheneum Pubs., 1970.
Each animal is shown looking silly in clothing.

Hutchins, Pat. *1 Hunter.* il. by author. Greenwillow Bks., 1982.
Colorful animals are stalked by an unsuccessful hunter.

Jeschke, Susan. *Angela and Bear.* il. by author. Holt, 1979.
Angela draws a picture of a bear and the bear walks off the page to become a companion.

Noble, Trinka Hakes. *The Day Jimmy's Boa Ate the Wash.* il. by Steven Kellogg. Dial Press, 1980.
Funny story about a class field trip gone awry.

Rice, Eve. *Sam Who Never Forgets.* il. by author. Greenwillow Bks., 1977.
Has Sam, the zookeeper, forgotten to feed the elephant?

Spier, Peter. *Gobble, Growl, Grunt.* il. by author. Doubleday, 1971.
An animal picture and sound dictionary in picture-book form.

Wegen, Ron. *Where Can the Animals Go?* il. by author. Greenwillow Bks., 1978.
Shows wild animals in conflict with civilization. Excellent introduction to a Save-the-Animals plea.

Wildsmith, Brian. *Wild Animals.* il. by author. Oxford, 1979.
Full-color animal portraits.

ANIMAL POETRY:

Cole, William, comp. *An Arkful of Animals.* il. by Lynn Munsinger. Houghton, 1978.

Cole, William, comp. *I Went to the Animal Fair; a Book of Animal Poems.* il. by Colette Rosselli. Collins [distributed by Philomel Bks.], 1958.

Eichenberg, Fritz. *Ape in a Cape; An Alphabet of Odd Animals.* Harcourt, 1952.

Kuskin, Karla. *Roar and More.* Harper, 1956.

Yolen, Jane. *All in the Woodland Early: An ABC Book.* il. by Jane Breskin Zalben. Collins, 1979.

Yolen, Jane. *How Beastly! A Menagerie of Nonsense Poems.* il. by James Marshall. Collins, 1980.

BOOK BANKS

This is a bank to help save money to buy books.

YOU NEED: an empty tennis-ball can or other reusable can with a plastic lid
book jackets or original art
rubber cement
clear varnish or acrylic finish, or other protective coating
a knife

HOW TO: Glue the jacket or picture to the can.
Cover the picture with protective finish.
Cut a coin-size slit in the plastic cover.

HINTS: If you don't have a tennis-playing friend who will save empty cans for you, ask the local tennis club or public court pro to save some.

ACTIVITIES— EARNING MONEY TO BUY BOOKS

You can find a book to read on almost any subject at the library. Sometimes, however, it's nice to own a book so you can reread it at your leisure. These days you can find many titles in paperback. Ask your bookseller to order your favorites. Meanwhile, here are a few ideas to earn a little money to pay for them. Pin this list on the bulletin board.

1. Address Christmas cards for families with long lists.
2. Clean carrots and celery and sell them to dieters for snacks.
3. Wash dogs.
4. Wrap Christmas presents.
5. Babysit.
6. Plant-sit.
7. Mow lawns.
8. Dog-sit.
9. Repaint outdoor furniture.
10. Wash cars or just whitewall tires.
11. Retrieve tennis balls for players at the local tennis court for a small fee.
12. Polish shoes or boots.
13. Clean and polish saddles and bridles for horse owners.
14. Rake leaves.
15. Shovel snow.
16. Clean the gutters.
17. Clean a garage.
18. Wash windows.
19. Collect and return bottles.

20. Build a tree house for a family.
21. Decorate a rural mailbox.
22. Clip pictures from magazines and greeting cards to sell to people who do découpage.
23. Telephone-sit for someone who is expecting a call.
24. Paint house numbers.
25. Provide decorations, bake a cake, organize games, and/or tell stories at birthday parties.
26. Plant a garden; sell the produce.
27. Wear a sandwich board to advertise the goods or services of a local business.
28. Bake cookies or snacks to sell to nondieters.
29. Decorate an outdoor trashcan for a business.
30. Make greeting cards.
31. Perform magic tricks at parties.
32. Develop film.
33. Find something, anything, that others don't like to do and do it.

HINTS: Suggest that each person in your class or group buy one book. Then exchange books with each other.

Always explain to your prospective employers that you need the money to buy books. They will be more receptive to giving you work.

Don't always charge for your services. Sometimes people will give you a book for your generosity.

Write an essay telling how you would earn money to put in the bank. Make a list of books to buy with money from the bank.

BOOKLIST

Books that feature money.

Aleichem, Sholem. *Hanukah Money.* tr. and adapted by Uri Shulevitz and Elizabeth Shub. il. by Uri Shulevitz. Greenwillow Bks., 1978.
Matt and his brother prepare for Hanukah in a picture story.

Allan, Ted. *Willie the Squowse.* il. by Quentin Blake. Hastings House, 1978.
Willie lives in a hole in a wall and changes the lives of two families.

Amazing Life Games Company. *Good Cents: Every Kids' Guide to Making Money.* il. by Martha Hairston and James Robertson. Houghton, 1974.
A compilation of ideas for children on how to earn money.

313

Asch, Frank. *Good Lemonade.* il. by Marie Zimmerman. Watts, 1976.
Advertising doesn't always work. Picture book.

Bates, Betty. *My Mom, the Money Nut.* Holiday House, 1979.
Mom isn't interested in anything except money.

Brittain, Bill. *All the Money in the World.* il. by Charles Robinson. Harper, 1979.
Quentin's wish for all the money in the world comes true.

Bulla, Clyde Robert. *Shoeshine Girl.* il. by Leigh Grant. Crowell, 1975.
Having to take a little responsibility turns out to be worthwhile after all.

Cleary, Beverly. *Ramona and Her Father.* il. by Alan Tiegreen. Morrow, 1978.
Ramona thinks up money-making schemes to help the family.

Fodor, R. V. *Nickels, Dimes, and Dollars: How Currency Works.* Morrow, 1980.
A brief overview of our monetary system.

James, Elizabeth and Carol Barkin. *How to Grow a Hundred Dollars.* il. by Joel Schick. Lothrop, 1979.
A true story about Amy's business venture, in narrative.

Lipsyte, Robert. *Summer Rules.* Harper, 1981.
Bobby Marks spends the summer at Happy Valley Day Camp as a junior counselor.

Merrill, Jean. *The Toothpaste Millionaire.* il. by Jan Palmer. Houghton, 1974.
Twelve-year-old Rufus and his friend Kate become millionaires by selling toothpaste.

Morgan, Tom. *Money, Money, Money: How to Get and Keep It.* il. by Joe Ciardiello. Putnam, 1978.
Money management through examples.

Pinkwater, Daniel M. *The Last Guru.* Dodd, 1978.
Harold Blatz, age 14, is the third richest person in the entire world.

Seuling, Barbara. *You Can't Count a Billion Dollars & Other Little Known Facts About Money.* il. by author. Doubleday, 1979.
A book of trivia about money. Good for introducing a money program.

GAME

Allowance Game. Milton Bradley, Springfield, MA 01101.
"Learn how to handle money" board game.

GOODNIGHT SHADE

Decorate a lampshade with a picture from your favorite book. Use the lamp in a child's room at home or in the reading corner of your classroom or library.

A window shade decorated in the same manner can be used in a child's room or as a roll-up exhibit.

YOU NEED: a plain white lampshade or window shade
a favorite picture book
tracing paper or some other translucent paper
water-base paints or nonpermanent-ink felt-tip pens
scissors
glue

Translucent paper and water-base colors work well because the light will shine through the picture and make it glow.

HOW TO: Trace or draw a picture of a book character or scene on translucent paper. Cut around the picture and glue it on the shade. Alternatively, you can paint directly on the shade with acrylic paints or felt-tip pens. (The latter method is best for the window shade project.)

HINTS: If you save the original plastic cover that the lampshade was packed in, it will help hold and protect the picture.

BOOKLIST

Goodnight books for the preschool or primary-grade child.

Brown, Margaret Wise. *Goodnight Moon.* il. by Clement Hurd. Harper, 1947.
A sleepy bunny says goodnight to all the objects in the room.

Coatsworth, Elizabeth. *Good Night.* il. by Jose Aruego. Macmillan Pub. Co., 1972.
A star watches a little boy secretly take a kitten to bed.

Dabcovich, Lydia. *Sleepy Bear.* il. by author. Dutton, 1982.
Short text; splashy pictures show a bear going to sleep for the winter.

315

Funazaki, Yasuko. *Baby Owl.* il. by Shuji Tateishi. Methuen, 1980.
A little owl looks for playmates in the night woods. Large format, black and white drawings and a short text.

Goffstein, M. B. *Sleepy People.* il. by author. Farrar, Straus, 1966.
A land of sleepy people who may inhabit your own bedroom slipper. The tiny size prohibits use with a large group, but is perfect for one, two, or three children.

Hoban, Russell. *Bedtime for Frances.* il. by Garth Williams. Harper, 1960.
Frances finds ingenious ways of stalling at bedtime.

Hush Little Baby: A Folk Lullaby. il. by Aliki. Prentice-Hall, 1968.
A gentle picture-book version of a folk song with a colonial setting.

Hutchins, Pat. *Good-Night Owl!* il. by author. Macmillan Pub. Co., 1972.
Owl is kept awake by noisy birds, animals, and insects. He gets his revenge at night, when everyone else is trying to sleep.

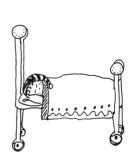

Kraus, Robert. *Night-Lite Storybook.* il. by N. M. Bodecker. Windmill Bks., 1975.
One-page stories to read aloud.

Marzollo, Jean. *Close Your Eyes.* il. by Susan Jeffers. Dial Press, 1978.
A lavishly illustrated lullaby.

Massie, Diane Redfield. *The Baby Beebee Bird.* il. by author. Harper, 1963.
The new Beebee bird keeps all the zoo animals awake while he dances and sings. Works well with a puppet.

Mayer, Mercer. *There's a Nightmare in My Closet.* il. by author. Dial Press, 1968.
A little boy invites his nightmare to bed. All ages.

Murphy, Jill. *Peace at Last.* il. by author. Dial Press, 1980.
Papa Bear finds it impossible to sleep when his family and nightime noises keep him awake.

Rice, Eve. *Goodnight, Goodnight.* il. by author. Greenwillow Bks., 1980.
Everyone is saying "goodnight goodnight."

Rukeyser, Muriel. *More Night.* il. by Symeon Shimin. Harper, 1981.
Jacob's grandmother describes night in a poetic picture book.

Ryan, Cheli D. *Hildilid's Night.* il. by Arnold Lobel. Macmillan Pub. Co., 1971.
Hildilid tries everything she can think of to get rid of the night.

Segal, Joyce. *It's Time To Go To Bed.* il. by Robin Eaton. Doubleday, 1979.
Animals are pictured giving the usual "I don't want to go to bed" excuses.

Waber, Bernard. *Ira Sleeps Over.* il. by author. Houghton, 1972.
Ira can't decide if he should take his teddy bear to Reggie's house.

Watson, Clyde. *Midnight Moon.* il. by Susanna Natti. Collins, 1979.
A poem revealing the secrets of the night. Small size picturebook.

Zalben, Jane Breskin. *Norton's Nightime.* il. by author. Collins, 1979.
Norton, the raccoon, is afraid of the dark.

Zemach, Margot. *Hush Little Baby.* il. by author. Dutton, 1976.
A broadly humorous interpretation of a lullaby.

PLACEMATS

Liven up the dinner table with placemats featuring books. (And consider a poetry dinner, as described on page 236.)

YOU NEED: Pictures cut from discarded books, original art, book jackets, posters featuring books, or covers cut from book catalogs.
Clear contact paper and dry-mount press are optional.

HOW TO: Draw or cut out a book design. Seal the picture in plastic with contact paper or a dry-mount press.

HINT: Clear plastic placemats designed as envelopes to hold pictures can be ordered from: Matmaker Corporation
2031 Winding Brook Way
Westfield, NJ 07090

BOOKLIST These books feature food or eating. Share one aloud before you do this as a group project.

PICTURE BOOKS: **Barrett, Judi.** *Cloudy with a Chance of Meatballs.* il. by Ron Barrett. Atheneum, 1978.
In the town of Chewandswallow it rains food.

317

Carle, Eric. *The Very Hungry Caterpillar.* il. by author. Collins [distributed by Philomel Bks.], 1970.
A caterpillar eats through a week of food.

Heller, Linda. *Lily at the Table.* il. by author. Macmillan Pub. Co., 1979.
Lily imagines herself the same size as the food on her plate in a wordless picture book.

Kent, Jack. *The Fat Cat; a Danish Folktale.* tr. and il. by author. Parents Mag. Press, 1971.
A greedy cat eats a variety of people and animals until a woodcutter outwits it.

Marshall, James. *Yummers!* il. by author. Houghton, 1973.
Emily Pig takes a walk to lose some weight and eats herself into a tummy-ache.

Paterson, Diane. *Eat!* il. by author. Dial Press, 1977.
When Martha's pet frog refuses to eat, she finds herself acting just like her exasperated parents.

Peck, Robert Newton. *Hamilton.* il. by Laura Lydecker. Little, 1976.
"The fatter he grew, the more Hamilton ate. Fat was his future. Fat was his fate."

Wallner, Alexandra. *Munch: Poems and Pictures.* il. by author. Crown, 1976.
Eating and snacking are the subjects of a collection of happy poems.

Watanabe, Shigeo. *What a Good Lunch!* il. by Yasuo Ohtomo. Collins, 1980.
Little bear learns to eat properly.

Yaffe, Alan. *The Magic Meatballs.* il. by Karen Born Anderson. Dial Press, 1979.
Marvin's parents change into roast beef and chicken after ignoring his warning.

LONGER BOOKS:

Catling, Patrick Skene. *The Chocolate Touch.* il. by Margot Apple. Morrow, 1979.
Everything that John touches turns to chocolate.

Hurwitz, Johanna. *Much Ado About Aldo.* il. by John Wallner. Morrow, 1978.
Aldo becomes a vegetarian after watching an experiment in school.

SWITCHPLATE

Every time you turn on the light, think of a book.

YOU NEED: a switchplate (available from a hardware store, or remove an existing one in your home)
acrylic, watercolor, or tempera paint
clear varnish or acrylic finish

318

HOW TO: Paint a picture of a book character or scene from a book or story on the switchplate.
Cover the design with a protective coating.

HINTS: If possible, try to incorporate the switch into your design. Remember to paint the heads of the screws that will hold the plate to the wall. The switchplate can also be decorated by the découpage process (see page 308).

BOOKLIST (MIDDLE GRADES): IN THE DARK

Any favorite book character can be used to decorate a switchplate, but keep in mind some of these books that explore dark places: caves, tombs, and underground caverns. Wouldn't children be delighted to be able to turn on the light with a homemade light switch?

Babbitt, Natalie. *Goody Hall.* il. by author. Farrar, Straus, 1971.
A night visitor to a tomb is part of a delightful melodrama.

Baumann, Hans. *The Caves of the Great Hunters.* il. with photographs. Pantheon Bks., 1962.
The true story of the discovery of prehistoric cave paintings in France.

Budney, Blossom. *After Dark.* il. by Tony Chen. Lothrop, 1975.
The sights and sounds of the night (picture book).

Dickinson, Peter. *Annerton Pit.* Little, 1977.
Martin and his brother Jake, who is blind, are trapped in an abandoned mine with their ghost-hunting grandfather.

Eldridge, Roger. *The Shadow of the Gloom-World.* Dutton, 1978.
Fernfeather, living underground, finds that it takes courage to be different.

Glubok, Shirley. *Discovering Tut-Ankh-Amen's Tomb.* illustrated. Macmillan Pub. Co., 1968.
A step-by-step account of the discovery of treasures in an ancient Egyptian tomb.

Hoover, H. M. *This Time of Darkness.* Viking, 1980.
Two children who have spent their whole lives inside the giant city complex explore outside.

319

Household, Geoffrey. *Escape into Daylight.* Little, 1976.
Kidnapped and held for ransom in a windowless dungeon, Mike and Carrie try to escape.

LeGuin, Ursula. *The Tombs of Atuan.* il. by Gail Garraty. Atheneum Pubs., 1971.
Arha must choose between a life of darkness in an endless labyrinth and a world unknown to her.

Pope, Elizabeth. *The Perilous Gard.* il. by Richard Cuffari. Houghton, 1974.
Kate Sutton is captured by fairy folk and forced to live underground.

Snyder, Zilpha Keatley. *Below the Root.* il. by Alton Raible. Atheneum Pubs., 1975, and *And All Between.* Atheneum Pubs., 1976.
Two communities—one that lives in the trees of Greensky, and one that lives underground in Erda—must learn to live together.

Steele, Mary Q. *Journey Outside.* il. by Rocco Negri. Viking, 1969.
An underground river and a search for a world outside make mysterious reading.

Twain, Mark. *The Adventures of Tom Sawyer.* il. by C. Walter Hodges. Dent, n.d.
Becky and Tom are lost in a cave in one adventure in this American classic.

JIGSAW PUZZLE

Make these puzzles to stimulate interest in a particular book or as an activity before or after booktime.

METHOD A

YOU NEED: a book jacket or picture
posterboard or cardboard of the same size
rubber cement
an X-acto knife, scissors, or jigsaw, depending on the thickness of cardboard
spray varnish

HOW TO: Glue picture onto cardboard.
Trim cardboard to fit picture.
Cover picture with spray varnish and let dry.
Cut puzzle shapes from picture with X-acto knife, scissors or jigsaw.
Store the puzzle in its own envelope or box.

METHOD B

YOU NEED: a picture or book jacket
¼″ plywood
rubber cement or white glue
a jigsaw
sandpaper

HOW TO: Cut plywood to fit picture or book jacket
Glue picture to plywood.
Cover picture with spray varnish and let dry.
Cut jigsaw puzzle pieces using jigsaw.
Smooth the edges of the puzzle pieces with sandpaper

HINTS: If you have access to a dry-mount press, you can laminate the picture instead of using varnish.
Children can draw their own pictures for the puzzles.
The older the children, the more complicated you will want to make the puzzles.

USE: If you will be using the same book to read aloud, let one or two children work the puzzle before booktime begins. If you have more than one puzzle, let all the children work them together. The first, or last, puzzle done represents the book you will read.

BOOKLIST: MYSTERIES

Solving a mystery is like doing a jigsaw puzzle in your head.

Arthur, Robert. *Mystery and More Mystery.* il. by Saul Lambert. Random House, 1966.
Ten stories originally published in *Ellery Queen's Mystery Magazine.*

Baudouy, Michel Aimé. *Secret of the Hidden Painting.* tr. by Anne Carter. Harcourt, 1965.
Stolen paintings and a gamecock are two puzzles that intrigue Parisian children spending a summer on the coast of Brittany.

Bennett, Jay. *Say Hello to the Hit Man.* Delacorte Press, 1976.
Who would want to kill Fred?

Bonham, Frank. *Mystery of the Fat Cat.* il. by Alvin Smith. Dutton, 1968.
A large tomcat is enjoying the wealthy estate that seems rightfully to belong to the Dogtown Boys' Club.

Carle, Eric. *The Secret Birthday Message.* il. by the author. Crowell, 1972.
A code is followed to find the surprise.

Corbett, Scott. *The Cave Above Delphi.* il. by Gioia Fiammenghi. Holt, 1965.
Mountain climbing, a cave, and a museum are elements in one of Corbett's exciting mysteries.

Garfield, Leon. *Mister Corbett's Ghost.* il. by Alan E. Cober. Pantheon Bks., 1968.
An old-fashioned ghost story.

George, Jean Craighead. *Who Really Killed Cock Robin? An Ecological Mystery.* Dutton, 1971.
A robin's sudden death causes alarm in a town dedicated to clean environment.

Hitchcock, Alfred, ed. *Alfred Hitchcock's Sinister Spies.* il. by Paul Spina. Random House, 1966.
Short stories chosen by the master of suspense.

Hutchins, Pat. *The Mona Lisa Mystery.* il. by Laurence Hutchins. Greenwillow Bks., 1981.
A slapstick mystery.

Newman, Robert. *The Case of the Baker Street Irregular.* Atheneum Pubs., 1978.
Sherlock Holmes–style mystery.

Peyton, K. M. *A Midsummer Night's Death.* Collins, 1978.
Jonathan Meredith wonders about the "suicide" of a teacher.

Raskin, Ellen. *The Mysterious Disappearance of Leon (I Mean Noel).* Dutton, 1971.
A wacky mystery involving Caroline Carillon's search for her husband Leon (Noel).

Raskin, Ellen. *The Westing Game,* Dutton, 1978.
Sixteen people are invited to unravel Samuel Westing's will.

Robertson, Keith. *The Money Machine.* il. by George Porter. Viking, 1969.
The proprietors of the Carson Street Detective Agency attempt to uncover a counterfeiting ring.

Sobol, Donald J. *Encyclopedia Brown, Boy Detective.* Elsevier/Nelson Bks., 1963.
The reader gets a chance to solve these mysteries along with Leroy Brown.

Stevenson, Robert Louis. *The Strange Case of Dr. Jekyll and Mr. Hyde.* Dodd, 1961.
The classic story of a doctor turned monster.

Wells, Rosemary. *When No One Was Looking.* Dial, 1980.
A mystery with a tennis-tournament setting.

Westall, Robert. *The Watch House.* Greenwillow Bks., 1978.
Anne feels the watch house is watching her!

PENDANTS

Wear a pendant to symbolize your favorite book or fictional character.

YOU NEED: sheets of shrink art plastic (available in hobby shops)
permanent-ink felt-tip pens
a paper hole punch
an oven with a window

HOW TO: Trace a picture from a book on the plastic, or draw your own design to advertise your favorite book. Cut around the design to shape your pendant.
Make a hole in the pendant with a paper punch, so that a chain or string can go through it.
Place your piece on a Teflon cookie sheet or a piece of aluminum foil. Bake in a pre-heated 350–400° oven.
Watch through the window as the magic takes place. Your design will curl up and shrink to a third of its original size, so make sure to start out with a large design.

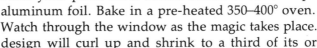

323

As soon as it is flat, remove the pendant with a spatula and let it cool on a flat surface.

HINTS: Shrink art plastic can be obtained from Artis, Inc., 9123 E. Las Turas Drive, Temple City, CA 91780 or from your local hobby shop. You can also use "liver lids," which can usually be obtained in quantity from your local butcher at a nominal cost. Clear plastic cups will also work.

Sometimes while the design is in the oven, it curls up so that the ends stick together. You can reach into the oven and pry the ends apart gently. The oven process takes less than a minute, so don't go off to read a book.

This activity is perfect to do while you are preparing a meal. While the soup is heating, make a pendant.

USE: Use shrink art to make necklace pendants, holiday decorations, pins, place cards, signs, or parts of a mobile.

BOOKLIST

In these books for the intermediate grades, symbols are an important part of the story.

Bosse, Malcolm J. *Ganesh.* Crowell, 1981.
Jeffrey is called after an Indian elephant-headed god in a story about an American boy in India and America.

Cooper, Susan. The Dark Is Rising sequence: *Over Sea, Under Stone,* Harcourt, 1966; *The Dark Is Rising,* Atheneum Pubs., 1973; *Greenwitch,* Atheneum Pubs., 1974; *The Grey King,* Atheneum Pubs., 1975; *Silver on the Tree,* Atheneum Pubs., 1976.
A series of five fantasies filled with the signs and symbols of the Old Ones.

Eager, Edward. *Half Magic.* il. by N. M. Bodecker. Harcourt, 1954.
A coin turns out to be an ancient talisman filled with magic.

Garner, Alan. *The Owl Service.* Collins [distributed by Philomel Bks.] 1979.
Strange patterned plates are the center of strange happenings.

Hurwitz, Johanna. *Once I Was A Plum Tree.* il. by Ingrid Fetz. Morrow, 1980.
The Jewish Star of David is important in this story.

Twain, Mark. *The Prince and the Pauper.* il. by Robert Hodgson. Dutton, 1968.
The king's seal becomes the key to a mystery of identification.

CROCHET BOOKWORM

Use the bookworm as a reading prize, a bookmark, or a favor at a party or a program of stories about worms or caterpillars.

METHOD A
by Nonie Borba

YOU NEED: knitting worsted
a crochet hook
craft eyes
a 2″ pipe cleaner

HOW TO: Leaving a 2″ piece of yarn (to attach bow), chain 75 stitches.
Double-crochet *twice in same stitch*. Continue until 8″ of chain stitch remain. The double crochet is the head; the chain is the tail.
End with two slip stitches.
Measure 12″ of yarn for bow on end of tail.
Tie bow on tail; glue eyes on head.
Insert pipe cleaner for antennae.
Twist your worm.

METHOD B

YOU NEED: a 5″ length of velvet ribbon
craft eyes
felt material

HOW TO: Cut out a round head from the felt material and glue on craft eyes and a felt mouth. Glue the head onto the ribbon.
This is a particularly good worm to make when you need a large number.

BOOKLIST

PRIMARY: **Carle, Eric.** *The Very Hungry Caterpillar.* il. by author. Collins [distributed by Philomel Bks.], 1970.
The enormous appetite of a caterpillar makes a delightful picturebook story.

Lionni, Leo. *Inch by Inch.* il. by author. Obolensky, 1962.
A clever inchworm measures his way out of a scrape.

O'Hagan, Caroline. *It's Easy to Have a Worm Visit You.* il. by Judith Allan. Lothrop, 1980.
Short introduction to worms.

325

INTERMEDIATE: **Ahlberg, Janet and Allan Ahlberg.** *The Little Worm Book.* Viking, 1980.
Original worm jokes in a small picture book.

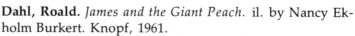

Carroll, Lewis. *Alice's Adventures in Wonderland.* il. by John Tenniel. Watts, 1964.
An intelligent caterpillar is a leading character in this classic.

Dahl, Roald. *James and the Giant Peach.* il. by Nancy Ekholm Burkert. Knopf, 1961.
An earthworm and a silkworm accompany James on a journey in a giant peach.

Darling, Lois and Louis Darling. *Worms.* il. by authors. Morrow, 1972.
A nonfiction introduction to worms.

Pinkwater, Daniel. *The Worms of Kukumlima.* Dutton, 1981.
A search in remote Africa for an intelligent earthworm who plays chess.

Rockwell, Thomas. *How to Eat Fried Worms.* il. by Emily McCully. Watts, 1973.
A bet forces Billy to eat fifteen worms in fifteen days. See also *How To Eat Fried Worms and Other Plays.* il. by Joel Schick. Delacorte Press, 1980.

BOOK CRAFT PROJECTS

A few quick crafts for your group to try.

BOOK PLATES

EX-LIBRIS

To identify books at home, it's nice to have book plates that have been created especially for you. These make nice gifts as well. Ask your local printer for gummed stock. Or use drawing paper or wallpaper and glue your own.

I still think EX LIBRIS (from the library of) should be on the bookplate with the owner's name but, of course, there are no rules.

EASY PRINTING TECHNIQUES:

Use tempera paint in a glass casserole. Dip one of the following into the paint and print on the book plate.

1. Cardboard or poster board designs cut out and glued onto a piece of cardboard so that a raised pattern is created.
2. Poster board designs glued on a rubber roller or a cardboard tube to make a continuous design.

3. Objects glued on cardboard: pipecleaners, leaves, buttons, pennies. Print directly from the objects.
4. A halved potato with a design cut in it.

BOOK JACKETS

The shelves of your library have many books that have lost their paper and plastic jackets. Put your book club to work. Let each child choose a book without a jacket, *read it,* and design a jacket for it.

The jackets should include the name of the author, the title, and a relevant picture or design. Suggest that the jackets have a summary of the book and a note about the author on the flap.

Use shelf paper or drawing paper. If you are pleased with the results, you will want to invest in plastic covers to keep the artistic efforts protected. Watch your circulation rise with the new look to your books.

BOOKMARKS

Bookmarks range from plain to fancy, but as far as I'm concerned, no one has figured out a way for the bookmark to be near at hand when you need it. (I may not be typical, however.) Maybe you could put bookmarks all over the house or the library where people usually read; when not in use, they make good decorations. Or put them in a can or jar (decorated with a book theme, of course) right with the books on the shelf.

FLOWER BOOKMARKS:

Press early spring flowers. An easy way is simply to place the flowers in a large book between two sheets of paper and replace it on the shelf. In a week your flowers are ready to use. Place the flowers between two sheets of clear contact paper. Trim to bookmark size. These are attractive enough to give as gifts, too.

BOOKBAGS

Plastic garbage bags make sturdy protective bags in which to transport books in bad weather. Decorate with fabric scraps held on by white glue.

CALENDAR

Make a calendar with one page for each month.

Choose twelve of your favorite books. For each month of the year, draw a picture to represent one of the books. Or, if you have a favorite book, decorate the calendar with pictures and quotes from just this one book. Use quotes from the book or books to decorate the pages.

327

If you are not artistic, you can use pictures from a discarded book or from a paperback edition, or you can trace pictures using an overhead projector and then color them in.

MURAL

Hang a piece of wrapping paper or newsprint around the room. Read, or better still, tell a story. Let the children suggest scenes from the story and put them in order. Mark off a portion of the mural for each scene. Divide the group into smaller groups or assign each person one scene of the story to illustrate. Provide crayons and/or paint for the mural. (Be sure to place newspaper on the floor to catch the paint drippings.)

SHIELDS

Design your own or your family's "a morial bearings." These are the figures, shapes, and colors that were carried on banners and shields or used as decoration during the Middle Ages.

REFERENCE: **Uden, Grant.** *A Dictionary of Chivalry.* il. by Pauline Baynes. Longmans, 1968.

JOLLY ROGER

Create your own Jolly Roger. This was the flag flown on pirate ships.

REFERENCES: **Cochran, Hamilton and Robert I. Nesmith.** *Pirates of the Spanish Main.* American Heritage, 1961.

Pyle, Howard. *Book of Pirates.* Harper, 1921.

VII. EXHIBITS

Exhibits and bulletin boards are great ways to publicize the library and its resources and programs. An imaginative display with a coherent theme will stimulate interest, where a hodge-podge is likely to evoke a "so what?" reaction. (Our local supermarket has so many signs plastered over its plate glass windows that most shoppers simply ignore them.)

My rules for bulletin boards and exhibits are simple:

1. Every exhibit, even a poster, must have something to do with books.

2. Exhibits should be changed often. Although you can enjoy the same picture in your house for thirty years, the life of an exhibit is about nine days.

3. Any exhibit that takes more than eight minutes to create must be reusable.

4. Placement of exhibits should vary. Don't always use the bulletin board. Try the ceiling, the floor, the door, or the desk tops.

5. Books, the actual physical books, should be available near the exhibit.

MISS BIANCA
by MARGERY SHARP

Miss Bianca again gives up her life of luxury to work for the cause of the Mouse Prisoner's Aid Society in Miss Bianca, sequel to The Rescuers. This time she is to lead the Ladies Guild into the Diamond Palace, treacherous domain of the cruel and heartless Grand Duchess. It is to save the life of eight-year-old Patience that the mice again risk their lives.

CARD A BOOK

Have you read a good book? Type up an intriguing notice on an index card and display it with the book to encourage browsing.

Feeling independent? Read about four who dared to be different. Browse through the book and read some of Muggles's Maxims:

"Trout made into fish cakes is still trout."
"When you say what you think, be sure to think what you say."
"The best thing to do with a bad smell is to get rid of it."

The Gammage Cup, by Carol Kendall. il. by Erik Blegvad. Harcourt, 1959.

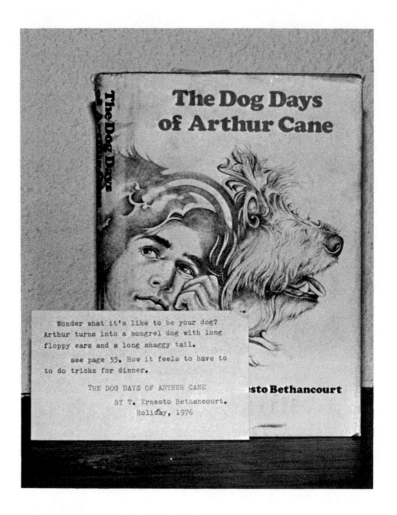

Wonder what it's like to be your dog? Arthur turns into a mongrel with floppy ears and a long, shaggy tail. Check page 35 to see how it feels to have to do tricks for dinner.

The Dog Days of Arthur Cane, by T. Ernesto Bethancourt. Holiday House, 1976.

Bobbie loves to eat. See page 18 for a description of how to enjoy breakfast.

One Fat Summer, by Robert Lipsyte. Harper, 1977.

CHALKBOARD SPECIAL

Hang a small chalkboard near the entrance of the library. Make it part of the daily routine to chalk up TODAY'S SPECIAL. Find the time to place today's books on a nearby table.

> LOVE HORSES?
>
> *My Mane Catches the Wind*
> and
> *The Poetry of Horses*
> (poems about horses)

My Mane Catches the Wind; Poems About Horses, comp. by Lee Bennett Hopkins. il. by Sam Savitt. Harcourt, 1979. *The Poetry of Horses,* comp. by William Cole. Scribner, 1979.

> THE GREAT APES
>
> 200 photographs
> large picture book format
> Browse through and love
> our "nearest kin"

The Great Apes, by Dan Freeman. Putnam, 1979.

> SAVE A RIVER
>
> with 76-year-old Ella and Reetard
>
> LET A RIVER BE!

Let a River Be, by Betty Sue Cummings. Atheneum Pubs., 1978.

CLOTH BULLETIN BOARDS

This is an oft-repeated scenario from my years as a school and public librarian: Get absolutely wonderful idea for bulletin board. Spend hours cutting out paper letters and pictures to go onto board. Put up bulletin board, carefully positioning the letters and pictures. Enjoy exhibit. Take pictures down very carefully, planning to re-use them next year. Store letters and pictures in storage cupboard. Forget the pictures are there and sling filmstrip projector into storage cupboard, ruining paper cutouts.

Now my life has changed—I've discovered fabric. It takes the same time to make a fabric bulletin board as a paper one. I still have to cut out the letters, but now I use a fabric background and attach fabric cut-outs to illustrate the theme. The cut-outs can be appliqués or the iron-on type with invisible webbing. It takes no time at all to put up the bulletin board since everything is already permanently attached to the background. Fabric looks more professional than paper and, best of all, when I've finished using the display, I fold up the cloth and store it for another time. Unfold it and it's ready to go.

THE LOUDSPEAKER—A BULLETIN BOARD FOR THE EARS

I hated the loudspeaker at school. "Attention! Attention! Will all students who ride the bus report to the office immediately. Immediately!"

Don't hate the loudspeaker. Use it. It's like having your very own radio station.

POETRY

Have each child read a poem over the loud-speaker at least once during the school year.

BOOKTALKS

Give oral annotations of new and old books of interest.

BOOK BREAKS

Read a chapter a day over the loudspeaker. Don't forget the "commercials" for the library, reading programs, authors, etc. Invite guests—parents and visiting authors—to read a story or talk about their favorite books.

READING GROWTH CHART

Hilary didn't read at two or two-and-a-half, unlike some of the children of my graduate students. I'd get so jealous. "Can Jeremy *really* read?" I'd ask Karen. "Oh, yes," Karen would say, picking up the newspaper and handing it to her three-year-old. Jeremy could hardly hold up the paper, but in a high voice he would start reading the daily news. At first I just turned green with envy when Hilary refused to even try the "read-alone" and "I-can-read" books.

I stood by gritting my teeth and telling my professional self that she wasn't ready to read. But the Mommy part of me broke down, and toward the end of second grade (see, I *was* patient) I bribed her. "Listen, if you read one of these books I'll give you a prize." We were standing in front of the children's paperback rack in a local bookstore.

It would be lovely to report that Hilary's first full-length book was *Swann's Way* or *The Decline and Fall of the Roman Empire*, but it was *Wednesday Witch*, by Ruth Chew. She read it happily and received her prize. (The Present Closet: If I see something on sale or in a mail order catalog that I think might make a good present someday, I buy it and put it in our Present Closet. When I need a house gift, birthday present, or a prize, there is always something handy.) On this "first book" occasion I found a Class-A present—a Japanese doll—and Hilary was very impressed to discover that reading brought such tangible rewards. Almost immediately she read a Beverly Cleary and got another prize. She was on her way and really didn't need any more outside stimulation.

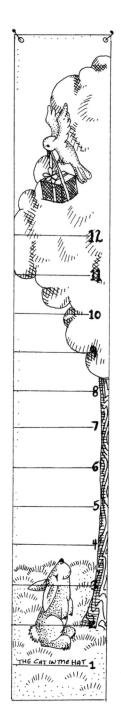

I think it's a pity, though, to bribe children up to a standard and then, when they reach the desired level, to stop giving praise or prizes. I decided to give a prize after Hilary had read ten books. I had been making cloth bulletin boards (see p. 332) and promised that if she read ten books I'd make her one too.

I purchased a child's growth chart in the gift section of a baby shop. Naturally I chose a book character one: *The Cat in the Hat.* Beginning at the bottom of the chart, each time Hilary read a book she wrote down the title. She never did reach the top—or was it that she never got her prize? I don't remember, but in our relaxed, informal, messy, and disorganized household that project never was completed. However, it works fine in a library or classroom. Children can make their own lists on adding machine tape. It's not necessary to require a certain number of books; just tell them to write down books they have read and enjoyed. Exhibit the lists on a classroom wall or in a hallway to encourage other children to read.

Now Hilary reads all the time. And I complain because she refuses to read my particular favorites. Parents are terrible.

PICTURE POCKET SMOCK

Once you've made a pocket smock like the one shown in the photograph, you'll have an instant exhibit that can be changed quickly and that will incidentally protect your clothes. You'll be able to save the money you would have spent on a new shirt and buy books instead.

A smock or an apron can be purchased ready-made at a kitchen or housewares shop, or you can make one yourself. Acetate for the pocket is

available at fabric and housewares stores. The acetate comes on rolls; it is

produced in various weights, so make sure that you purchase stock that is heavy enough to withstand abuse but light enough to be pliable. The letters on the smock in the photograph were printed at the local T-shirt printing shop.

Fill the pocket once or twice daily with a different book or book jacket and presto! you are a walking, talking advertisement for books.

Hint: When stitching on pockets, reinforce the acetate by folding the edges over one quarter inch and stitching them down, before attaching the pocket to the smock. This will give you a double-stitched look and a pocket that will hold more weight.

PICTURE POCKET TOTE

Display a book jacket or book picture on the outside of a tote bag.

YOU NEED: a simply-styled canvas tote
transparent pliable acetate (available at fabric or housewares store)
needle and thread or sewing machine

HOW TO: Stitch a large acetate pocket to the outside of a tote bag.

USE: Use the tote bag to carry your storyhour supplies, including the books to be shown and the artifacts to be exhibited. Use the transparent pocket to display a book jacket, a picture of a book character, or a printed sign announcing the theme of a program.

LITERATURE MAP

My daughter can articulately describe a peninsula or explain longitude and latitude, but she has a difficult time telling me whether Chicago is a city, state, or county.

335

To give children a clearer sense of place, hang a map of the United States or the world in your library or classroom. Every time a child reads a book that is set in an identifiable city or state, he or she can write the book's title on a piece of paper and pin it to the map. (See also Map Games, p. 282. Circles on the literature map in the photograph show the variety of states represented in one library's book collection.)

LAURA INGALLS WILDER LOG CABIN

A good old-fashioned house-raising can be a project for the entire class. The log cabin can be used as the focal point of a pioneer celebration, such as Laura Ingalls Wilder Day or Lincoln's Birthday.

YOU NEED: FOR THE HOUSE FRAME
cardboard for walls and roof
sheet (about 18" x 18") of ¼" plywood for house platform
scissors
Scotch tape

FOR LOGS
a variety of thin pretzels—
approximately   3 bags of pretzel rods about 7" long
1 bag of pretzel sticks
1 bag of pretzel rings
1 bag of pretzel nuggets
1 bag of pretzel TV juniors
a serrated knife

FOR MORTAR
whites of 3 eggs
4½ cups confectioners' sugar
This recipe makes enough mortar to build an 8" x 10" house.

HOW TO: Measure the pretzels and cut out a simple cardboard house to use as the frame.
Lay out the pretzels on the cardboard to make sure they fit.
Trim the logs as necessary with the serrated knife.
Using Scotch tape, put the cardboard frame together. Stand the house frame on the piece of plywood, anchoring it with tape.
When you are ready to build, mix the mortar.
In a large bowl, mix egg whites until smooth. Blend

with 2 cups of confectioners' sugar. Gradually beat in remaining sugar. Cover the icing in the bowl with a damp towel while you work on the cabin.

With a spatula, cover the walls and roof of the house liberally with icing. Press logs firmly into place. Do one side at a time.

Use the remaining mortar to cover the platform (snow).

HINTS: When the mortar is ready, work quickly so that the icing doesn't dry out.

Shop for the pretzels before you begin creating the cardboard frame. The types of pretzels available may determine the architecture of the house.

BOOKLIST (MIDDLE GRADES): AMERICAN HISTORY

Avi. *Night Journeys.* Pantheon Bks., 1979.
Peter protects two runaway indentured servants in colonial Pennsylvania in 1767. A sequel is *Encounter at Easton* (Pantheon, 1980).

Benchley, Nathaniel. *Gone and Back.* Harper, 1971.
Obadiah's father searches for success during the opening of the Oklahoma Territory.

Bond, Nancy. *The Best of Enemies.* Atheneum Pubs., 1978.
A twentieth-century reenactment of the Battle of Concord of the Revolutionary War.

Brink, Carol Ryrie. *Caddie Woodlawn.* il. by Trina Schart Hyman. Macmillan Pub. Co., 1973.
An adventure-loving tomboy grows up in Wisconsin in the 1800s.

Clapp, Patricia. *Constance: A Story of Early Plymouth.* Lothrop, 1968.
A fifteen-year-old girl gives a firsthand account of the settlement in Plymouth.

Fritz, Jean. *The Cabin Faced West.* il. by Feodor Rojankovsky. Coward, McCann & Geoghegan, 1958.
Ann Hamilton faces the Pennsylvania frontier.

Lobel, Arnold. *On the Day Peter Stuyvesant Sailed Into Town.* il. by author. Harper, 1971.
The governor of New Amsterdam makes some changes in the small town of the 1600s that will become New York.

O'Dell, Scott. *Sarah Bishop.* Houghton, 1980.
During the Revolutionary War, fifteen-year-old Sarah sets up housekeeping in a cave in the wilderness.

337

Tunis, Edwin. *Frontier Living.* il. by author. Crowell, 1976.
"Every significant aspect of daily life on the American frontier brought to life in text and more than 200 drawings."

Turkle, Brinton. *The Adventures of Obadiah.* il. by author. Viking, 1972.
A young Quaker boy and his family are introduced in this delightful picture book.

Wilder, Laura Ingalls. *The Little House in the Big Woods.* il. by Garth Williams. Harper, 1953.
The first in a series of the author's own pioneer childhood.

ARTIFACTS

Souvenirs, a slide set, quilt patterns, dolls, and recipes relating to Laura Ingalls Wilder are available from the Laura Ingalls Wilder Home and Museum, Mansfield, MO 65704.

"AUSTRALIA"

Design an "Australia" for your classroom or library. In Judith Viorst's *Alexander and the Terrible, Horrible, No Good, Very Bad Day* (il. by Ray Cruz. Atheneum Pubs., 1972) the boy who is having the bad day keeps threatening to go to Australia.

Make a corner of your room (or a giant carton) into a place where children can go to think, read, and have a little private time. Hang a sign over the corner: AUSTRALIA.

PET ROCK HOUSE

Try to capitalize on successes in the commercial world by incorporating their themes into book programs. Remember the "pet rock"? A clever manufacturer sold millions of cardboard boxes containing plain old ordinary rocks. Packaged with the rock was a booklet for training the rock. It told how to teach your rock to sit, lie down, stay, and behave like a good-mannered pet.

Now, you might ask, what does this have to do with children's books? Well, you can find your own pet rock. Use reference books in the library to identify your rock. Then create a home for it and place it on exhibit with books about rocks and stones.

YOU NEED: a cardboard box
(This is a good way to get rid of all those shoeboxes, cottage cheese containers, and jewelry boxes that you've been saving because you are sure that someday they'll be useful art materials.)
a rock

HOW TO: Simply use your own ingenuity to create a hut or a palace for your pet. (I got really carried away with this and had a friend make a wooden house for my pet rock.)

HINTS: The pet rock can be an inspiration to potential poets and novelists.

He or she or it (the rock) can dictate a letter or write an autobiography.
Pet rocks and magic pebbles love to give interviews to school news magazines.

BOOKLIST

Books to use with the pet rock.

Baylor, Byrd. *Everybody Needs a Rock.* il. by Peter Parnall. Scribner, 1974.
Ten rules for finding a friend.

Brown, Marcia. *Stone Soup; An Old Tale.* il. by author. Scribner, 1947.
Three soldiers make soup using stones (picture book).

Epstein, Anne Merrick. *Good Stones.* il. by Susan Meddaugh. Houghton, 1977.
"That's my stone. When I die, I go into that stone."

Gackenbach, Dick. *McGoogan Moves the Mighty Rock.* il. by author. Harper, 1981.
A Master Guitar Player and Singer of Songs befriends a talking rock. Charming story to tell or read aloud.

George, Jean Craighead. *All Upon a Stone.* il. by Don Bolognese. Crowell, 1971.
Journey of an insect (picture book).

339

Kooiker, Leonie. *The Magic Stone.* tr. from the Dutch by Richard and Clare Winston. il. by Carl Hollander. Morrow, 1978.
Chris finds the magic stone in Frank's grandmother's wheelchair and learns that magic is not all fun.

Meyer, Carolyn and Jerome Wexler. *Rock Tumbling: From Stones to Gems to Jewelry.* photographs by Jerome Wexler. Morrow, 1975.
Making something out of an ordinary stone.

Steig, William. *Sylvester and the Magic Pebble.* il. by author. Windmill Bks. [distributed by Simon & Schuster], 1969.
A donkey turns into a rock in this amusing picture book.

Simon, Seymour. *The Rock-Hound's Book.* il. by Tony Chen. Viking, 1973.
Rock collecting.

CALLING CARDS

If characters in books had their own calling cards, what would they say? Exhibit these, or your own creations, along with the books.

> WESLEY
> The great,
> the one and only,
> world-famous
> Count Dario
> of the Dardanelles

The Frog and the Beanpole, by Charles Kaufman. il. by Troy Howell. Lothrop, 1980.
Wesley is an invisible frog who performs in a circus with Marveline, a ten-year-old orphan.

> HARVEY
> mean and nasty

Rolling Harvey Down the Hill, by Jack Prelutsky. il. by Victoria Chess. Greenwillow Bks., 1980.
Poems about a gang of boys: Harvey (selfish as a pig), Cheerful Tony, Lumpy (causes trouble), Will (acts like a chimpanzee).

> GEORGIE HALL
> I fly

The Fledgling, by Jane Langton. il. by Erik Blegvad. Harper, 1980.
A Canada goose teaches a young girl to fly.

> MRS. PIGGLE-WIGGLE
> Cures for slowpokes,
> show-offs, and bullies

Hello, Mrs. Piggle-Wiggle, by Betty MacDonald. il. by Hilary Knight, Lippincott, 1957.
Mrs. Piggle-Wiggle has amusing and effective cures for the common faults of children. One of a series.

<table>
<tr><td>

JANE ELIZABETH
LONGMAN

Spy

</td></tr>
</table>

Journey into War, by Margaret Donaldson. il. by Joanna Stubbs. Andre Deutsch, 1980.

Janey, an English girl, is separated from her father in France during the summer of 1940. Along with Polish twins, she becomes a spy and saboteur against the Germans.

REPORT CARDS

At the end of the school term, when everyone is worrying about grades, ask the children to make up report cards for characters in books that they have read. Then exhibit the report cards on the bulletin board and display the books on a table nearby.

EXAMPLES

REPORT CARD

Name: Ollie Herdman   Teacher: Miss Hemphill

Grades: Reading _F-_   Fighting _A+_

Hitting _A+_   Keeping Secrets _O-_

Math _C-_

Comments: Ollie is torture to the class. I hope you do something about him. I'm sure if he tried he would get all A's.

(by Hilary, 5th grade)

The Best Christman Pageant Ever, by Barbara Robinson. il. by Judith Gwyn Brown. Harper, 1972.

REPORT CARD

University of Mordor

Name: Sauron   Teacher: Ms. Shelob

Grades: Black Magic _A++_   Reading _B+_

Goldworking _A+_   Seismographics _A_

Languages _B_   Agriculture _F-_

Comments: Sauron would be an all-around prodigy if he paid more attention. Shortly after vacation he stopped turning his classmates into Nazguls and is now getting along with Gollum very well. He is having problems with existing languages but shows great originality in composing his own. His seismographic studies are progressing steadily, and he is already planning a volcano named Mount Doom. His ideals are high.

(by Nathan, 5th grade)

The Lord of the Rings, 2d ed., by J. R. R. Tolkien. Houghton, 1967 [© 1966].

341

STAFF FAVORITES

Collect childhood pictures of teachers and administrators. Put the pictures on a bulletin board, and write under each the title of a book (still in print) that the person liked as a child, when the picture was taken.

REFERRAL STICKERS

Refer a reader from one book to the next. On the back cover glue a strip that says "Like this book? Try _____" and list another book that is similar in style or subject.*

EXAMPLES FOR GRADES 6–8

The Road from Home: The Story of an Armenian Girl, by David Kherdian. Greenwillow Bks., 1979.
Some of Us Survived: The Story of an Armenian Boy, by Kerop Bedoukian. Farrar, 1979.

The Armenians escape from Turkey—two views.

What Happened in Hamelin, by Gloria Skurzynski. Four Winds, 1979.
Time Piper, by Delia Huddy. Greenwillow Bks., 1979.

Two stories, one old and one modern, based on the legend of the Pied Piper of Hamelin. *See also* the Robert Browning poem:
The Pied Piper of Hamelin, by Robert Browning. il. by Kate Greenaway. Warne, 1880.
or
The Pied Piper of Hamelin, by Robert Browning. il. by C. Walter Hodges. Coward McCann & Geoghegan, 1971.

Watership Down, by Richard Adams. Macmillan Pub. Co., 1974.
The Private Life of the Rabbit: An Account of the Life History and Social Behavior of the Wild Rabbit, by R. M. Lockley. Macmillan Pub. Co., 1974.

Adams used the Lockley book for his research.

PUBLISHERS' POSTERS

Buy a large plastic picture frame—the type that is easy to use. Place conference materials, postcards, or greeting cards in the frame. Change the materials frequently for a professional-looking classroom or library exhibit.

---

*This doesn't always work. Once a girl asked me for a book like *Alice in Wonderland.* I recommended another fantasy, and she said, "Oh, I'm not reading fantasies. I'm reading books with heroines called Alice."

PUBLISHERS' CATALOGS

Several publishers send out user surveys on their twice yearly catalogs. What *do* librarians do with that lavish promotional tool, the publisher's catalog?

Perhaps others use them for ordering information; I use them for crafts, bookmarks, games, and exhibits. Most catalogs have illustrations from the new books and long, well-written annotations. Keep the catalogs on file by publisher during the year. When the new catalogs arrive, cut up and use the old ones instead of discarding them.

BOOKMARKS

Mount the annotations on paper and use as bookmarks.

GAMES

Mount the annotation, author's name, and title on one side of a card, the illustration on the other. Children guess which book is represented by the picture.

Mount the annotation on one card, and the picture, author's name, and title on the other as a matching game.

343

PROMOTION AND EXHIBITS

As the actual books arrive, put a few selected catalog pages in a folder marked "New Books" for browsing.

Use selected folder pages on a "New Books" poster.

Post selected book titles and annotations on washroom mirrors, on cafeteria walls, or under school bus windows. (Think of places where students congregate.)

Use the annotations in the library newsletter.

PROJECT CARDS

Glue the picture and annotation on a card. On the reverse side, or under the annotation, type possible activities. This is another packaging idea for a library or book report activity, so make it fun. Children who complete the projects on five cards win five points.

SAMPLE PROJECT CARD QUESTIONS

PICTURE BOOK: *The Knight and the Dragon,* by Tomie de Paola. Putnam, 1980.
Find a folk story about a dragon. Read it and write a plot summary.
Discussion question: Do you think dragons ever existed? Why or why not?

NONFICTION: *I Skate!,* by Margaret Faulkner. Little, 1979.
List the events in a day in Karen's life.
Find Jill Krementz's *A Very Young Skater* (Knopf, 1979) in the library. Read both books. Which book did you like best? Give three reasons for your opinion.

MOVIE TITLE: *The Black Stallion Picture Book.* Random House, 1979.
Find Walter Farley's *The Black Stallion* (Random House, 1941) in the library. Read *The Black Stallion Picture Book* and *The Black Stallion.* Which did you enjoy more? Why? See the film *The Black Stallion.* Compare it with the original book. How does the film differ from the book?

PICTURE-BOOK
BIOGRAPHY: *Freddy My Grandfather,* by Nola Langner. il. by author. Four Winds, 1979.
Compare the girl's grandfather with your own grandfather or another older man you know.
Write an essay describing your grandfather or grandmother.

WHERE TO OBTAIN PUBLISHERS' CATALOGS

From the publishers! Write them requesting to be put on their mailing list.

A current listing of juvenile publishers and their contacts can be obtained by sending a self-addressed, stamped envelope to The Children's Book Council, 67 Irving Place, New York, NY 10003; or refer to *Literary Marketplace*.

PACKAGING THE BIBLIOGRAPHY

You *can* just duplicate an annotated booklist that you have developed and place it on a table, but why not package it to "sell" more books? Draw pictures on the list. Cut it out in an interesting shape, or print it on colored paper. Use your imagination to make an attractive, eye-appealing bibliography.

DOG BIBLIOGRAPHY

METHOD A

YOU NEED: thin plywood
a jigsaw or coping saw
paint
yarn
glue
a permanent felt-tip pen or
　　press-on letters
a plastic dog dish

HOW TO: Cut out plywood in the shape of bones.
Paint the bones.
Trim the borders with yarn.
Letter book titles on the bones.
Decorate the dog dish.
Place the bibliography (dish and bones) on a table with dog books around it.

METHOD B   YOU NEED: cardboard
acrylic paints
gesso—acrylic
permanent felt-tip pen or press-on letters

HOW TO: Cut out bone shapes from the cardboard.
Paint with acrylics.
Let dry thoroughly.
Letter book titles onto bones.
Coat with gesso.
Display as in Method A.

BOOKLIST—DOGS: These are picture books. See pages 26–7 for additional books about dogs, for grades 4–6+.

Asch, Frank. *The Last Puppy.* il. by author. Prentice-Hall, 1980.
The puppy seems to be last in everything until he becomes a boy's *first* puppy.

Cleary, Beverly. *Ribsy.* il. by Louis Darling. Morrow, 1964.
Ribsy is lost and finds a number of temporary homes. (See p. 284 for a *Ribsy* game)

Landshoff, Ursula. *Okay, Good Dog.* il. by author. Harper, 1978.
An "I Can Read" book about dog training.

Muir, Frank. *What-a-Mess.* il. by Joseph Wright. Doubleday, 1977.
A puppy gets in trouble. For further adventures, read *What-A-Mess, the Good* (Doubleday, 1978).

Parker, Nancy Winslow. *Cooper, the McNally's Big Black Dog.* il. by author. Dodd, 1981.
A big black dog is FOR SALE until he becomes useful.

Parker, Nancy Winslow. *Poofy Loves Company.* il. by author. Dodd, 1980.
A loveable poodle shows off his "company manners."

Wagner, Jenny. *John Brown, Rose and the Midnight Cat.* il. by Ron Brooks. Bradbury, 1977.
A sheepdog is jealous of Rose's affection for a cat.

346

HORSE BIBLIOGRAPHY

Keep changing the titles on the horses for an attractive bulletin board display.

YOU NEED: felt   scissors
labels   glue

HOW TO: Make a large horse out of felt and attach to bulletin board.
Cut out a number of small felt horses.
Print or type the title of a book and its author's name on labels and glue to each horse.

USE: Show the number of horse stories available by adding a new miniature horse each day.

BOOKLIST—HORSES:

Bødker, Cecil. *Silas and the Black Mare.* Tr. from the Danish by Sheila La Farge. Delacorte Press, 1978.
Silas lives by his wits and wins a spirited black mare. Boldly drawn characters. Also, *Silas and Ben-Godik* (1978) and *Silas and the Runaway Coach* (1978).

Brady, Irene. *America's Horses and Ponies.* il. by author. Houghton, 1969.
Fifty horses are studied in meticulous drawings and text. Nonfiction.

Cole, Joanna. *A Horse's Body.* Photographs by Jerome Wexler. Morrow, 1981.
The physiology of the horse in photographs accompanied by a short text.

Cole, William. *The Poetry of Horses.* il. by Ruth Sanderson. Scribner, 1979.
Poems featuring horses.

Hall, Lynn. *The Horse Trader.* Scribner, 1981.
Karen has a crush on a con man who cheats her when she buys a horse from him.

MacClintock, Dorcas. *Horses As I See Them.* il. by Ugo Mochi. Scribner, 1980.
Shadow portraits accompany a brief text on horse breeds and their work. Nonfiction.

O'Connor, Karen. *Working With Horses: A Roundup of Careers.* Photographs by Kelle Rankin. Dodd, 1980.
Blacksmith, jockey, trainer, veterinarian, and more.

347

SELLING THE LIBRARY

Be as visible as possible and the library can become the center of your community.

ALICE AND THE WHITE RABBIT

The Chicago Public Library has a collection of full-size, professionally tailored book character costumes. Children and adults adore the characters.

Liz Huntoon, the coordinator, cautions you to be sure to get the publisher's clearance for copyrighted characters' costumes. Also, be prepared for costume repair and provide ventilation holes so nobody expires from the heat that could otherwise build up inside the costume.

GROCERY BAGS

The Portland (Oregon) Public Schools enlisted the cooperation of a large local grocery/variety store chain to promote family reading aloud during Children's Book Week. Each checkout counter had a short read-aloud bibliography that customers could take home, and the store's grocery bags were imprinted with the Reading Club's mascot, Albert Alligator, and the following message:

> Have you read to a child today?
> Read today . . .
> . . . for tomorrow
> Albert Alligator says, "Read aloud!
> It's fun . . . it's relaxing . . . it's a togetherness time."

(A message from your public schools, courtesy of Fred Meyer)

LICENSE PLATES

Does your state allow name license plates? Order one for your car that says BOOKS or READ.

TARANTULAS

In Reno, Nevada the librarian at Wooster High School asked a friend to loan his pet tarantula to the library. In complete secrecy, signs were taped up in the bathrooms and on students' lockers in a four-day sequence:

TARANTULA!

TARANTULA IS COMING!

TARANTULA IS COMING! WHEN???

TARANTULA IS HERE! WHERE???

Just in time for Halloween the female spider was brought to the library. A "Name the Tarantula" contest was held. Everyone came into the library to look at the tarantula and of course at the books on display about spiders.

If you don't have a tarantula, maybe you can bring your elephant. . . .

APPENDIXES

What to Read: The Juvenile Lists

SINCE READING everything published is impossible, you must be selective in your choice of books. A good way of wading through the recent publications is to consult year-end lists. Several journals and organizations compile their own lists of best books published in the preceding year. If you read these books, you will have at least a general idea of the trends in juvenile publishing, and ready access to titles to use in your recommendations. Of course, you will be reading the books a year after they have been published, but in the children's book world this is not necessarily a disadvantage. There are many books that get a lot of attention when they are first published but are not really worth your precious time. The booklists will eliminate most of these "morning glories." And since worthwhile children's books tend to stay in print longer than adult bestsellers, books published a year ago will still be available.

Out of the two thousand or so children's books published each year in the United States, fewer than a hundred are likely to be rated "very good" or "excellent." These are usually short books; surely you can read forty or fifty of them each year.

My suggestion is that you choose your reading from one or more of the juvenile lists. *School Library Journal* publishes a spring list and a yearly list of best books. To help you catch up, *SLJ* has published an annotated list covering twelve years of "Best of the Best" books selected from their annual "Best Books of [the Year]" column. The list is available from the R. R. Bowker Company, Order Department, Box 1807, Ann Arbor, MI 48106, for $1.00. It appeared in the December 1979 issue of *School Library Journal*.

A list that is usually shorter is published in the June *Horn Book* magazine. Called "Fanfare," it is a highly selective bibliography of outstanding juvenile books.

Two important lists—"Notable Children's Books" and "Best Books for Young Adults"—are compiled annually by divisions of the American Library Association: the Association for Library Service to Children (ALSC) and the Young Adult Services Division (YASD). These lists are available from ALA and are also reprinted in *School Library Journal* and *Booklist*, in the March or April issues.

Longer retrospective bibliographies are published by the Association for Childhood Education International, the International Reading Association, and the National Council of Teachers of English.

The Bulletin of the Center for Children's Books provides balanced book reviews throughout the year.

ADDRESSES

Unable to find the above publications in your local library? Write directly to the sources.

PUBLICATIONS:

Booklist
American Library Association
50 E. Huron
Chicago, IL 60611

Bulletin of the Center for Children's Books
5801 Ellis Avenue
Chicago, IL 60637

The Horn Book
Park Square Building
31 St. James Avenue
Boston, MA 02116

School Library Journal
1180 Avenue of the Americas
New York, NY 10036

Subscriptions:
R. R. Bowker Company
P.O. Box 67
Whitinsville, MA 01588

ORGANIZATIONS:

American Library Association
50 E. Huron
Chicago, IL 60611
(The American Association of School Librarians, the Association for Library Service to Children, and the Young Adult Services Division are the pertinent divisions.)

Association for Childhood Education International
3615 Wisconsin Avenue NW
Washington, DC 20016

Child Study Children's Book Committee
Bank Street College
610 W. 112th Street
New York, NY 10025

International Reading Association
P.O. Box 8139
800 Barksdale Road
Newark, DE 19711

National Association for the Education of Young Children
1834 Connecticut Avenue NW
Washington, DC 20009

National Council of Teachers of English
1111 Kenyon Road
Urbana, IL 61801

DIRECTORY OF PUBLISHERS

A.L.A. American Library Association, 50 E. Huron St., Chicago IL 60611

Abelard-Schuman. *See* Harper

Abingdon Press. Abingdon Press, 201 Eighth Ave. S., Nashville, TN 37202

Addison-Wesley. Addison-Wesley Publishing Co. Inc., Reading, MA 01867

Astor-Honor. Astor-Honor Inc., 48 E. 43 St., New York 10017

Atheneum Pubs. Atheneum Publishers, 597 Fifth Ave., New York 10017

Avon. Avon Books, 959 Eighth Ave., New York 10019

Bodley Head. Chatto, Bodley Head & Jonathan Cape, 99 Main St., Salem, NH 03079

Bonim Bks. *See* Hebrew Pub.

The Bookstore Press. The Bookstore Press, Box 191, RFD 1, Freeport, ME 04032

Bowker. R. R. Bowker Company, 1180 Ave. of the Americas, New York 10036

Bradbury Press. Bradbury Press Inc., 2 Overhill Rd., Scarsdale, NY 10583

Caxton Printers. The Caxton Printers Ltd., Box 700, Caldwell, ID 83605

Clarion. Clarion Books, 52 Vanderbilt Ave., New York 10017

Collins. William Collins Publishers, Inc., 2080 W. 117th St., Cleveland, OH 44111

Coward, McCann & Geoghegan. Coward, McCann & Geoghegan, Inc., 200 Madison Ave., New York 10016

Crane, Russak. Crane, Russak & Co. Inc., 3 E. 44 St., New York 10017

Cricket Magazine. Cricket Magazine, Box 100, La Salle, IL 61301

Crowell. *See* Harper

Crown. Crown Publishers Inc., One Park Ave., New York 10016

Delacorte Press. *See* Dell

Dell. Dell Publishing Co. Inc., One Dag Hammarskjold Plaza, New York 10017

Andre Deutsch. *See* Dutton

Dial Press. The Dial Press, One Dag Hammarskjold Plaza, New York 10017

Dodd. Dodd, Mead & Co., 79 Madison Ave., New York 10016

Doubleday. Doubleday & Co Inc., 245 Park Ave., New York 10167

Dover. Dover Publications Inc., 180 Varick St., New York 10014

Dutton. E. P. Dutton, Inc., 2 Park Ave., New York 10016

Elsevier/Nelson. *See* Dutton

Evans, M. & Co. M. Evans & Co. Inc., 216 E. 49 St., New York 10017

Faber & Faber. Faber & Faber, Inc., 99 Main St., Salem, NH 03079

353

Farrar, Straus. Farrar, Straus & Giroux Inc., 19 Union Square W., New York 10003

Feminist Press. The Feminist Press, Box 334, Old Westbury, NY 11568

Follett. Follett Publishing Co., 1010 W. Washington Blvd., Chicago, IL 60607

Fontana Lions. *See* Collins

Four Winds. Four Winds Press, 50 W. 44 St., New York 10036

Garrard. Garrard Publishing Co., 1607 N. Market St., Champaign, IL 61820

Golden Press. *See* Western Pub. Co.

Greenwillow. Greenwillow Books, 105 Madison Avenue, New York 10016

Grosset. Grosset & Dunlap Inc., 51 Madison Ave., New York 10010

Harcourt. Harcourt Brace Jovanovich Inc., 757 Third Ave., New York 10017

Harper. Harper & Row, Publishers Inc., 10 E. 53 St., New York 10022

Hastings House. Hastings House, Publishers Inc., 10 E. 40 St., New York 10016

Hebrew Pub. Hebrew Publishing Co., 100 Water St., Brooklyn, NY 11201

Heinemann. Heinemann Educational Books Inc., 4 Front St., Exeter, NH 03833

Lawrence Hill. Lawrence Hill & Co. Publishers, Inc., 520 Riverside Ave., Westport, CT 06880

Hodder-Stoughton. Hodder-Stoughton Educational, 47 Bedford Sq. London WC1B 3DP England

Holiday House. Holiday House, Inc., 18 E. 53 St., New York 10022

Holt. Holt, Rinehart & Winston General Book, 521 Fifth Ave., New York 10175

Houghton. Houghton Mifflin Co., One Beacon St., Boston, MA 02107

Knopf. Alfred A. Knopf Inc. 201 E. 50 St., New York 10022

Seymour Lawrence. Seymour Lawrence, Inc., 61 Beacon St., Boston, MA 02108

Lippincott. *See* Harper

Little. Little, Brown & Co., 34 Beacon St., Boston, MA 02106

Longmans. Longman, Inc. 19 W. 44 St., Suite 1012, New York 10036

Lothrop. Lothrop, Lee & Shepard Books, 105 Madison Ave., New York 10016

McGraw. McGraw-Hill Book Co., 1221 Ave. of the Americas, New York 10020

McKay. David McKay Co., Inc., 2 Park Ave., New York 10016

Macmillan Pub. Co. Macmillan Inc., 866 Third Ave. New York 10022

Meredith. Meredith Corp., 1716 Locust St., Des Moines, IA 50336

Methuen. Methuen Inc., 733 Third Ave., New York 10017

Morrow. William Morrow & Co., Inc., 105 Madison Ave., New York 10016

Obolensky. *See* Astor-Honor

Oxford. Oxford University Press, Inc., 200 Madison Ave., New York 10016

Pantheon. Pantheon Books, Inc., 201 E. 50 St., New York 10022

Parents Mag. Press. Parents Magazine Press, 685 Third Ave., New York 10017

Parkside Press. Parkside Press, 2026 Parkside Ct., West Linn, OR 97068

Philomel Books. *See* Dutton

Platt & Munk. *See* Grosset

Prentice-Hall. Prentice-Hall, Inc., Englewood Cliffs, NJ 07632

Putnam. G. P. Putnam's Sons, 200 Madison Ave., New York 10016

Raintree Pubs. Raintree Publishers, Inc., 205 W. Highland Ave., Milwaukee, WI 53203

Random House. Random House, Inc., 201 E. 50 St., New York 10022

Scholastic. Scholastic Book Services, 50 W. 44 St., New York 10036

Scribner. Charles Scribner's Sons, 597 Fifth Ave., New York 10017

Seabury. The Seabury Press Inc., 815 Second Ave., New York 10017

Sierra Club/Scribner. *See* Scribner

Simon & Schuster. Simon & Schuster, The Simon & Schuster Bldg., 1230 Ave. of the Americas, New York 10020

Sisters' Choice Press. Sisters' Choice Press, 2027 Parker St., Berkeley, CA 94704

Sterling. Sterling Publishing Co., Inc., 2 Park Ave., New York 10016

Tuttle. Charles E. Tuttle Co., Inc., 28 S. Main St., Rutland, VT 05701

Univ. of London Press. *See* Hodder-Stoughton

Univ. of Washington Press. University of Washington Press, Seattle, WA 98105

Van Nostrand. Van Nostrand Reinhold Co., 135 W. 50 St., New York 10020

Vanguard. Vanguard Press, Inc., 424 Madison Ave., New York 10017

Viking. The Viking Press, 625 Madison Ave., New York 10022

Walck, H. Z. *See* McKay

Warne. Frederick Warne & Co., Inc., 2 Park Ave., New York 10016

Watts, F. Franklin Watts Inc., 730 Fifth Ave., New York 10019

Western Pub. Co. Western Publishing Co., Inc., 1220 Mound Ave., Racine, WI 53404

Whitman, A. Albert Whitman & Co., 560 W. Lake St., Chicago, IL 60606

Wilson, H. W. The H. W. Wilson Company, 950 University Ave., Bronx, NY 10452

Windmill. Windmill Books Inc., The Simon & Schuster Bldg., 1230 Ave. of the Americas, New York 10020

Workman Pub. Workman Publishing Co. Inc., One W. 39 St., New York 10018

INDEX